MASS MEDIA RELIGION

COMMUNICATION AND HUMAN VALUES

Series editors

Robert A. White, Editor, Centre for the Study of Communication and
Culture, London, UK
Michael Traber, Associate Editor, World Association for Christian
Communication, London, UK

International editorial advisory board

Binod C. Agrawal, Development and Educational Communication, Space
Applications Centre, Ahmedabad, India
Luis Ramiro Beltrán, UNESCO, Quito, Ecuador
James W. Carey, University of Illinois, USA
Marlene Cuthbert, University of Windsor, Canada
William F. Fore, Communication Commission, National Council of
Churches of Christ, New York, USA
George Gerbner, University of Pennsylvania, USA
James D. Halloran, University of Leicester, UK
Cees Hamelink, Institute of Social Studies, The Hague, The Netherlands
Neville D. Jayaweera, World Association for Christian Communication,
London, UK
Emile G. McAnany, University of Texas, USA
Walter J. Ong, St. Louis University, USA
Breda Pavlic, Culture and Communication Sector,
UNESCO, Paris
Miquel de Moragas Spa, Autonomous University of
Barcelona, Spain

Also in this series

Media and Politics in Latin America:
The Struggle for Democracy
edited by Elizabeth Fox

The Mass Media and Village Life: An Indian Study
Paul Hartmann with B. R. Patil and Anita Dighe

World Families Watch Television
edited by James Lull

MASS MEDIA RELIGION

The Social Sources of the Electronic Church

Stewart M. Hoover

269.26
H789

SAGE PUBLICATIONS
The Publishers of Professional Social Science
Newbury Park   London   New Delhi

For information address:

SAGE Publications, Inc.
2111 West Hillcrest Drive
Newbury Park, California 91320

SAGE Publications Ltd.
28 Banner Street
London EC1Y 8QE
England

SAGE Publications India Pvt. Ltd.
M-32 Market
Greater Kailash I
New Delhi 110 048 India

Printed in the United States of America

Library of Congress Cataloging-in-Publication Data

Hoover, Stewart M.
    Mass media religion : the social sources of the electronic church
  / Stewart M. Hoover.
      p.   cm. — (Communication and human values)
    Bibliography: p.
    Includes index.
    ISBN 0-8039-2994-3.   ISBN 0-8039-2995-1 (pbk .)
    1. Television in religion—United States.   2. 700 Club.
  3. Evangelicalism—United States—History—20th century.   4. United
  States—Church history—20th century.   I. Title.   II. Series:
  Communication and human values
  BV656.3.H66 1988
  269′ .2—dc19   87-36859
                                                                  CIP

SECOND PRINTING 1989

Contents

List of Figures

There is not as yet on the horizon of religious broadcasting the program that will compare in "success" with the mass evangelist of earlier days. The danger is that there will be. The danger is that some creative genius will develop the program that is so "successful" by the standards of the commercial users of the media that the fundamental purposes of the Christian church will be ignored or denied.

Everett Parker, David Barry, and Dallas Smythe (*The Television-Radio Audience and Religion,* 1955)

Foreword

Few topics in the study of religion have received as much attention during the past decades as religious broadcasting. The impetus for the dozens of books and thousands of articles dealing with the "electronic church" came first from recognition, during the mid-1970s, that evangelical Christianity was a vital and growing component of American religion, and that at least part of its vitality and growth seemed traceable to its extensive use of radio, television, and other modern methods of communication. A more important stimulus was the rise to prominence of the Christian "new right" during the 1980 election campaigns. Journalistic and academic observers and analysts of religious broadcasting have focused on the personalities and careers of key practitioners, theological and political commonalities and differences among broadcasters and their supporters, the finances of broadcast ministries, the size and composition of the listening and viewing audience, the implications of religious broadcasting for the more conventional activities of local churches, and, of course, the potential for social change represented by a sizable aggregate of people who give regular attention to charismatic spokespersons of fairly well-defined social and political viewpoints. Much of the early subjective and impressionistic work on these topics caricatured the broadcasters, exaggerated the size of the audience, emphasized its ostensibly monolithic character, and sounded alarmist or triumphalist notes about its political and social role.

With the passage of time, the carrying out of more careful studies, and the resultant accumulation of evidence, many of the subjective generalizations and exaggerations have been modified or corrected, so that we now have a reasonably balanced and informed view on most of the major questions. We know there are differences between broadcasters and their audiences. We have a much clearer understanding of how broadcasters raise their money, how much they raise, and how they spend it. We know that the audience for religious broadcasts is substantial, though not nearly so large as once was claimed, and we know much about its demographic characteristics and its theological and political views. We know that most viewers are church members and that religious broadcasts constitute an addition to their participation in local congregations rather than a substitute for it. In short, we can fill in many of the blanks with considerable confidence. Notably lacking, however, has been a detailed look at the ways individual viewers perceive and use the religious broadcasts they watch and support. With the publication of *Mass Media Religion: The Social Sources of the Electronic Church*, Professor Stewart Hoover has taken a significant step in correcting this situation.

As one of the principal investigators in the landmark survey conducted in 1983 by the Gallup Organization and the Annenberg School of Communications at the University of Pennsylvania, Professor Hoover has already helped draw the most widely accepted outline of the size and nature of the audience of religious broadcasts. With this book, he has begun to fill in this outline. By conducting numerous and extensive interviews with viewers and supporters of the most innovative and perhaps the most important of the broadcasts, the *700 Club*, the flagship program of Pat Robertson's Christian Broadcasting Network, Hoover enlarges our understanding of such issues as why individuals begin and continue to attend to religious programming, how regular audience members resemble and differ from each other in the ways they receive and use the messages produced by broadcasters, and what religious, political, and other social effects are likely—or unlikely—to result from participation in the electronic church. He helps us understand Pat Robertson's attractiveness to millions of Americans. He demonstrates that, as with other media, viewers do not simply accept whatever they hear on a religious broadcast, but filter it according to their own predispositions and convictions. He contends that, while a religious program such as the *700 Club* can serve as a sophisticated and articulate voice for conservative Christianity, thereby giving viewers a greater sense of their potential influence and power as a distinct segment of society, it can and often does produce a broadening rather than a narrowing of identity and identification, a movement in the direction of universalism rather than sectarianism, toward the freer-flowing mainstream rather than toward brackish and stagnant backwaters.

It is important that we understand these matters as well as possible because, despite the embarrassingly troubled times religious broadcasters have experienced as this book was being completed, mass-mediated religion is clearly here to stay. It can be a force for demagoguery and an instrument to turn people from serious engagement to simplistic solutions, but it can also strengthen and deepen the faith of viewers by providing them with instruction, exhortation, inspiration, hope, encouragement, entertainment, example, and opportunity for service. It also performs a symbolic function of great importance, in that it has been a major means of serving notice to the nation that evangelical Christians are no longer content to be treated as a peculiar and obscurantist minority, but are a force with which to reckon, socially, politically, and theologically. Folk to whom a medium has meant so much will not readily abandon it in time of trouble.

—William Martin
Professor of Sociology,
Rice University

Introduction

Religious broadcasting has moved, over the past decade, from the margins of social and religious life to center stage. Once a feature of late-night and small-market Bible Belt radio, religion is now available on television in every region of the United States and, increasingly, the world. What does this new religious broadcasting represent? Is it merely a new kind of broadcasting, or is it also a new kind of religion? There have been some sweeping claims made about its significance—claims that it transcends both broadcasting and religion and has assumed a place of unprecedented power and prominence in culture, politics, and society.

Television is itself a cultural medium. It is often central to ongoing processes of cultural and symbolic formation. A form of television that embodies a radically, self-consciously *cultural* reality—religion—must be seen to have at least the potential of transforming society.

The broad question is, then, what kind of religious culture are we creating in this era of great social and institutional change? The postwar period of prosperous stability has been replaced by upheaval. First came the social revolution of the 1960s, followed by a period of realignment in the 1970s, and then a new surge of social and political consciousness—this time of a decidedly conservative nature—in the 1980s. Television is thought to have been involved in each of these eras in concrete ways. It was the stage on which the social drama of the 1960s was played out for most Americans (it is thought). It has been central, in the form of the new religious broadcasting, to the resurgent "right" in the 1980s.

It is the purpose of this book to consider the implications of religious television primarily on a cultural level. What are the symbols and values projected by these programs? How does "electronic church" broadcasting affect the way American culture deals with the major problems of the day, such as racism, militarism, the urban crisis, the drug crisis, the feminization of poverty, and broader social change?

In the past, the impact of religious broadcasting on such issues has been considered trivial. I contend, however, that it is far from trivial, that for many people and subcultures, religious broadcasting represents a powerful center of affinity and orientation. The audience is not as large or significant as some fear. The quality of that audience—its loyalty and depth of involvement—is a different matter, however. My goal is to push the debate beyond discussions of quantity to considerations of the qualitative, cultural significance of the electronic church.

Religion is a difficult field to study. There are complex problems in analyzing a phenomenon that makes substantive, transcendent claims. Wherever one looks for evidence of its characteristics, it can always claim to be something beyond them. It is—as one of my former professors, Larry Gross, was fond of saying—in a special "reservation" on the boundary of social and cultural life. It is accorded certain privileges, including that of being ultimately unmeasurable. These privileges have their costs, however, not the least that religion is therefore easily discounted or even dismissed as a dimension of social and cultural analysis.

Some social theorists have dealt with religion through "secularization." Religion—it was thought—will shrink in the face of modernity because social progress will bring personal rationalism and a set of pragmatic social structures that make religion less relevant to daily life. Daniel Lerner's description of "the passing of traditional society" was a model of such theory. I don't think it is unfair to say that Lerner suggested that Islam, as a faith and as a social system, probably might not survive the influence of modernization.

Lerner was writing about Iran, which in the 1980s has experienced the resurgence and ultimate political triumph (temporary or not) of an antimodernist Islam. Similar movements, which are religious, or at least religiocultural, at their roots, have also arisen elsewhere in recent years. So much for "secularization," at least for now.

My father is a minister, and religion is the "family business," in a way. As a result, I have always had an interest in religion, particularly the type that was typical of the Bible Belt when I was growing up. Now I am a communication researcher, and I find that that religion has gone "big time." Because of my background, I know enough to maintain a healthy skepticism about the claims of Bible Belt evangelicalism (a skepticism not shared by secular media such as the *Wall Street Journal*). But I also know that expressive religion is an important part of life for many people. A type of communication that appears to be transcending religion—and being transformed by it—deserves serious attention.

My early experiences with religious diversity, and my own study of theology and phenomenology have given me, I believe, a certain understanding of, or empathy with, deeply religious people. While I may disagree completely with the worldviews and values expressed, I have endeavored, successfully I think, to engage in discussions that reveal their sources. Perhaps, then, the research reported in this book reflects a *verstehen* that other observers might not have had.

Communication theorists as disparate as George Gerbner, Horace Newcomb, and James Carey have advocated a multilateral approach to theory building. What Carey calls a "cultural studies" approach places communicational phenomena in their social, cultural, historical, and institutional contexts. He has argued that such an approach makes even the existential meaning of death a matter that can be understood, in a way, within the research process.

It was clear to me from the beginning that such a contextual approach was necessary if I were to do anything to extend our understanding of the meaning of the electronic church. The phenomenon has a history. It came from somewhere, both culturally and institutionally. It exists in a broader culture and society. Its meaning and messages are bound by those contexts. The movements of which the electronic church is a part also have their own institutional structures, and those contribute to its meaning. Finally, the electronic church is consumed by—and imbued with meaning by—people. Previous quantitative studies have firmly established the broad outlines of who these people are, and what they seem to get out of their viewing.

There is more to the story, however. Much of what is available from earlier studies simply does not answer all of the questions. Therefore, the core of this study is a series of interviews with people who are members of one of the most important electronic church ministries—the *700 Club*. The analysis of the interviews refers consciously to the earlier quantitative work in a methodology I have come to call "elaboration." The basic questions are as follows: What can we learn about the meaning of those quantitative data by talking with the viewers themselves? What can we learn about the limitations of those other approaches? What insights can we gain into formerly confusing relationships?

These are questions that could be applied to research on television in general. A recent conference in Tubingen, Germany, on qualitative approaches to television was called "Re-thinking the Audience." A number of scholars who want to push beyond surface relationships to deeper meanings in our analysis gathered there to compare notes. There were those who began with a radically "cultural" premise—that television analysis is largely a theoretical and critical, not an empirical, process. There were those who held the opposite—that the starting point needs to be empirically verifiable evidence. Overall, though, there was the sense that we were converging toward a common point—that television analysis has much to gain from each perspective, and that a fusion of them is necessary if we are to further our understanding of its meanings. The work described here, which bases interviews with the audience on both empirical and critical foundations, thus represents what I see to be a positive current trend in the field.

Analyzing such interviews is—not surprisingly—a complex task. Much of what we want to know is available simply by listening to what the viewers have to say. Where religious broadcasting fits in their lives with other activities and how their lives are different because of it tells us much about its meaning for them. The interviews are data—not evidence—but they reveal much that can help us build theory about religious broadcasting *and* about mass media in general, and they can become evidence through careful analysis.

The unique contribution of this study is its analytic methodology, that of qualitative accounts of these viewers' "histories." The term *faith history* is a meaningful one—a term of art—in some theological circles, and is a concept that was quite comfortable to these viewers. These "histories" are not, however, "testimonies" (elaborated accounts of transcendent meaning). They are qualitative accounts of interacting elements of lives and consciousness in process. They beg the question—because of the self-conscious objectives of this study—of where the electronic church "fits in." Most previous research has begun with a presumption of either power or impotence on the part of these programs in individual lives. Neither perspective is fully justified, as these interviews show.

To encapsulate these interacting dimensions, I have presented a diagram for each viewer or couple interviewed. These "trajectories" are explained in some detail in Chapter 5. They resemble path diagrams, but they are not quantitative or objective. They are subjective and have only one dimension— time—that connects the various elements in them from left to right. They are not intended to "prove" anything by themselves (except perhaps that, for everyone I spoke with, religious broadcasting came *after,* not before, their other involvements in religion). Instead, they are intended to give the reader insight into the often complex set of factors that make up the religious consciousness of these viewers.

The approach taken is interdisciplinary. These issues must be seen in their historical context. They must be understood as social and cultural phenomena, based in a certain place and time. They must also be evaluated with attention to earlier empirical study. Any one of these directions could have been (and has been, in other studies) the sole direction taken. I have attempted to bring them together, to deepen and strengthen the analysis.

I share with many others a sense of ambivalence about the electronic church. I am not personally in sympathy with its worldview. It should be clear that I find its actual impact and appeal more limited than its advocates claim, and that it has a dubious claim to the sort of social and political significance it has recently been accorded. At the same time, it seems to touch the lives of real people and help them through crisis. It offers genuine satisfactions for many of them. I hope that this book will further our understanding of it and of the cultural meaning of mass media (and their satisfactions) in general.

Ray Birdwhistell, another of my former teachers, was very influential.

From his perspective as an anthropologist, he constantly challenged us—whom he saw to be nascent positivists—to consider that the real question about a social or cultural phenomenon is not "*what* is it?" but "*where* is it?" That is, we know it exists—on a certain level—because we can name it. The real question is *where* it fits into the cultural environment. The question is one of *meaning,* not measurable "significance." The question addressed here, then, is not so much "*what* is the electronic church?" as it is "*where* is the electronic church?" We will build a description of this phenomenon as it exists in the interaction between individuals and their sociocultural environments. Its ultimate meaning can only be known through such contextualization.

Acknowledgments

All books represent the hard work of many people aside from their authors. This study has stretched over five years, and involved several distinct phases. Many people have made contributions to it in each of these phases, and therefore there are a large number who must be acknowledged, with my gratitude.

I would like to thank, first of all, the academic and scholarly advisers who assisted with portions of this work done during my graduate study at the Annenberg School. George Gerbner, Larry Gross, Carolyn Marvin, Charles Wright, Robert Lewis Shayon, and Robert Hornik all were invaluable to the direction and scope of the study. In addition, comment and criticism from James Carey and Elihu Katz have amplified important elements of the work of that period.

A number of people involved in the world of religious broadcasting have also been most helpful and encouraging. William Fore has been very supportive and insightful throughout. Everett Parker and Dallas Smythe have helped focus my research through their willingness to reflect on their own landmark work of so many years ago. Early phases of the study, in particular, would not have been possible without the assistance of a number of staff at Christian Broadcasting Network itself, who agreed to be interviewed. In spite of our differences of opinion, Ben Armstrong of NRB has been consistently encouraging of my efforts.

The core of the book depended heavily on the willingness of a number of viewers of the *700 Club* to talk with a stranger about experiences and motivations of a deeply personal nature. The book simply would not have been possible without their cooperation, and I thank them.

The book also would not have been possible without the active involvement, interest, criticism, and advice of its series editor, Robert White, and the support of his institution, the Centre for the Study of

Communication and Culture in London. He has been a tireless consultant and advocate for this project over many, many months, and it exists in large measure because of his hard work.

Many of my colleagues also have been very understanding when this project made me less than available and focused in my academic responsibilities. I thank all of them, but particularly my two chairmen, Alex Toogood—a good friend and adviser who passed away in the midst of this project, and whom I will sorely miss—Herb Dordick, who made many concessions to my work on this project; and my assistant in the Temple London Program, Joan Dicks.

In the final stages, when the fatigued author thinks that the work is done, but the work of actually producing a usable manuscript is just beginning, a number of people step in. I want especially to thank my editor, Larry Elveru, and his collaborator, Sherrill Franklin, for putting other things aside for several weeks of intense work on the manuscript. Karen Evans, my word-processing specialist, and Liz Arter contributed keyboard time to the final push. Derrick Williams produced the trajectory diagrams.

Finally, and most important, I wish to thank my wife, Karen. I am no manager of detail, but she is, and just as the project needed a manager finally to carry it to fruition, she was eager to do so. Her tireless efforts, support, and encouragement, particularly in the final months, make the final product also hers.

If I have overlooked someone, I hope to be forgiven. Whatever value there may be in this work is a result of the combined efforts of these people.

—Stewart M. Hoover
Wallingford, Pennsylvania

1

Religious Television and the New Religious Consciousness in America

We know now that the period between World War II and the era of social revolution we have come to call "the '60s" was an unusual interval of quietude in the midst of otherwise turbulent times. "The '50s" has entered our cultural vocabulary denoting a time of normalcy. Seen in the context of the great changes that have taken place in the decades since the war, however, that time of relative stability and calm was the exception, not the rule. Change has been the rule, and, by the decade of the 1970s, this change had found its way into all levels of personal, social, political, and cultural life.[1]

Religious faith, practice, and institutions have been involved in, and affected by, these changes. The 1950s seemed to be the heyday of the mainline, establishment religions of the "middle." Postwar church attendance and income confirmed this time as one of power and prestige for these churches.[2]

Different religious forms began to emerge in the 1960s. Interest in Eastern mysticism, in intentional communities, in noninstitutional, often nonformal religious expression was strong among the youth counterculture of that era. This so-called new religious consciousness[3] largely rejected older, established religious institutions, seeing them as "part of the problem," not "part of the solution." This rejectionism even found formal theological expression in such intellectual movements as the briefly popular "death of God" theology.

In the 1970s, the formerly dominant mainline Protestant groups continued a decline in membership that began in the 1960s, while a number of independent congregations and "evangelical" denominations recorded impressive growth.[4] It has been this "evangelical revival," more than anything else, which has typified the evolving religious climate of recent years. A major magazine proclaimed 1977, the year an evangelical Christian became president of the United States, "The Year of the Evangelical." By 1980, Martin Marty points out, this movement "could claim the loyalty of all three major presidential candidates, along with entertainers and entrepreneurs, athletes and beauty queens. Obviously, such a subculture can hardly be described as marginal."[5]

The rise of a new, "neo" evangelicalism was also felt *within* the mainstream churches. Newly prominent evangelical interests and entirely new "charismatic renewal" movements arose in most major denominations, as well as in the Roman Catholic church. The formerly dominant and self-reliant institutions of the religious establishment therefore found themselves needing to account for significant theological disarray among their constituents.[6]

Neoevangelicalism and resurgent fundamentalism[7] also captured the attention of the media and the secular establishment. Based in the founding of the National Association of Evangelicals in 1942, and growing out of the Lausanne conferences of international evangelicalism, a cooperative movement arose around such figures as Billy Graham, resulting in "Key '73" and other evangelism campaigns during the early 1970s.[8]

While many evangelical churches and groups responded to their increased prominence with purely pietistic motives, a sociopolitical agenda also emerged. In a 1976 exposé, the liberal-evangelical journal *Sojourners* reported on an evolving "Plan to Save America" being organized by prominent conservative politicians and evangelical Christians.[9] Among those early planners were such now-famous preachers as Jerry Falwell and Bill Bright of Campus Crusade for Christ.

By 1980, the political arm of the evangelical movement had evolved into a broad-based, multimillion-dollar political organization, or group of organizations, responsible for such things as annual "Washington for Jesus" rallies, where thousands would gather for prayer and exhortations reminiscent of the mass events of the civil rights and antiwar movements. Most prominent among these groups were The Religious Roundtable and The Moral Majority—organizations committed to forwarding an agenda of "traditional values" in politics.[10] While the full extent of their impact on politics is not clear, such organizations have played important roles in all general elections since 1980. The newly politicized evangelicals found forceful allies in the secular new right and a champion in Ronald Reagan, while he and other conservative politicians found in these groups steadfast support for a new social agenda.

The role of the media

This "awakening" of evangelical political and religious consciousness in the past decade has been typified by many things, not least its involvement in the political and public spheres. One central factor has attracted more attention than any other, however: This movement (if that is what it is) has derived a great share of its strength, organization, and momentum from its electronic media ministries.

Electronic media have been at the center of the resurgence of religious and social consciousness since the 1960s. Their role is both one of shaping the consciousness of participants in the movement, and one of convincing the American public that the country is in the midst of great cultural and religious change. The media became central to these processes, the stage on which they were experienced by most Americans.

The leaders of the social revolution of the 1960s were masters of the so-called media event. Cult figures like Timothy Leary, the Guru Maharaj Ji, and Abbie Hoffman knew how to grab the attention of the dominant, establishment media. Major social events such as the urban riots of the 1960s and the political upheavals of 1968 onward were acted out on a "media stage." Antiestablishment media also emerged, and the era seemed to evolve within a consciousness that, in the words of an important analyst of the time, "the whole world [was] watching."[11]

The civil rights and antiwar movements readily captured media attention, and, at the same time, the religious roots of those movements often pervaded the news coverage. Martin Luther King, Jr. regularly preached to the entire nation during the evening news, as did the Reverend William Sloane Coffin and the Berrigan Brothers on occasion. Billy Graham also enjoyed evening news exposure, though from a different point of view, becoming the informal White House chaplain during the Vietnam era.

This era of change brought with it an awareness of the crucial role of the mass media in social and political change. Far from being neutral and observing society from the sidelines, the media, particularly the electronic media, were increasingly seen as dominant factors in the evolution of social thought and public opinion during the Vietnam and Watergate years. More recently, the press, especially the electronic press, have found themselves under scrutiny, from both the right and the left, for their alleged biases.[12]

The medium of "the right"

The lesson that electronic media can play a major role in massive social and cultural changes was not lost on the developing religious and secular movements on the "right" during the 1970s. Both the social and the religious agendas of the neoevangelical movement have been well served by the development of the highly visible, newly sophisticated religious broadcasting and multimedia institutions that have come to be called the "electronic church." Since these ministries first rose to national prominence in the early 1970s, they have drawn increasing attention from supporters and critics alike.

Fear and euphoria abound. Supporters say the electronic church represents a new era for religion—the capture, by faith groups, of the "new media" which will replace print media as the major purveyors of faith in a postindustrial age. Some suggest that they are merely ancillary to the more basic working out of the evangelical revival. Others fear that they pose a serious threat to all churches by taking away members and income. Detractors charge that most of them are merely thinly veiled political or social-reform organizations, hiding behind a mask of religion and tax exemption to bring about a conservative political agenda. Still others argue that they are a sort of sleight of hand, a public relations shell surrounding financial empires built on direct mail fund-raising, serving and supported by a relative handful of already committed Christians who are being deceived into bankrolling "ministries to the world." Some even say that they are only a flash in the pan, a momentary sideshow that will fade as their novelty wears off.

This book will explore the significance of this new type of broadcasting. Growing as it has from a variety of roots, we will need to evaluate it in several ways.

Religious broadcasting is, first of all, a religious activity, produced and viewed by people who share common symbols, values, and a "moral culture" they celebrate. Second, electronic church broadcasting is embedded in the wider neoevangelical and fundamentalist revivals of recent years. As such, it is tied to both the conservative and the more mainstream wings of American religion. Third, the electronic church is a form of broadcasting. It shares formal and informal elements with all of broadcasting, and its meaning is partially shaped by that context. Fourth, religious broadcasting has its own institutional and political structure. The organizations that produce these programs have their own histories and polities, and we must try to understand them. Fifth, religious broadcasting has come to have an influence on all religious institutions in America, even outside its fundamentalist and evangelical roots. Finally, religious broadcasting has influence on American culture itself. Such religiously based revitalization movements historically have had social and political implications beyond their spiritual bases.

The religious character of the recent eras of change

Evaluations of these ongoing changes in religion and society have tended to describe them as deep and profound. The major work on the religious aspects of the "social revolution" of the 1960s saw a "new religious consciousness" pervading the social consciousness of the youth counterculture.[13] The interest in Eastern and other nontraditional religions on the part of the youth movements seemed to be brought on by a desire to resolve the dissonance between the materialism and superficiality of the "Sunday spirituality" of their parents' generation and the crisis of modern lives that seemed empty of meaning. Eastern spirituality challenged these new adherents to examine their values and the totality of the meaning systems in which they lived and to make a religion or spiritual system the basis of their values. This new religious consciousness implied that spiritual involvement was essential to a worldview encompassing personal ethics, community relations, and social action.[14]

Émile Durkheim described individual involvement in religious practice as having this sort of integrative, global nature.[15] When we speak of religion in formal terms, we tend to speak of just such totalities of experience. Religions are systematic and offer all-encompassing explanations. Clifford Geertz has described religion as

(1) a system of symbols which acts to (2) establish powerful, pervasive, and long-lasting moods and motivations in men by (3) formulating conceptions of a general order of existence and (4) clothing these conceptions with such an aura of factuality that (5) the moods and motivations seem uniquely realistic.[16]

Religious consciousness, as it has been used by most observers, and is used here, is a term that attempts to describe the individual's relationship to such systems, symbolic and real, and the moods and motivations that evolve with that involvement.

Changes in consciousness are also implied by nonreligious systems of meaning. Raymond Williams has attempted to describe the profound cultural change in Britain in the mid-twentieth century through the changing shape of consciousness.[17] He sees this changing consciousness (which he calls a "structure of feeling") as based on sociopolitical and economic changes. But he sees the mass media as a "text" through which the ramifications of these changes can be worked out in the minds and experiences of members of the culture, in much the same way we have described the role of media in the movements of the 1960s.

Others have gone further, suggesting that the nature or structure of consciousness itself has changed over time, being shaped by the media through which individuals experience cultural change. Marshall McLuhan has been identified with this approach, but it has been given a more systematic statement by Walter Ong.[18] Ong holds that the very change in the media through which we experience our culture has in turn affected the nature of that experience, and that a different consciousness may evolve with a change from oral to more modern modes of communication.

A clear definition of *religious consciousness* is difficult. It is usually meant to imply a broad integration of faith and experience. As the term is most often used, it does not carry a clear idea of its own boundaries or limits. Our purpose here is to look at the implications of the development of the electronic church for neoevangelicalism and broader religious, social, and political movements of recent years. How profound is the difference the electronic church has wrought in religious consciousness? Testing whether it is involved in real *change* at such deep levels of experience is the most severe standard we can devise. It is a test suggested both by the claims made about the impact of the phenomenon (that it is having profound social, cultural, and political effects), *and* by the growing body of thought (represented by Williams) that media have unique and powerful roles as systems conveying cultural meaning.

As the term *religious consciousness* has been used to describe the movements of recent years, it has acquired several clear implications. First, it suggests that a set of central religious or meaning *symbols* organize belief systems. These symbols may be fixed, traditional ones; they may be ideas; they may be practices; or they may be figures, such as the Guru Maharaj Ji or Martin Luther King, Jr.

Second, the term *consciousness* usually implies a *totality of worldview*, a set of "root paradigms," and a constellation of values surrounding this worldview. The "New Age Consciousness" in vogue in California in the 1980s evokes for its followers a system of values surrounding peace, justice, and understanding. These deep values and paradigms become organizing principles for adherents.

Third, the term *new consciousness* is normally applied to systems, such as the ones we have been discussing, where there is a search for new religious meaning and validation. William McLoughlin[19] has described the consciousness that underlay the movements of revitalization during the Protestant "Great Awakenings" in American history (a subject to which we shall return). These revitalization movements derive a good deal of their momentum from their "newness." Their very reason for being is as a reaction to the status quo and a presentation of new cultural symbols and forms. Thus religious or spiritual consciousness usually has a dimension of newness, of a fresh approach to resolving the disparities between belief systems and day-to-day life.

Fourth, there are also personal and social implications to change in consciousness. New types of consciousness emerge in individual cognitive structures and psychological processes. Changes in consciousness, as Williams has said, and Glock and Bellah observed in the social movements of the 1960s, result from social and cultural shifts and the associated tensions felt by individuals.

**The social origins of changing
religious consciousness and the
new religious movements**

The movements and media of the "left" in the 1960s and the movements and media of the new religious and politically active "right" in the 1980s have their sources in what observers have seen as a crisis in traditional social and religious institutions brought on by modern life. This "crisis of modernity" is based in the ongoing evolution of late industrial and postindustrial society, where traditional structures have been undermined by physical, social, and economic changes. According to Peter Berger:

> While modernization brings promises and tangible benefits, it also produces tensions and discontents both institutionally and psychologically. In addition to the external institutional dislocations resulting from changes in the economic and political structures, there is massive alienation as a result of the loss of community and the turbulent upheavals caused by social mobility, urbanization, and the technological transformations of everyday life.[20]

Robert Bellah suggests that modern society has undermined the traditional base of consciousness in local community by cutting the roots of the "moral culture" on which people depend for normative guidance:

> We have moved from the local life of the nineteenth century—in which economic and social relationships were visible and, however imperfectly, morally interpreted as part of a larger common life—to a society vastly more interrelated and integrated economically, technically, and functionally. Yet this is a society in which the individual can only rarely and with difficulty understand himself and his activities as interrelated in morally meaningful ways with those of other, different Americans.[21]

Berger is convinced that the "new consciousness" counterculture of the 1960s and the neoevangelical movement of the 1970s and 1980s represent the two major groups of discontents resulting from this crisis. The counterculture has now faded, but its legacy has survived in the form of interest in Eastern mysticism, in various cults, and in the "therapies" of "personal growth" and "encounter" movements. Berger also points out that there is a class basis for these two reactive movements. While the modern therapy counterculture has continued to be a phenomenon among the more intellectual and professional classes, the lower classes, which traditionally were dominant in evangelical piety, not surprisingly have found the neoevangelical movement powerful and attractive.[22]

Sociologist Wade Clark Roof has proposed that the merging of "therapeutic" approaches with religious practice, through the sanctioned involvement of clergy and laity in them, has been a result of the ongoing crisis in the mainline church. Forces on the religious right have gone a different direction. Their critique is based on a call for a return to America's biblical roots and a turn away from purely "humanistic" solutions to human problems. Self-actualization, whether carried out within a mainline church or in a secular counseling center, would look to them like pure humanism, bereft of biblical rootedness.

Roof agrees with Berger that the "rising tide of religious conservatism" is deeply rooted in the social climate of crisis, and has resulted in impressive growth among the evangelicals and fundamentalists. These groups have adhered to a stance of "strictness," he says, and have stressed "absolutist beliefs, social and moral conformity, enthusiasm, and missionary spirit."[23]

Roof describes these developments as the "collapse of the middle." While mainline churches have lost members and social power in recent decades, movements on both flanks have flourished. On the left, the nontraditional, non-Christian, even secular movements of "spiritual therapy" have evolved. On the right, neoevangelical, fundamentalist, and charismatic movements and churches have grown rapidly.

The role of the media in revitalizing the religious right has been emphasized by many observers. Roof too points to conservative religious involvement in the media, and the evolution of the electronic church, as underlying the new social and political prominence of these movements. While he stops short of calling these media a new form of religion, he agrees that they have played an important role.[24]

What is the electronic church?[25]

Previous assessments of the electronic church have avoided ascribing sociological significance to the phenomenon in favor of more superficial analysis. The questions have revolved around two central issues, the size and significance of the audience and the programs' potential for political impact. Representatives of the electronic church ministries have claimed ever-increasing prominence and power for them. Critics of the electronic church in conventional churches have been concerned with whether these programs might be hurting local church attendance and income. Critics outside of religion have focused on the obvious political implications of the programs, and have wondered whether they might form the basis of a purely political movement. But for all interested parties, it has been essential to establish how central or marginal the audience is.[26]

Because we wish to look at this phenomenon in a social and cultural context, we are concerned with a different set of questions. First, what role do the media play in the movement? Have they really been central, or are they more peripheral? Second, what attracts viewers to the electronic church? Do the content and form of religious broadcasting reconstruct religious worldviews? That is, to what extent does it alter religious consciousness? How deep or profound is its role? Third, has the emphasis on mass media by the neoevangelical movement had a significant impact on religious belief and religious institutions in general? These programs may constitute a movement of their own within the broader one. They may have a lasting impact on broader evangelical traditions and institutions, on mainline religious institutions, and on American culture, politics, and society in general, as has been feared by many critics. The question of the nature and size of the audience is only fully meaningful when these more basic questions have been addressed.

Analyzing the electronic church as part of a religious revitalization movement

Religious phenomena lend themselves particularly well to a type of communication analysis James Carey has called "cultural." Mass media traditionally have been studied under the assumption of a "transportation" model, where the concern is with instrumental transmission of "messages." Carey points out that media are, instead, cultural systems, consumed in specific places and in specific ways, often inconsistent with the intentions of those who craft their content. What is needed, he maintains, is a "ritual" definition of media, which places their use in social and cultural context.[27]

The development of the electronic church makes such an analysis, an examination of social and cultural context, necessary. It is not enough to know that the audience of the electronic church is of a certain size. Are these viewers merely viewers, or are they caught up in the broader cultural and social changes we have discussed? What constitutes involvement in the electronic church? If we are concerned with *how* the audience is involved with these broadcasts, the fact that they "attend to" the program may not tell us very much. There is much more going on here than can be described in terms of communication *messages*.

We are concerned with communication media and their integration into culture. We are concerned with meaning. Carey quotes anthropologist Clifford Geertz:

> Believing with Max Weber that man is an animal suspended in webs of significance he himself has spun, I take culture to be those webs, and the analysis of it to be therefore not an experimental science in search of law, but an interpretive one in search of meaning.[28]

Investigating the meanings that underlie the electronic church has implications for both the questions we ask and the means by which we will address them.

The "cultural" approach to communication studies draws much from the anthropological tradition of ethnography, to which Geertz has been an important contributor. Ethnographic studies reveal webs of meaning through a thoroughgoing analytic process Geertz calls "thick description." Only analyses that place phenomena in their social and cultural contexts afford us a full understanding of them. In calling for a model of communication studies that focuses on ritual, Carey challenges us to recognize media in modern life as an integral part of the larger culture.

Geertz's approach to the study of religion describes his cultural method of analysis well:

> The anthropological study of religion is therefore a two-stage operation: first, an analysis of the system of meanings embodied in the symbols which make up the religion proper, and, second, the relating of these systems to social-structural and psychological processes.[29]

The obvious effects of media messages are not the central question, according to this view. Deeper questions of how media are embedded in the broader currents of individual and cultural change are. The questions surrounding "new consciousness" and "new movements" we have proposed dictate such an approach. We must look to historical, cultural, religious, and cognitive sources of these movements and ideas in order to understand them fully. Data of a less "cultural" sort, such as statistics on growth patterns, viewing behavior, church contribution patterns, political beliefs, and demographic characteristics of adherents to these new movements and to the electronic church are important to our understandings. They must, however, be lodged in these larger contexts before we can understand the process by which these movements in general, and religious television in particular, contribute to the construction of meaning by their followers.

The religious "new right" and the electronic church as movements of revitalization

The changing religious climate since the 1960s has had as its central dynamic the development of movements that are reactions to cultural changes. William McLoughlin has suggested that these movements may be evidence of an emerging "Fourth Great Awakening" in the American religious experience. He proposes that, as in the earlier awakenings, the stresses and strains of a cultural search for coherence and meaning are yielding to movements of revitalization.[30]

Anthropologists have observed, across human societies, that revitalization movements crop up when cultural patterns can no longer adjust to new circumstances—when new conditions arise for which traditional ways of thinking and acting are no longer appropriate. McLoughlin cites anthropologist Anthony Wallace:

> A great awakening occurs, Wallace says, when a society finds that its day-to-day behavior has deviated so far from the accepted (traditional) norms that neither individuals nor large groups can honestly (consistently) sustain the common set of religious understandings by which they believe (have been taught) they should act. When parents can no longer adequately guide their own lives or their children's, when schools and churches provide conflicting ethical guidelines for economic and political behavior, and when courts impose sanctions upon acts commonly recognized as necessary (or accepted) deviations from the old rules, then a period of profound cultural disorientation results.[31]

This describes the contemporary "crisis of modernity" rather well, as McLoughlin notes, and the movements that have resulted, particularly those on the right.

Following such periods of dislocation and "individual stress," according to McLoughlin, comes the gradual deterioration of traditional patterns of culture. They begin to lose their meaning and efficacy in new situations, and "a new culture must be written to suit the 'actual state of affairs.'"[32] This period of "cultural distortion" often yields movements of reaction and fundamentalism, points of view that see a return to tradition as the only solution. Such groups, according to McLoughlin, may prefer the stresses of cultural dissonance to the unknown, a transformed culture that deals with new realities.

Revitalization movements prosper when leaders arise who clearly articulate the cultural crisis. America's Protestant awakenings have not focused on individuals, according to McLoughlin, but have been movements instead with a number of spiritual leaders. He cites Peter Worsley's analysis of charisma to explain this process:

> "It is a legitimation grounded in a relationship of loyalty and identification in which the leader is followed simply because he embodies values in which the followers have an 'interest.' . . . The followers . . . in a dialectical way, create, by selecting them out, the leaders who in turn *command* on the basis of this newly accorded legitimacy. . . . He articulates and consolidates their aspirations."[33]

Such leaders can serve transformation *or* reaction. They can embody the needed revitalization or a reactionary fundamentalism tied to old shibboleths. A telling characteristic of the electronic church is that the programs revolve around one or more central figures, who become symbolic of the worldview represented by the program.[34]

Anthony Wallace emphasizes, in a way McLoughlin does not, the importance of communication to the revitalization process. An essential element is a new pattern of communication, based in the formation of "codes" that convey revitalized symbols of reform to others in hopes of converting them to the cause. The preaching of this code is an "evangelistic" activity, Wallace points out, one that develops new networks and new affinities. Some who are reached come to identify with the revitalization process in more depth than do others. Some become "disciples," committed to the evangelistic process. Some are merely followers. Thus networks of prophets, disciples, and followers develop.[35]

This type of communication creates appeals that cut across the particularist lines of the "old ways" to create new ones. Initially, the core adherents of these movements project their appeals to the larger society in hopes of obtaining converts to the cause. The intention is a global one. It is to transform society. Thus, as McLoughlin has shown, the Great Awakenings had political as well as cultural implications.

Revitalization moves beyond reaction only when these movements include adherents who are willing to experiment with new cultural forms. They may become ecstatically involved in their newfound consciousness. This process brings about a cultural change that links old symbols and values with new social conditions.

We will look for evidence of these forms of revitalization in the electronic church. These ministries may be serving such a "communication" function for broader processes of revitalization. They make some claim to be doing just that, as we will see. They may also be moving beyond fundamentalism and reaction to begin experimenting with new cultural forms.

Dimensions of transformation

Transformations of consciousness in movements seem to involve three distinct dimensions or contexts. They are, first of all, *personal* processes, which are dependent on individual powers of cognition, and on individual spiritual and personal experience. The countercultural movements of the 1960s and the conservative Christian movements of the 1980s have been animated by the desire of individuals to recapture lost identities in the face of larger social and cultural change.

One particularly useful approach to investigating how individuals develop such consciousness of religious meaning has been undertaken by James Fowler, who has conceived of this dimension in terms of its *cognitive* bases.[36] The development of religious consciousness or religious faith takes place alongside other individual developments and is dependent on an interaction between personal and contextual factors for its direction.

Fowler's work, as well as that of McLoughlin and Wallace, assumes that personal awareness most often occurs in a second context: *local communities of reference*. Robert Bellah and his associates see the basis for the crisis of modernity in the absence of communities of shared memory.[37] The counterculture and revitalization movements of the past have created communities for their disciples.

A nontraditionalist today may seek out an established sect, or find community in the therapeutic movement. A traditionalist or fundamentalist, on the other hand, may find community in a growing independent Baptist or community church. In each case, evolving consciousness takes place with reference to a community of faith and support, in what Bellah calls the "historical conversation" between culture and character.[38]

The community is the arbiter of culture for the individual in that it is the most accessible reference group through which he or she can understand his or her culture. An individual lives within more than one community of reference, of course, and a community consciousness can and often does develop with reference to any one or all of them.[39] The community context, for McLoughlin, can provide the content of authentic values, the prophetic witness that organizes the reform process, and the object of reform itself, in the case that community or movement values are found to be unable to provide meaning.

Finally, religious consciousness seems to recognize a more impersonal *social structure* or set of structures that provide the broad context or universe within which the individual or *personal*, and the group or *community*, dimensions relate to one another. In the age of the counterculture of the 1960s, the hypocrisy of conventional social mores or of establishment religion was obvious only when seen within this larger context. Mainline religion seemed to pander to status and power—values of the larger, secular setting—repudiating personal piety and communitarian values. The neoevangelical critique calls for a reaffirmation of traditional values in the face of secularization—a process of accommodation to "society" and "the world."[40] This profane world becomes the turf on which the struggle for a revitalized new society takes place.

Tracing the development of the role of the electronic church in consciousness and revitalization

The electronic church has complex roots and an involved history, in both social and cultural terms. In the coming chapters, we will evaluate this phenomenon in these contexts, looking for its meaning in its individual, cultural, social, and political sources.

In Chapter 2, we will review the historical origins of the fundamentalist and neoevangelical response to the crisis of modernity and the social and cultural sources of these movements. We also need to understand the roots of their orientation toward communication media. It is clear that conservative Christian movements have been particularly adept at using the media, but this proclivity has not been without its tensions.

In Chapter 3, we look at the history of religious broadcasting. We attempt to understand the development of the electronic church and its various forms in response to sociocultural change in America, within the larger neoevangelical and fundamentalist movements, and in the context of "conventional" broadcasting and the mass media.

In Chapter 4, we look at the specific history of the most prominent of these broadcasting organizations, the Christian Broadcasting Network, and its flagship program, the *700 Club*. This program represents, for many observers and viewers, the very core of the electronic church. Its history represents, in many ways, the development of the wider reality of new religious communication and its role in evolving religious consciousness.

Chapter 5 sets the stage for our interviews with viewers of the *700 Club*. If we are to bring together our interest in this phenomenon with an understanding of the meaning of the wider movements and developments it represents, we must do so with a systematic attention to detail. We lay out the schema whereby these analyses will take place in subsequent chapters. Interviews will present life histories of these viewers, and we will attempt to see within those histories the stages of interaction of major experiences of their lives, both social and spiritual.

In Chapters 6 through 8, we will hear from the viewers themselves. We will want to know about their beliefs, experiences, central symbols, and their worldviews. What factors have drawn them into this expression of religious consciousness? What have been the catalytic experiences of conversion that have brought them to their current stage of religious consciousness? What trajectories of development can we see in their lives? Most important, we want to know what role their involvement in broadcast religion has played in these other aspects of their lives.

In Chapter 9, we will consider the symbols and values that seem most important to these viewers. To understand fully the role of religious broadcasting in the neoevangelical and "new right" movements, including its potential political impact, we need to examine its role in shaping a new cultural context for its viewers. We will look at the various dimensions of interaction revealed by their faith histories, and will discuss the major symbols and values the *700 Club* conveys for them. The interviews and histories reveal a wide range of experiences. We will attempt systematically to analyze the commonalities and differences there, in order to draw some conclusions about the meaning of the program to its viewers on the individual, community, and societal levels of consciousness.

Chapter 10 looks at these developments in wider contexts. The electronic church has had specific effects on religious broadcasting as an activity. What have we learned about its effects on that previously marginal area of communication? The electronic church plays a central role in the current evangelical and fundamentalist revival. How has it affected that wider movement? The electronic church has had effects on religious groups outside the evangelical realm. It has changed the balance of power between the establishment and evangelical churches. What are the implications of these developments for the policies and communication plans of conventional denominations? To what extent does the existence of television in general, and religious television in particular, affect the way all religious organizations and movements must now see themselves? The electronic church gives us insights into the meaning of television in general. To what extent is all television—as a central ritual of meaning in contemporary life—"religious"? Finally, these effects of the electronic church in American religious culture also have implications for American culture in general. America is a religiously rooted culture. The movements of evangelicalism and fundamentalism have cultural change as their goal. How is the electronic church serving this purpose?

The story here is not only the story of personal religious development or the story of institutional relationships between conventional and electronic religious organizations. It is not only the story of political or social "effects" of these programs. It is the story of how the electronic church has become an evolving social and religious culture unto itself. We intend to map personal experience, institutional relationships and meanings, and media meanings and functions through the eyes, ears, and experiences of the viewers themselves.

Notes

1. Many accounts of these changes have described them in epochal terms. Particularly influential has been Daniel Bell's *The Coming of Post-Industrial Society* (New York: Basic Books, 1973).

2. Wade Clark Roof, "America's Voluntary Establishment: Mainline Religion in Transition," in *Religion and America*, ed. Mary Douglas and Steven Tipton (Boston: Beacon, 1982), p. 136.

3. See Charles Y. Glock and Robert N. Bellah, eds., *The New Religious Consciousness* (Berkeley: University of California Press, 1976) for a discussion of this period.

4. Dean M. Kelley, "Why Conservative Churches Are Still Growing," *Journal for the Scientific Study of Religion* 17, no. 2 (1978): 165-72.

5. Martin E. Marty, "Religion in America Since Mid-Century," in *Religion and America*, ed. Mary Douglas and Steven Tipton, p. 281.

6. For a complete discussion of this "two-party" dimension of American Protestantism, see Martin E. Marty, *Righteous Empire* (New York: Dial, 1970), pp. 177-87.

7. See discussion in Chapter 2 for the distinction between fundamentalism and evangelicalism.

8. William Newman and William D'Antonio, "'For Christ's Sake:' A Study of Key '73 in New England," *Review of Religious Research* 19, no. 2 (Winter 1978): 139-53.

9. Jim Wallis and Wes Michelson, "The Plan to Save America," *Sojourners* 5 (April 1976): 5-12.

10. For a concise description of these developments, see Peggy L. Shriver, *The Bible Vote* (New York: Pilgrim, 1981).

11. Todd Gitlin, *The Whole World Is Watching: Mass Media and the New Left, 1965-70* (Berkeley: University of California Press, 1980).

12. Herbert J. Gans, "Are U.S. Journalists Dangerously Liberal?" *Columbia Journalism Review* (November/December 1985): 29-33.

13. Glock and Bellah, eds., *The New Religious Consciousness*.

14. For a complete discussion of the salience of Eastern mysticism for those involved in the youth counterculture, see Glock and Bellah, eds., *The New Religious Consciousness*, in particular, pp. 1-72.

15. Émile Durkheim, *The Elementary Forms of the Religious Life* (New York: Free Press, 1965), pp. 402 ff.

16. Clifford Geertz, *The Interpretation of Cultures* (New York: Basic Books, 1973), p. 90.

17. See Raymond Williams, *The Long Revolution* (New York: Columbia University Press, 1961), *Communications* (London: Chatto & Windus, 1969), and *Culture* (Glasgow: Fontana Paperbacks, 1981). For an interpretation of Williams's approach, see Lawrence Grossberg, "Strategies in Marxist Cultural Interpretation," *Critical Studies in Mass Communication* 1 (1984): 392-421.

18. Walter Ong, *The Presence of the Word* (New Haven, CT: Yale University Press, 1967).

19. William G. McLoughlin, *Revivals, Awakenings, and Reform* (Chicago: University of Chicago Press, 1978).

20. Peter L. Berger, "From the Crisis of Religion to the Crisis of Secularity," in *Religion and America*, ed. Mary Douglas and Steven Tipton, p. 15.

21. Robert N. Bellah et al., *Habits of the Heart* (Berkeley: University of California Press, 1985), p. 50.

22. Berger, "From the Crisis of Religion," pp. 16-17. These "therapeutic movements" have received much attention in accounts of the modern era, and will be of some concern to us, as well. See discussions of the therapeutic realm in Christopher Lasch, *The Culture of Narcissism* (New York: Warner Books, 1979) and Bellah et al., *Habits of the Heart*.

23. Roof, "America's Voluntary Establishment," p. 134, is paraphrasing Kelley, *Why Conservative Churches Are Growing* (New York: Harper & Row, 1972).

24. Roof, "America's Voluntary Establishment," p. 133.

25. It should not be inferred that the use of this term here implies that the phenomenon of modern, syndicated religious broadcasting is, in fact, a "church" in any sense. A convenient label for the phenomenon has proven useful, and among the many that could have been chosen ("televangelism" or "the electric church," for instance) "electronic church" seems to have been the most widely used.

26. For a complete discussion of these issues, see Stewart M. Hoover, "The Religious Television Audience: A Matter of Significance, or Size?" *Review of Religious Research* 29, no. 2 (Winter 1987).

27. James W. Carey, "Communication and Culture," Review Essay of *The Interpretation of Cultures*, by Clifford Geertz, in *Communication Research* (April 1975): 173-91.

28. Carey, "Communication and Culture," p. 184.

29. Geertz, *Interpretation of Cultures*, p. 125.

30. McLoughlin, *Revivals, Awakenings, and Reform*, pp. 9 ff.

31. Ibid., p. 12.

32. Ibid., p. 14.

33. Ibid., p. 17.

34. The potential pitfalls of this tendency are obvious, but have been publicly affirmed by the periodic "crises of legitimacy" that have rocked some of these ministries from time to time, most notably the scandal that erupted around the *PTL Club* in 1987.

35. Anthony F.C. Wallace, *Culture and Personality*, 2d ed. (New York: Random House, 1970), pp. 192-96.

36. See James W. Fowler, *Becoming Adult, Becoming Christian* (San Francisco: Harper & Row, 1984), and *Stages of Faith* (San Francisco: Harper & Row, 1981).

37. Bellah et al., *Habits of the Heart*.

38. Ibid., pp. 27 ff.

39. Robert Redfield has considered this issue of the relationship between the various communities of reference within which the individual resides. He points out that it is both the consciousness of each of these, and the relationship between them, that shapes the individual's self-understanding, an issue to which we will return later. See Robert Redfield, *The Little Community* (Chicago: University of Chicago Press, 1956).

40. For a discussion of the worldview of the movement surrounding its social witness, see George M. Marsden, "Preachers of Paradox: The Religious New Right in Historical Perspective," in *Religion and America*, ed. Mary Douglas and Steven Tipton, pp. 150-68.

2

Popular Communication in American Protestant Revitalization Movements

In the early 1800s, Alexis de Tocqueville observed that the young nation of the United States had developed into a strongly and self-consciously religious one.[1] The religiosity of the colonial era had spawned a variety of Protestant sects, which collectively constituted the religious culture of the new country. This culture accepted a certain amount of religious diversity, but was committed to the idea that expressions of piety were essential to the common life and to the extension of Western civilization.

Debates about the essentially Christian character of the founding fathers notwithstanding, it is clear that conscious religiosity was the rule, rather than the exception, in the cities, towns, and villages of eighteenth-century America. Because of the relative religious diversity that accompanied colonial settlement (which, indeed, was the reason for it in some cases), a rather diffuse Protestantism came to be the cultural religion of the new nation, a Protestantism steeped in the sociocultural context of its adherents' northern European and British roots.[2]

Max Weber noted that the development of religious institutions reflects their sociocultural context. Class ideology and conflict, economic and demographic changes, and political upheavals all contribute to changes in religious institutions, both formal and informal.[3] In the case of American Protestantism, change has been the rule, reflecting the massive shifts in the character of society that have accompanied national development over the past two centuries.

One of the most dramatic religious changes coincided with expansion westward during the mid-nineteenth century. Now called the "Second Great Awakening," this period was marked by the rapid development of a unique American contribution to religious piety and polity: evangelicalism. While there is some disagreement among scholars about the causes of this religious evolution,[4] it is generally agreed that, during the postcolonial period, established churches underwent great change. Because of the massive migration to the western frontier in that period, the churches' traditional hold on the social and moral climate of the nation was weakened. New communities and cultures developed rapidly in the West, communities that were largely bereft of the "moral culture" of established and "establishment" religion.[5] The social conditions that underlay this change included both the large percentage of emigrants in the West from the lower classes in the eastern cities, and the presence among them of large numbers of recent immigrants.

The response of establishment churches in the East to these developments on the frontier was twofold. First, the tradition of Wesleyan revival in Britain armed them with a model of theology that stressed personal, as opposed to institutional, salvation. A personalized religious consciousness, which was "self-contained," better fit the physical limitations of life on the frontier, where formal religious institutions were scarce. It also formed a powerful synthesis with the dominant frontier ideal of individualism. Second, British experience with Wesleyan and other evangelical revivals indicated that *denominationalism* for its own sake was not only not relevant, but could be an absolute hindrance, to the spreading of the gospel.[6]

New England cleric Lyman Beecher was instrumental in the development of nondenominational approaches. Cooperative interdenominational societies (called "voluntary societies") developed, including Sunday school societies, Bible societies, and societies devoted to social progress of many kinds.[7]

While much more could be said about the theological claims of evangelicalism, one major characteristic is important to our task here. In contrast to the structured orthodoxy of establishment churches and the Roman Catholic church, evangelicalism has stressed a theology of the word. Whereas orthodox theology has tended to stress liturgy and various sacraments as significant, particularly as they are rooted in the local community of the church, evangelicalism sees its theological roots in the power of "the word" itself. Preaching, "witnessing," and otherwise sharing the "good news" is the major objective. Ecclesiastical and institutional structures are less important.

Such a theology seems to be particularly prone to take up new means of communication. Religious media scholar Quentin Schultze has observed that the impulse of evangelicalism toward communication technology is based both on theology that stresses proclamation and on a cosmology in which new technology holds a special place, as God-given tools intended to extend the reach of "the word."[8] Evangelicalism in the eras of the Great Awakenings was concerned with forms of communication more than with communication technology, however.

One such form, the cultural phenomenon known as the "revival" (while not new) evolved new significance in this period. Itinerant ministers, many (but not all) of whom were more or less self-appointed, traveled the back roads and byways of the growing frontier, spreading this individualistic piety. Arriving in each new place, they would set up a series of preaching services devoted to eliciting individual professions of faith and salvation.

The establishment of churches in these communities was a goal, but perhaps secondary to the goal of bringing about personal transformations. Revivalism further contributed a form, almost a syntax, to this expressive evangelicalism. These meetings were, in a sense, the popular communication of their time, steeped in the ideals of the frontier.[9] Their relationship to popular media such as the penny press has also been noted by historians. Even before the turn of the century, evangelicalism seemed to be open to using the media of the secular world to meet sacred ends.[10]

This period of ferment had major effects on the religious climate for American Protestantism. The faiths of the frontier, especially the Methodists and Baptists, grew quickly and displaced the formerly dominant denominations of the colonial period in numerical and intellectual prominence.[11] There was great ferment *within* these and other denominations as well, resulting in reformation in some of the most austere and insular establishment groups.[12]

The major legacies of the period before World War I have been a continued ideological commitment, even within the denominations of the establishment classes, to evangelical witnessing and interdenominational cooperation; the development of major denominations out of this period of ferment (most of which later achieved "establishment" status on their own); and a uniquely American commitment to the role of the *individual* in religion, often at the expense of the established religious community and structure. Evangelicalism, as an institution, emerged from this era with independent ministers and congregations, various cooperative "voluntary societies," and many publishing and other organizations continuing in a loose, nondenominational fashion to carry forward the ideals of the earlier movement.[13]

The rise of fundamentalism

The Second Great Awakening of the mid-nineteenth century came in a context of social and cultural stress and change brought about by frontier migration and related events. It carried with it an accommodation to those events, a realignment, not a rejection of the "modernity" of that era. Among its legacies, however, was an individualistic and noninstitutional religious culture that was well fitted to a period of rejectionism that followed.

The Protestant establishment (including the newer establishment—Baptists, Methodists, and other groups that formed during the Great Awakening) emerged from the nineteenth century with more commitment to evangelistic action than to theological contemplation. The frontier largely had been tamed by the turn of the century, but that experience left its mark on Protestant churches. The revivalism of the Great Awakening, for instance, had infused many of the new churches and their converts with a commitment to a religion of "the heart" at the expense of a synthesis in "the head." Thus when even greater periods of change and dislocation occurred early in the twentieth century, Protestantism was not in any sense a unified polity or theology. The unity of Protestantism in the 1800s—the evangelical impulse—was to become its diversity in the decades that followed.

Just as the migration west created the context for the emergence of evangelistic piety, further social and cultural change set the stage for evolution after 1900. After the turn of the century, Protestantism clearly was no longer the *only* American religion. Widespread immigration from Europe (and later Asia) introduced new and important competitors to established Protestantism, most notably Catholicism. The complacency that typified the "Protestant era" in America before 1900 became unsettled by the gradual realization that a pluralistic society was forming.[14]

An industrial society also emerged, bringing with it social and cultural dislocations and realignments. Dominant Protestant thought accounted for industrial and scientific culture by developing a "new theology" of "progressive revelation." Even such prima facie challenges to naive Protestant faith as the theory of evolution and other scientific advances were interpreted by some prominent theologians as part of a growing (progressive) understanding of a still God-centered universe.[15] This theological ferment was a challenge to the powerful tenets of the earlier evangelical revival. Evangelicalism was "Bible-centered," and had a theology of the word. The authority of the Bible was the pillar of Protestant piety in the Great Awakening. "Christian Modernism" of the early twentieth century, in its movement toward accounting for an emerging dynamic and pluralistic culture and society, was seen as undermining biblical authority.[16]

A new "awakening"—*fundamentalism*—was the direct reaction to these tendencies. Growing out of a more moderate movement to reaffirm biblical authority within a modern context, the term itself was soon captured by forces of premillennialist activism forged at postrevivalist era "'Prophetic' Bible conferences" in the late 1800s.[17]

Scholar Winthrop Hudson suggests that this infusion of rejectionist ideology into fundamentalism reduced the controversy with modernism to a few basic tenets. Fundamentalism held as absolutes against the encroachment of modernist revisionism the Genesis account of creation, the Virgin birth, Jesus' substitutionary atonement, Jesus' physical resurrection, and Jesus' imminent bodily return to earth. The so-called social gospel of the modernists was a direct challenge to these "fundamental" beliefs.[18]

More important than the exact nature and logic of its theology was the fact that fundamentalism became a broader critique of modernist, secular society in general. Hudson notes:

> Fundamentalism can probably be best understood as a phase of the rural-urban conflict [of that era], representing the tendency of many who were swept into a strange new urban environment to cling to the securities of their childhood in rural America. In this sense, Fundamentalism was much more cultural than religious in its orientation, and frequently exhibited, as H. Richard Niebuhr has observed, "a greater concern for conserving the cosmological and biological notions of older cultures than for the Lordship of Jesus Christ."[19]

Niebuhr and others have observed the tendency for fundamentalism, from the very first, to subscribe to the most conservative and nativist social and political views. Whether this can be traced to its sociocultural origins in what the Bergers[20] have called "demodernist" discomfort with secular culture, or to its lack of a well-articulated theology of culture to complement its clearly stated biblical tenets, fundamentalism has always been a piety with a strong sociocultural flavor. It promotes a social philosophy rooted in demodernism. Billy Sunday, its most prominent leader, is said to have equated salvation with "manliness, decency, and patriotism."[21]

George Marsden sees the roots of fundamentalist political beliefs in the cultural crisis following World War I. The political developments in prewar Germany could be traced to an intellectual and philosophical base of rationalism and humanism. American fundamentalists looked with great apprehension for signs of a similar undermining of traditional Christian values at home once the war was over.

> Preachers made the most of such analogies after the war when the nation seemed threatened by labor unrest, a "Red menace," and revolutionary outbreaks of public displays of sexuality in new dances, movies, tabloid newspapers, and advertising. Worse still, some Protestant denominations were embracing these modern trends.[22]

The frontier experience accounts for much of this cultural conservatism. The frontier revival era engendered concern about outward expressions of piety—specifically, life-style proscriptions in dress, and against gambling, smoking, drinking and "entertainments." The nondenominationalism of the frontier period and the threat posed by formal denominations teetering toward secularism led fundamentalists to see mainstream churches as needing reform—as part of the problem, not part of the solution.

The crucible of the revival tent left the fundamentalist movement with an expressive, outwardly emotional faith. But tensions inherent in Wesleyan and later evangelical theology led to controversies, the most prominent being whether it is necessary for a "second Baptism," or conversion, also to entail "gifts of the spirit" such as speaking in tongues, or the gift of physical healing.[23] (This "Holiness" tension also has cropped up in the recent evangelical-fundamentalist revival that emerged in the 1970s as "charismatic" or "Holy Spirit" groups in Protestant and Catholic congregations.)

The fundamentalist movement fell on hard times following its popular repudiation during the Scopes "Monkey" Trial of 1925. Its anti-intellectualism and rural culture lost favor in a rapidly industrializing society. Its problems were partly, then, problems of communication. It had lost its ability to command public attention. Marsden shows that fundamentalism did not fade away, but rather regrouped its forces by consolidating as independent congregations when fundamentalists left denominational churches they considered "unscriptural." As a result, there was a renewed emphasis on the nondenominational "voluntary association" movement of the nineteenth century. Fundamentalist groups built networks of communication and solidarity through cooperative "transdenominational agencies," such as book, tract, and periodical publishers, and Christian schools.[24]

In the 1930s, the fundamentalist movement reemerged. Not only were fundamentalist churches and denominations growing, but their leaders were attracting national attention through their adept use of the "modern technology of the radio."[25] Joel Carpenter has said that this fundamentalist use of mass media was an example of a good match between medium and message.

> Fundamentalists were well-suited for the medium. Both their evangelistic messages and their gospel music were designed for mass appeal, and they presented themselves as promoters of a widely shared American tradition. Radio reached into homes, automobiles, and even bars and pool halls; and it bypassed denominational barriers. Persons who lacked the time, "church clothes," or disposition to attend religious services could easily tune in.[26]

The reemergence of fundamentalism was linked to use of the mass media, both publishing and broadcasting. The leading fundamentalist figure of the time, Charles Fuller, came to national prominence with a popular radio program called *The Old-Fashioned Revival Hour*.[27] Just as the evangelists of the earlier "awakenings" had used the popular media of their time (public rallies, tracts, newsletters, and so on), fundamentalist leaders came to see broadcasting, during this period, as a natural forum for their witness (a matter to which we shall return in the next chapter). All was not rosy with the movement, however, as fundamentalism itself split over theological and social questions. The basic issues were how militant the movement should be in demanding strict separation from establishment churches, and how strident fundamentalist social advocacy should be.[28]

Neoevangelicalism emerges

Gerald Sheppard has described the subsequent rise of a fundamentalist revitalization movement—"neoevangelicalism"—which was intended to overcome some of the particularism of its fundamentalist roots. As in the earlier eras, communication tools and techniques were integral to these plans.

> In the 1940s, a respectable evangelicalism emerged around the creation of such groups as the National Association of Evangelicals, seminaries like Fuller [Theological Seminary], the success of the Billy Graham Crusades, and magazines like *Christianity Today*. Such groups represent a moderate evangelicalism which wants to overcome the social naivete and rigidity of the earlier fundamentalists.[29]

Evangelical use of media was central in these moves. Theologically, there were grounds for involvement with powerful, modern tools of communication. Culturally, the nondenominational tradition of the crusade or revival found new use.

This "respectable evangelicalism," an establishment-oriented, moderate form, laid the groundwork for the later public, political ascendancy of the "new right." Distinct from a still-vibrant fundamentalist movement and a reemergence of the charismatic movement (the successor to the "Holiness" movement of earlier times), these "new evangelicals" were able to claim a broad middle ground. Marsden holds that Billy Graham personified the aspirations of this new evangelicalism.

> Behind Graham was a group of leaders with fundamentalist backgrounds attempting to forge a new post-fundamentalist coalition of America's evangelicals.[30]

This put neoevangelicalism, as the moderate wing of the Religious Right, in a position to challenge the mainline denominations' preeminence in America. This was done by stripping away some of the more stringent elements of the earlier movement to "universalize" its appeal and develop a more coherent critique of modernism.[31]

The "cultural crisis" of the 1960s proved to be a boon to neoevangelicalism. Many of the complaints of the counterculture—against centralized authority and the empty rituals of establishment culture—were appropriated by the movement, according to Marsden. But there were also benefits in maintaining a stern reaction against the specter of secularism and permissiveness. In the post-Vietnam era of anomie—the "crisis of confidence" spoken of by President Jimmy Carter—neoevangelicalism could reach to its roots and pull up decisive answers, answers that would play well in political, as well as religious, discourse.[32]

Political analyst Alan Crawford and others have observed that this new evangelicalism came to have a peculiarly populist political flavor. Stressing the interests of small business, small farmers, the "common, working" people, neoevangelicalism was consistent with, and an important part of, the overall political shift to the right of the 1980s.[33]

Like fundamentalism in its heyday, neoevangelicalism brings a social, as well as a theological, agenda to bear in contemporary culture. Marsden points out that, in the past, revivalism often took on "moral crusades," but that the traditional stance of fundamentalism has been one of separatism from social and political issues beyond those we might call "moral," such as pornography. The tension between a stance of separatism and one of social reform continues and has created a gulf between strict fundamentalist and the neoevangelical interests.[34]

Wade Clark Roof's "collapse of the middle" concept is based on this history. Formerly dominant religions—the mainline Protestant denominations and the Roman Catholic church—find themselves increasingly challenged by these developments on "the right." Neoevangelicalism, a movement aimed at bringing about broad religious and social reforms, is more palatable than the fundamentalist critiques of the past.[35] There is a nascent fundamentalist right wing of this movement, but the force of the centrist neoevangelism has been felt by social and religious institutions alike in the past decade. A range of political "social issues" have been articulated by evangelical churches and organizations and, on the religious front, the liberal denominations have borne the brunt of the continuing conservative critique.

The neoevangelical movement within churches: The "two parties"

The twentieth century has seen an uneasy coexistence between establishment denominations—which continue to be repositories of "modernist" tendencies in theology—and evangelical and fundamentalist denominations, churches, and interests. Mainline Protestant denominations are accused by their evangelical and fundamentalist counterparts of evolving from earlier evangelism to a complacent establishment status typified by accommodation to the secularism and pluralism of the modern era. The growth, beginning in the 1940s, of the "Ecumenical Movement" among mainline churches has come to symbolize this for the conservative movements. Ecumenical bodies like the National and World Councils of Churches are particular objects of their scorn.[36]

Still, evangelical and fundamentalist interests exist within these same mainline denominations. Called the "two-party system of American Protestantism" by Martin Marty,[37] this phenomenon has been described by empirical studies[38] as having two foci. Both *within* and *between* denominations, there exists a clear disagreement on theological and social issues. Earlier disagreements about biblical and ecclesial authority have been joined by controversies over abortion, capital punishment, materialism, and national defense. This "two-party" controversy is one of clashing symbolic *and* political worldviews.

Louise Bourgault has described what she calls the "symbolic worlds" of contemporary modernist and conservative Protestantism.

> The symbolic world of mainline Protestantism, with its quiet, intellectually toned, ritualized and regularized worship services, its dependence on family-based church participation, its economic and social participation in secular culture, its embrace of scientific theory, its intellectual and analytical approaches to biblical teachings. . . . This cast is what the fundamentalists disparagingly refer to as "the denominational churches with their 'Sunday religion.'"

On the other "side,"

> The symbolic world of fundamentalist religion, with its emotional style, its conversion experiences, its literal interpretation of the Bible, its rejection of the prevailing culture with its scientific approaches to human creation, its ascetic intolerance of the larger secular society, its poor and "old fashioned" looking members—all of these form a symbolic cast.[39]

Weber introduced a class basis for differentiating between movements, characterizing religions of the "dispossessed," such as fundamentalism, as religions of "magic." To use Weber's formulations, the "lower" and "working" classes, who can be said to have been drawn to fundamentalism's "other-worldly asceticism," contrast with bourgeois modernism's "practical rationalism in the conduct of life . . . and inner-worldly asceticism."[40] Modernism has been the trend in urban, Protestant churches, including the Protestant Episcopal, Unitarian Universalist, and Christian Congregational denominations. Fundamentalism, on the other hand, traditionally found its expression in independent, rural, and frontier faiths, such as the Methodist, Disciples of Christ, and Baptist movements. Today, the latter groups have evolved into formal denominations and are among the largest of the mainline groups. Even the Southern Baptist Convention, long a conservative and fundamentalist stronghold, has become "establishment" in the South and Southwest.

There have been major points of differentiation between these "two parties" (fundamentalist and evangelical impulses on the one hand, and mainline or modernist groups on the other) in the personal, community, and social contexts we introduced in Chapter 1. Evangelicalism and fundamentalism have evolved as highly personalistic expressions. The individual and his or her faith is the central focus of polity and piety. The rise of fundamentalism derived its power from the challenge such piety can make to established church structure. The current evangelical revival has similar implications for established religious institutions.

Evangelicalism and fundamentalism are further typified by the type of *community* they have become. Fundamentalist rejection of denominationalism and of institutionalized religion led to the adoption of a diffuse and informal nonecclesial structure, based on the "voluntary society" movement and the later development of publishing and mass media networks. Throughout the country, the expression of evangelical and fundamentalist faith has created communities in diaspora. Each community structures and reinforces the piety of its members. Among them, a consistency of belief and behavior has resulted in a de facto evangelical or fundamentalist "nondenominational denominationism."

Their relationship to society prompted both the creation of these religious cultures and their recent ascendancy in religion, politics, and society. Just as turn-of-the-century adherents to "the fundamentals" established their identity through a radical critique of modernism's accommodation to society,[41] the sociopolitical agenda of the neoevangelical revolution has linked established mainline religion with the "secular humanism" of the broader society.[42]

The neoevangelical movement and popular religious communication

Evangelical and fundamentalist use of mass media is not new to the electronic age. Harry Stout and Nathan Hatch have described the rise of the religious press in the eighteenth and nineteenth centuries in ways strikingly similar to the most common accounts of the power of the electronic church.[43] It is also possible, even necessary, to see preaching and popular revival as mass communicational phenomena in colonial and frontier America. In his history of the colonial pulpit, Stout cites the case of George Whitefield, who preached to massive audiences throughout New England, achieving a public and secular as well as "sectarian" influence.[44]

Hatch and Stout see the mass communication enterprise as having affected the content of popular religion. Aimed at the broad public, tracts, newspapers, and books adapted to common vernacular, away from formal theological discourse.

> In such an audience-centered culture, much of American Christianity ordered its system of values around the issue of communication. . . . Popular reception itself could serve as a divine imprimatur. Radically dependent upon popular support,

evangelical editors and authors also came to wed commercial and religious instincts.[45]

The use of popular communication media by conservative Christians derives from the unique characteristics of these movements and has had clear consequences beyond its effect on content.

As we have seen, evangelicalism and fundamentalism developed as interdenominational and interchurch phenomena. Beginning with the voluntary associations of the Second Great Awakening, continuing with the transdenominationalism of the fundamentalist awakening of the 1930s, and appearing today in "parachurch" agencies such as schools and publishing houses, they have not been institutional in the same way conventional churches have. They have rejected institutional structures of denominations in favor of independent congregations and independent-minded groupings of congregations. They developed a freewheeling, independent character, supported by loose networks of associations and agencies, many of them involving communication activities.

The revivals of the Great Awakenings were, first and foremost, popular events, intentionally steered to the nomenclature and concerns of their audiences. Salvation, in these revivals, came about as the result of a communicational experience that was made relevant to the cultural concerns of adherents. These revivals were the popular media of their time for many, providing an entertaining diversion in local settings.

The use of this form of communication was tied to the theology behind these movements. These were religions of the "heart," not the "head," and the emotionalism of the popular revival was seen as an authentic way of coming to new consciousness through salvation. This had broader implications. If what mattered was personal salvation, then formal church structure was irrelevant, or even a hindrance. The popularity of the movements was based in part on their ability to cut across traditional institutional lines.

The popular communication of these ideas depended on the influence of powerful, charismatic personalities. George Whitefield, Lyman Beecher, Dwight Moody, Billy Sunday, Charles Fuller, and Billy Graham are part of a long tradition of leaders who came to embody the aspirations of the religious reform movements. A kind of "star system" has always been at the heart of evangelical and fundamentalist outreach. Each epoch of its development is marked by the contribution of a specific figure. These preachers, and the lesser lights of the era, also had to develop management skills to match their preaching skills. Nonchurch organizations needed to develop independent structures, and independent sources of financial support, and the revivalist era saw much progress in the development of *direct* financial support.

There also is a marked tendency for these movements to appeal to nativist American values. Simplicity in theology and in social critique always has been a basic tenet of fundamentalism as it appeals to those who are troubled by the intellectualism of modernity. Popular communication styles and approaches have always favored such simplicity. As Marsden puts it with regard to the development of new communication activities in the past decade,

> If there is a rule of mass communications that the larger the audience the simpler the message must be, fundamentalists and similar evangelicals came to the technological age well prepared. . . . For better or worse, fundamentalism is a version of Christianity matched to its age.[46]

The particular simplicity of fundamentalism and neoevangelicalism looks to visions of "old-time" America, to the values of a dimly remembered past. The social and political agenda of these movements is based on a desire to return society to these beliefs.

Neoevangelicalism and fundamentalism thus contain many of the elements McLoughlin suggests are basic to revitalization movements in general. There is a basic critique of society, a sense that a new cultural structure must be written to integrate belief and practice in the crisis of modernity. Leaders and submovements have emerged that have begun to articulate a new "code": a new set of social and theological symbols and values. There is a nativist or reactionary tendency in some of the rhetoric that might serve to set back the movement. The leaders who have emerged have been "charismatic" in the way McLoughlin uses the term—they have embodied the aspirations of their movements, symbolizing those aspirations themselves.

In the following chapter, we will see how these conditions have supported the development of a new type of popular religious communication, religious broadcasting. The "television preachers" of today have much in common with the revivalists and movements of the past. Their power and prominence derives from a history of controversy and realignment in American Protestantism. They are playing a part in writing a new chapter in that history. Just how important a part they are playing is the central question here.

Notes

1. Alexis de Tocqueville, *Democracy in America*, trans. Henry Reeve, rev. ed. (New York: Colonial, 1900).

2. For a complete discussion, see George M. Marsden, "Preachers of Paradox: The Religious New Right in Historical Perspective," in *Religion and America*, ed. Mary Douglas and Steven Tipton (Boston: Beacon, 1983), pp. 150-68.

3. Max Weber, *The Sociology of Religion* (Boston: Beacon Press Paperback, 1964).

4. For a discussion of this period, see Linda K. Pritchard, "Religious Change in Nineteenth-Century America," in *The New Religious Consciousness*, ed. Charles Glock and Robert Bellah (Berkeley: University of California Press, 1976), pp. 297-330.

5. A citation from Winthrop S. Hudson, *American Protestantism* (Chicago: University of Chicago Press, 1961), p. 85, is illustrative. The rapid development of the Mississippi-Ohio Valley was a source of great anxiety in the religious leadership of the established Northeast. "The initial alarm was raised by Samuel J. Mills when he reported, following his return from a tour of inspection in 1815, that some of the valley's inhabitants had never seen a Bible or heard of Jesus Christ."

6. For concise descriptions of these developments, see Hudson, *American Protestantism*, and H. Richard Niebuhr, *The Social Sources of Denominationalism* (New York: New American Library, 1975).

7. Hudson, *American Protestantism*, pp. 82-83.

8. Quentin J. Schultze, "The Mythos of the Electronic Church," *Critical Studies in Mass Communication* 4, no. 3 (September 1987): 245-61.

9. For an excellent recent discussion of the history of preaching and revivals as popular communication and popular culture, see Harry S. Stout, *The New England Soul: Preaching and Religious Culture in Colonial New England* (New York: Oxford University Press, 1986).

10. See, in particular, William McLoughlin, *Revivals, Awakenings, and Reform* (Chicago: University of Chicago Press, 1978); and Marsden, "Preachers of Paradox," p. 153.

11. Pritchard, "Religious Change," p. 326.

12. Hudson, *American Protestantism*, pp. 96 ff.

13. George M. Marsden, *Fundamentalism and American Culture* (New York: Oxford University Press, 1980), pp. 11-39.

14. Hudson, *American Protestantism*, pp. 128 ff.

15. Ibid., pp. 143 ff. See also William McLoughlin, "Is There a Third Force in Christendom?" in *Religion in America*, ed. William McLoughlin and Robert Bellah (Boston: Beacon, 1966), pp. 54 ff.

16. Marsden, "Preachers of Paradox," p. 151.

17. Hudson, *American Protestantism*, p. 147.

18. Ibid., pp. 143 ff.

19. Ibid., p. 148.

20. Peter L. Berger, Brigitte Berger, and Hansfried Kellner, *The Homeless Mind* (New York: Random House, 1973).

21. Hudson, *American Protestantism*, p. 148.

22. Marsden, "Preachers of Paradox," p. 152.

23. Hudson, *American Protestantism*, p. 160.

24. Marsden, "Preachers of Paradox," p. 153.

25. Ibid., p. 153.

26. Joel A. Carpenter, "Tuning in the Gospel: Fundamentalist Radio Broadcasting and the Revival of Mass Evangelism, 1930-1945" (Paper delivered to the Mid-America American Studies Association, University of Illinois, Urbana, April 1985), p. 5.

27. Marsden, "Preachers of Paradox," p. 153.

28. Ibid., p. 154.

29. Gerald Sheppard, published remarks to a symposium, *Reform Judaism* 9, no. 4 (March 1981), quoted in Peggy L. Shriver, *The Bible Vote* (New York: Pilgrim, 1981), p. 36.

30. Marsden, "Preachers of Paradox," p. 155.

31. Ibid., p. 158.

32. Ibid., pp. 156-57.

33. Alan Crawford, *Thunder on the Right* (New York: Pantheon, 1980), p. 256. See also Shriver, *The Bible Vote*, pp. 37-41.

34. Marsden, "Preachers of Paradox," p. 158.

35. For a theological discussion of this development, see Richard Quebedeaux, *The Worldly Evangelicals* (San Francisco: Harper & Row, 1978).

36. Hudson, *American Protestantism*, p. 164.

37. Martin E. Marty, *Righteous Empire* (New York: Dial, 1970), pp. 177 ff.

38. Most notably, see Dean R. Hoge, Everett L. Perry, and Gerald L. Klever, "Theology as a Source of Disagreement About Protestant Church Goals and Priorities," *Review of Religious Research* 19, no. 2 (Winter 1978): 116-38; and Dean L. Hoge and David A. Roozen, *Understanding Church Growth and Decline, 1950-78* (New York: Pilgrim, 1979).

39. Louise M. Bourgault, "An Ethnographic Study of the 'Praise the Lord Club'" (unpublished Ph.D. dissertation, Ohio University, 1980), pp. 38-39.

40. Weber, *The Sociology of Religion*.

41. Marsden, "Preachers of Paradox," p. 152.

42. Shriver, *The Bible Vote*, pp. 47-51.

43. Harry S. Stout and Nathan O. Hatch, "The Religious Press in Early America" (Paper delivered to the Craigville Consultation on Evangelicals and Communications, Craigville, MA, July 1986).

44. Stout, *The New England Soul*.

45. Stout and Hatch, "The Religious Press," p. 24.

46. Marsden, "Preachers of Paradox," p. 164.

3

Religious Broadcasting:
A Spark in the
Neoevangelical Revival

Evangelical and fundamentalist organizations were among the first to see the power of broadcasting as a proselytizing tool. But those who moved into broadcasting were by no means new to communications. Most had long been associated with Bible schools, religious publications, and revival ministries.[1]

There is a tendency to see fundamentalist and evangelical broadcasting as something new and as somehow responsible for the current neoevangelical revival. This idea deserves scrutiny. As historian Joel Carpenter observes,

> The evangelical coalition's mastery of mass communications, claims one observer, has been the matrix of its survival and success. I don't see it exactly that way. Rather, in an age of sight and sound, evangelicals have used the reality-establishing force of mass communications to convince themselves—and many others, apparently—that they are a real presence in American public life. They have transmitted their images into the "show windows of modern publicity."[2]

Evangelical and fundamentalist broadcasters have been widely heard, seen, and felt throughout the history of American broadcasting. The "received history" of modern broadcasting views religious uses in a rather truncated way, however. It is widely believed that religious conservatives—devoted to simplistic theology, on-air fund-raising, and saving souls at all costs—have overtaken mainline and establishment churches in the battle for the airwaves. The broadcasts of these latter groups, devoted to a modernist "social gospel" (or so this reasoning goes), are thought to be increasingly marginal in their appeal and influence.[3] History, however, reveals a more complex set of interacting religious, social, and policy relationships.

Early religious broadcasting

Carpenter has observed that a general malaise overtook fundamentalism in the 1930s. The great period of mass evangelism, typified by the work of Billy Sunday, had ended with the movement in disarray even before his death in 1935. In many ways, the discovery of radio was the spark that revitalized the movement. Early moves by churches and individual evangelists to build radio stations and begin programs were not without controversy, however. Carpenter reports that one Bible institute, for instance, built a radio station in 1923 only after it overcame the fears of its leaders that radio used airwaves that were the "realm of Satan, whom the Bible called 'the prince of the power of the air.'"[4]

Radio and fundamentalism were a good match for each other. The messages of fundamentalists were simple, straightforward, and represented a broadly conceived amalgam of conservative, nativist American cultural values. Radio gave these evangelists a reach they had never had before— into thousands of American homes. Just as Billy Sunday was the symbol of the prebroadcast era of fundamentalism, so Charles Fuller came to represent fundamentalism on the new medium. Originating in Los Angeles in 1930, Fuller's ministry grew, in just seven years, from a local broadcast to a national program, networked coast to coast.[5]

Others followed his lead, and most of them quickly learned that such broadcasts could be paid for by funds solicited over the air and from constituents who wished to support this new "ministry." Fuller, for instance, used a mailing list of listeners and other contributors to solicit additional support regularly with a newsletter. By paying for air time, radio ministers rapidly expanded their reach and increased their scheduling flexibility. According to Carpenter, Fuller achieved his greatest growth after 1937, when he began buying air time on the Mutual Broadcasting Network (the only national network that then would sell time for religious broadcasts).[6]

Many early radio ministers quickly learned another lesson that would serve them well in the era of televangelism. Religious broadcasting works particularly well when it is accompanied by nonbroadcast, direct-contact activities. Fuller, for example, held rallies in cities where his program was heard and gradually grew to national prominence as a religious spokesperson.[7]

The form and content of these early broadcasts was largely preaching and worship of the kind that had evolved on the revival circuit. The fact that they were on a new, national medium dictated some modification of that form, however. Carpenter reports that when Fuller founded his radio program, he sought out and hired the best musical talent he could find, even luring one group away from a rival religious broadcaster.[8]

Several dimensions of contemporary electronic church broadcasting thus stem from this early period of experimentation: The centrality of a figure such as Fuller, the tendency to lodge broadcasting within broader parachurch activities of a ministry, the importance of direct fund-raising, the importance of being able to purchase air time, and a concern with the form and sophistication of programs *as radio programs*.

The "establishment era" of religious broadcasting

This initial period of activity by evangelical and fundamentalist radio stations and widespread syndication of programs gave way to another form of religious programming after the passage of the Communications Act of 1934. So-called sustaining-time programs were either produced by religious groups themselves, or produced cooperatively by religious organizations and broadcasters and carried as "public affairs" in partial satisfaction of FCC mandates requiring nonentertainment (and, more important, *noncommercial*) programming. These programs ranged from locally broadcast church services to nationally distributed religious programs available from the radio networks and broadcast by local affiliates.

Early regulation of broadcasting encouraged this "sustaining-time" (as opposed to "paid-time") religion. In the period between the creation of the Federal Radio Commission in 1927 and the revision of broadcasting legislation in 1934, a movement arose that sought to set aside a certain portion of the broadcast spectrum for nonprofit, educational, and religious uses. But this effectively would have voided the licenses of some successful commercial stations that were already on the air in order to make enough space available in every city. This movement collapsed with the ill-fated Wagner-Hatfield Amendment, which failed in Congress by a close vote. A congressional compromise allowed the new Federal Communications Commission to forgo regulations allocating certain frequencies to noncommercial users, if its investigations showed that such allocations were not needed. Established broadcasters naturally went on their best behavior to the commission, promising that their service in the public interest would be exemplary without regulation, and that noncommercial uses would be given free air time.[9]

The need for some rational management of access to sustaining time at the national level produced agreements between networks and national, ecumenical bodies, such as the Federal Council of Churches, and later the National Council of Churches. The U.S. Catholic Conference, the New York Board of Rabbis, and the Southern Baptist Convention later joined as representatives of the nation's other religious interests in negotiating access to network sustaining time.

This was the period of preeminence of establishment religion, a period when Will Herberg could say of American religiosity, "To be a Protestant, a Catholic, or a Jew are today the alternative ways of being an American."[10] Nondenominational religious movements, including fundamentalism, were marginalized by the religious culture of the time and were not included in any of the major representative groups. Because they were more or less antagonistic toward the mainline Protestant establishment, and opposed to ecumenism, independent evangelicals found themselves outside the sustaining-time system.[11] It was also thought that evangelicals and fundamentalists could not claim a constituency much beyond the Bible Belt, and some particularly forceful independent religious broadcasters, such as Father Charles Coughlin, frankly scared the broadcasters with their controversial stands. Father Coughlin soon proved that a vibrant, nativist appeal could also play well among the urban working classes, but the development of such an appeal by conservative Protestantism, in areas outside the cities, was still some time off.

The sustaining-time system effectively segregated religious broadcasting by theological origin. Establishment, mainline religion found itself welcomed on network (and local) sustaining-time while conservative, evangelical, and independent groups became wedded to paid-time broadcasting.[12] With the exception of Billy Graham's early use of ABC, they were limited to off-network syndication because network exposure was available only through sustaining time.

The mainline, ecumenical churches were involved in a type of broadcasting far different from the revivalism that dominated the independent, conservative, paid-time broadcasts, typified by the self-conscious, and quasi-intellectual "instruction" of Fulton Sheen. Such nonemotionalist approaches to broadcasting fit better with mainline, establishment values. The major denominations each began radio broadcasting before 1940, and moved into television soon after its widespread introduction in the 1950s. The sustaining-time coalition set up by the National Council of Churches and the other national bodies moved into television as well.[13]

The first television program produced by a major denomination was the venerable *This Is the Life*, produced by the Missouri Synod Lutheran Church out of broadcasting funds raised for their successful radio program, *The Lutheran Hour*. The first ecumenical network production was titled *I Believe*. It was aired on Tuesday evenings (such prime-time exposure is nearly unheard of today) and featured theological discussions.[14] Other denominational and ecumenical programs followed, including the stalwarts *Lamp Unto My Feet* and the *Catholic Hour*.

In his history of mainline broadcasting, Harold Ellens suggests that the mainline churches early on became wedded to only one or two formats—basically variations on a sermon—and that this carried on into their productions for years. *National Radio Pulpit*, a radio program still produced by the National Council of Churches, set the standard for this form.[15]

There were suspicions early on that these new media held out the opportunity of doing things differently. Everett Parker, the dean of mainline denominational broadcasters, observed,

It is not sufficient to transpose a sermon from the pulpit to the microphone. The new medium requires a new approach. . . . By heightening the dramatic appeal of the program, we intend to increase its impact and add to its audience.[16]

The establishment churches saw three distinct approaches to religious broadcasting that typified the era before the emergence of the electronic church. There were the independent, paid-time broadcasters such as Fuller, Aimee Semple McPherson, and Robert Shuler (not to be confused with today's Robert Schuller). There were the traditional approaches taken by the Protestant and Catholic mainline broadcasts on the networks—dominated by a loyalty to the form of conventional Sunday worship. Finally, there was a sought-after, yet never-achieved desire for a more attractive "alternative." This latter quest never ended, even during the gradual demise of the network sustaining-time system in the 1970s.[17]

Several examples of successful nonevangelical, nonindependent paid-time broadcasting emerged, however. The most significant was Bishop Fulton Sheen, who in 1952 shifted from a sustaining-time basis, under the auspices of the National Council of Catholic Men, to a commercial program on the DuMont Television Network, sponsored by the Admiral Corporation. Realizing the power of the program, Admiral moved it to ABC (CBS and NBC turned it down due to corporate policies against accepting paid-time religious programming). Sheen's program is unique in the history of American broadcasting. It was, and is, the only religious program ever to have competed on a commercial basis on network television. It did so successfully until 1957 when Sheen was forced to leave television because of long-standing disputes with New York's archbishop, Cardinal Spellman.[18]

The format Sheen pioneered—instructive, inspirational chats—never found its way to commercial success again, though programs like the *Lawrence Welk Show* have been said to carry a similar ambience. A study done at the time of its greatest prominence found nothing unique about the theme or subject matter of Sheen's program, other than his style to which viewers from a variety of perspectives could relate.[19]

Harold Ellens found that there continued to be a good deal of searching for models after the demise of Sheen's program. He identified four approaches to religious broadcasting that have continued since that time. The "mighty acts of God" model mimics the successful revivalist formats of the fundamentalist broadcasters. The "pulpit" model is typified by the infatuation of many denominational broadcasters of the 1950s and 1960s with sermons. The "instructional" model, inspired to an extent by Sheen, is evident in documentaries and dramas, such as *This Is the Life*, the drama program produced by the Missouri Synod Lutheran Church.

In Ellens's final model, major denominational and ecumenical broadcasting agencies would insert messages into more conventional television programs, avoiding the stereotyping and expectations that had come to accompany self-consciously "religious" broadcasting. This approach, which Ellens called "leavening," appears today to have been an attempt to write a new definition of religious broadcasting, one that did not suffer from the genre's "prehistory."[20] It also may represent a distancing on the part of these groups from broadcasting activities that were coming to be less and less effective, satisfying, and central to the mission of the respective churches at a time when great social change was overtaking America.

The Federal Communications Commission and religion

The FCC's seemingly benign attitude toward religious broadcasting did not keep the peace. In the 1930s, Father Charles Coughlin became the first religious broadcasting figure to become enmeshed in national politics. Historian Erik Barnouw suggests that Coughlin's style, and particularly CBS's discomfort with him, was probably the major reason behind the FCC's controversial 1941 Mayflower decision, which attempted to impose a code of neutrality on all broadcasters.[21] In a second major incident, three decades later, a religious station in Red Lion, Pennsylvania, carried attacks on political figures by evangelist Billy James Hargis and attempted to use its religious basis to avoid granting equal time for replies from the subjects of the broadcast attacks. The Red Lion case found its way to the U.S. Supreme Court, where the court significantly expanded the responsibilities of all broadcasters to serve the public interest.[22]

Legal scholar Linda Lacey has concluded that, over the years, the FCC has shied away from religious broadcasting issues, and that this laissez-faire attitude may well have violated the establishment clause of the First Amendment by turning a blind eye to developments in paid-time religion.[23] Peter Horsfield has identified three FCC decisions that exempted paid-time religious broadcasters from FCC regulation. First, in 1960, the FCC decided that a station could fulfill public service obligations regardless of whether a given public affairs program was sustaining time or paid time. Second, though the FCC had specific rules regulating the fund-raising and "membership" activities of noncommercial broadcasters (the question being how such solicitations differ from commercial announcements, and whether fund-raising "telethons" were actually "program-length commercials"), it specifically exempted religious broadcasters from such scrutiny. Third, the commission decided that "religious" programs did not invoke the Fairness Doctrine (and thus require broadcasters to present opposing views) because, in their view, religion is not a matter of controversy.[24]

The FCC's skittishness about religion makes some sense in light of its most dramatic experience with religion—the Lansman-Milam Petition. In 1975, two independent consultants, Jeremy Lansman and Lorenzo Milam, filed a Petition for Rulemaking with the commission, asking that it reconsider its practice of allowing sectarian groups to hold noncommercial FM and TV licenses. Their reasoning was that the purpose of noncommercial broadcasting was not served by such licensees when their programming was essentially on one theme, was not broadly serving the public interest, and, more important, when many of these stations were operated as quasi-commercial entities, devoting much time to on-air fund-raising.[25]

The evangelical and independent religious broadcasters' trade association, the National Religious Broadcasters (NRB), was founded in 1944 to do battle against the sustaining-time system and is now a lobbying and advocacy organization for their interests. The NRB saw the Lansman-Milam Petition as an affront to its constituents and began a direct-mail and fund-raising campaign to fight it. Even though the intent of the petition was to ask for an FCC study, and then only of noncommercial policy, the NRB broadened the front by arguing that this was an attack on *all* religious broadcasting tied to a national antireligion trend typified by the famous atheist, Madeline Murray O'Hair.[26]

Linking of this issue with O'Hair fixed it in the minds of many people and resulted in a phenomenal amount of mail to the FCC. Letters, petitions, telegrams, phone calls, and visits by placard-carrying demonstrators began even as the FCC was deciding *not* to consider the petition and was quickly returning it. The mail did not stop, however. The Commission has received millions of pieces of mail about this one issue, has stopped answering that mail, and, even into the mid-1980s, was still trying to find a way to stop the flow.

The Lansman-Milam case made it clear, for the first time for many observers, how important religious broadcasting was to a great many Americans. About the same time, a number of newer evangelical television programs began to make their way to major cities via cable television and dedicated "religious" UHF television stations. A steady increase in license applications for radio and television stations by religious groups followed.[27]

The electronic church emerges

In the late 1960s, the time and money available to mainline groups through their sustaining-time relationships with the networks began to deteriorate.

The emergence of paid-time broadcasters desiring wider syndication accelerated the process.[28] These broadcasters found a hospitable climate because government and industry were relaxing earlier policies discouraging paid religious programming. They also found new technology increasing their access to television. Cable offered them increased market opportunities, as did the availability of dark (closed), unsuccessful UHF television stations. And, by leasing satellite transponders, national distribution of their programming was simplified by the late 1970s.[29]

This boom in paid-time religious television, along with the malaise in the ecumenical broadcasting world, led to a rapid decline in sustaining programs. Religion could be a profit center for broadcasting. At the networks, the flagships of the sustaining-time system, the sense grew that religious broadcasting needs were being met elsewhere as local affiliates increasingly decided not to carry network religious programs. By 1977, the National Council of Churches itself had changed its long-standing policy against purchasing air time for religious programs.[30]

The formats of the electronic church

Fundamentalist radio long had been dominated by preaching and music borrowed from the revival tent. Early evangelical television promised more of the same, with figures like Billy Graham and Oral Roberts adapting tried and true approaches to this new sight-and-sound medium. Graham was the first, and set many of the standards for the form, but he was more than just the first modern religious broadcasting phenomenon. He also represented the aspirations of a new, modern form of evangelicalism, as George Marsden has noted.[31]

Graham was not initially interested in broadcasting. Primarily a leader of urban crusades, he had to be convinced to try broadcasting some of his services. He began with radio, purchasing time on the ABC network in 1950 for a weekly program, *Hour of Decision*. In 1957, he also began a series of television specials.[32] Graham had started as a Youth for Christ crusader and gradually built his own reputation as a leader of revivals and crusades. By the time he was approached to start broadcasting, he already had built an international reputation, and had attracted the attention of such people as newspaper publisher William Randolph Hearst. Hearst is said to have been so taken with Graham's charisma (and perhaps with his political significance in the cold war era) that he ordered his papers to "puff Graham." Thus when Graham began broadcasting he was already the best-known evangelist of his time, and he had an extensive organization to support his broadcasting activities.[33]

Graham set a new standard for religious broadcasting, one of organizational sophistication and national prominence. Whereas religious broadcasting before 1950 had been steeped in the rural culture of the Bible Belt and thereby remained of marginal interest to the national media scene, Graham's program and his crusades charted a different course. He soon drew the attention of fundamentalist and evangelical leaders to the potential of national-level broadcasting. Graham's success, coupled with that of Fulton Sheen's program, heightened awareness of the benefits of religious broadcasting.

Graham's ministry became an early model for the ministries of the electronic church. He emerged out of the heart of the developing neoevangelical movement from a base in one of its major transdenominational organizations, Youth for Christ, and was connected with other parachurch institutions and agencies in the movement. By the time he started broadcasting, he had already developed a large public relations and fund-raising support structure. His ministry developed sophisticated systems of contact with supporters through direct mail and newsletters. His crusades had taken him repeatedly to major urban centers, where he enjoyed much public attention.

Graham carried the form and structure of his crusades to radio and television, thereby extending the reach of his "direct-contact" work. Most important, his message, as a moderate form of earlier fundamentalist truisms, was easily adapted to these media. He addressed the crisis of culture with the symbols and values of neoevangelicalism, becoming a major force for that perspective in the public realm. For Graham, as with most of the electronic church ministries that followed, there was more there than "met the eye" in his programs themselves.

The form and content of the electronic church ministries that gained prominence in the 1970s varied a good deal, as did their institutional structures. Where Graham has used broadcasting to enhance his activities outside the realm of the airwaves, these latter-day institutions seem to be based solely on electronic media. The following profiles of the major electronic church ministries illustrate this point, to a greater or lesser extent, but there is greater diversity in their structures and intent than is often assumed by observers.

Rex Humbard's You Are Loved

Rex Humbard was one of the first, if not the first, contemporary religious broadcaster to move into television broadcasting.[34] He started his program at his independent temple in Akron, Ohio, in the 1950s. As is the case with most of the others, his program format closely followed the structure of the religious services that had been his trademark. He and his family were musicians, and his crusades and his program relied heavily on music.

The *You Are Loved* format, which emerged in the mid-1970s at the onset of the electronic church era, moved out of the auditorium of the purpose-built Cathedral of Tomorrow that had been his home base in Akron since 1958. Filmed on location in Florida, the program prominently featured musical numbers sung by family members and occasionally included guests in outdoor settings. Humbard would present a brief homily, usually stressing a salvation message. He eschewed politics, and emphasized music where possible. For a time, Humbard was the most widely distributed of these programs. By the mid-1980s, however, he had pulled back significantly and was no longer a major national producer.

Oral Roberts and You

Oral Roberts probably predates Humbard on nationally syndicated television (Humbard was on television first, but on a local station), and vies with Graham for the title of elder statesman of evangelical use of the medium. Roberts began on television in the 1950s, and moved into the electronic church era with a new format in the late 1960s. He had had a long career as a revivalist and faith healer, and his television work began with the broadcast of his tent meetings in 1954. Denied network time because of the controversy that would accompany someone who claimed to heal terminal illnesses with his hands through prayer, his program was nonetheless a mainstay of Sunday mornings throughout the country in the 1950s.

The early program was memorable. Dark, black-and-white images of the interior of a revival tent brought Roberts, clad in shirtsleeves, perspiring, and bellowing over the sick and needy sitting in folding chairs, into millions of American homes. The image of the television faith healer grasping a forehead and exclaiming, "*Healed . . . Healed!*" was fixed in many impressionable young minds by Roberts.

In the mid-1960s, he left television, and the healing circuit, to start a university in Tulsa, Oklahoma. He returned to television in 1969 with a slickly produced entertainment-oriented music and preaching program called *Oral Roberts and You.* He had had a complete make-over. Gone were the tent and the hands-on healing. In their place were homilies, delivered directly to the camera, interspersed with exciting, "modern" arrangements of gospel tunes performed by well-scrubbed young people from his university. The format was almost like a variety program, though with a religious twist.[35] Controversy has followed Roberts through the 1980s, but his broadcast work has gone on unabated.

Jerry Falwell's Old Time Gospel Hour

Jerry Falwell's program is probably the most controversial of all of the new media ministries because of his frequent forays into politics. Falwell began as a fundamentalist pastor in an independent Baptist church in Virginia, but only came to prominence when his televised attacks on the evils of modern social and political life attracted press attention in the 1970s. Once convinced that preachers should leave politics to others, Falwell found that his media ministry put him in a position of influence and prominence.

The program, started within a year of the founding of his church in 1956, has always been a broadcast of his Sunday church service, complete with offering, preaching, announcements, and music. The program is taped in the sanctuary of a 17,000-member church, which was built with television in mind. As it is a church service, Falwell saves his most powerful and pointed political rhetoric for personal appearances. It is clear to the viewer, however, that this is a man with definite opinions about current events.

Among the guests who have shared his pulpit have been political, sports, and entertainment figures. Occasionally, there are location shots interspersed in the program. Falwell sometimes suspends the normal format to present a "special" of some kind—such as programs promoting the "right-to-life" movement, and special appeals for funds. As is the case with all of the electronic church genre, the latest production values, equipment, and techniques are used on the *The Old Time Gospel Hour*.

Like Oral Roberts, Falwell has created a college, Liberty Baptist College, and a number of other ministries. Viewers can make a pilgrimage to his church, Thomas Road Baptist, and to the college, where special seminars and services are often scheduled to accommodate such visits.

Robert Schuller's Hour of Power

In many ways, Robert Schuller's program is unique in modern television religion. It originates from the chancel of the Garden Grove Community Church in California, which was completed in 1980. It is a huge structure, made mostly of glass, that has become a landmark in the area. Schuller calls his church "The Crystal Cathedral." He built it to continue a tradition dating from his earliest ministry—as an accommodation for people who want to "drive in" to church, and attend services while parked in their cars.

The program begins with a swell of classical-style string music and fanfares of trumpets, introducing Schuller's invocation from the Psalms, "This is the day that the Lord has made, let us rejoice and be glad in it!" Music is a central feature of the program. Often, there will be a performance from the classical church repertoire. Rarely will there be the upbeat gospel music that typifies most of the other programs.

Schuller's taste in music reflects his taste in theology. He is the only one of the major electronic church figures who is actually a mainline pastor (of the Reformed Church of America), and his theological approach is more liberal and modernist-orthodox than is the case with his competitors. His program reflects this, presenting all the elements of his actual Sunday morning service, including such things as communion and the consecration of deacons for the congregation.

His sermons are full of anecdotes that illustrate the benefits of his major theme—"possibility thinking." He will often interview a celebrity guest about their success in life when they were in this state of mind. He has been identified with Norman Vincent Peale in his approach and philosophy, and is aggressively nonpartisan politically, presenting liberal as well as conservative spokespersons (on the rare occasions when the program delves into politics at all).[36]

Jimmy Swaggart

There actually are few religious television programs that are aired at any times other than the classic "religious ghetto" of weekend mornings and late nights. Jimmy Swaggart's is one of these, appearing in many markets on weekday mornings. The format of the program takes two distinct forms, and varies from week to week even in the "post-scandal" era.

The basic purpose of one format seems to be information. Swaggart teaches and preaches, in a studio, using blackboards, charts, and other visual devices. His themes are usually biblical prophecy and the problems of the present age. He has been accused of being particularly strident and judgmental about social, political, and religious issues. He has been most controversial for his attacks on Catholicism.

Swaggart's other format is based in his successful career as a gospel rhythm and blues artist. He travels the country holding crusades, and ceaselessly promotes them, his albums and tapes, and his books and pamphlets, in his program. When he is not holding forth in his "teaching" format, his program is a rebroadcast of one of his performances on the crusade circuit. When not singing and playing the piano, he prances back and forth, Bible held aloft, exuding the passion of the revival preacher, expounding on biblical prophecy.

Pat Robertson's 700 Club

The Christian Broadcasting Network's *700 Club* is perhaps the quintessential example of the electronic church genre. It evolved from a televised prayer and Bible-study program in the early 1960s into the first of the "Christian talk shows" of the electronic church era. CBN was also the first of the television ministries to lease satellite time to distribute the *700 Club* to cable television systems throughout North America. CBN has been a "group owner" of five television stations and five radio stations, though those properties were sold in 1985. CBN was among the first of the developing ministries to install telephone-counseling equipment, backed up by a computerized direct-mail and fund-raising operation.

The whole idea of new religious genres has been given a boost by CBN from time to time, as it has experimented with "Christian" programs to be distributed alongside the *700 Club* on its cable channel. The most famous of these other programs was probably *Another Life*, a "Christian soap opera" premiered in the early 1980s but later canceled. CBN has also introduced, and then canceled, a "Christian news program." More recently, CBN has begun to fill most of its non-*700 Club* cable channel time with innocuous "family programming"—mostly situation comedies and westerns from the 1950s, all commercially sponsored.[37]

A more complete description of the history of CBN and the *700 Club* follows in Chapter 4.

Jim and Tammy Bakker's PTL Club

Along with Jimmy Swaggart and the *700 Club*, the *PTL Club* (for "Praise the Lord Club") is a weekday religious program that has gained prominence in the era of the electronic church. It is the newest of the major television ministries—it started as a local program in 1974—but it has become one of the best known, for a number of reasons. First, it is one of the few programs that intentionally copies a commercial format—the variety talk show—and does not include the elements of worship services. Second, like the Christian Broadcasting Network, it operates a national satellite service to cable systems. Third, also like CBN, it has periodically experimented with other commercial broadcasting formats, including a cooking and housekeeping program called *Tammy's House Party*. Fourth, and perhaps most important, PTL has been embroiled in financial, legal, and personal controversy almost continually since its founding.

A major scandal erupted in 1987 causing PTL founding hosts, Jim and Tammy Bakker, to resign under a cloud of sexual and financial accusations. Before that time, the *PTL Club* had been the most effervescent of these programs, based in the charismatic pentecostalism of its hosts and performers. Shot in a state-of-the-art studio, the *PTL Club* mimics the format of programs like *The Merv Griffin Show*.

In their heyday, Jim and Tammy presided over the program, assisted by a sidekick named "Uncle Henry" Harrison. They engaged in free-form dialogue about faith and their lives, punctuated by guest testimonies. A major component of the program was music, with their "PTL Singers" providing a backdrop of mod-gospel charismatic music for Tammy's frequent solos. Other musicians were also regulars on the program.

The staple of the program, more so than with others, was fund-raising.

The *PTL Club* was always the most aggressive of the major electronic church shows, and was often accused of actually being the "Pass the Loot Club."

The PTL ministry was much larger than just the programs it presented. The Bakkers built a 1200-acre vacation and entertainment complex called "Heritage Village USA," including a hotel, a campground, a theme amusement park, a miniature Holy Land, and time-share condominiums. Tammy had pretensions to a recording career and her albums were often touted on the program.

While each of the electronic church ministries maintains a massive direct-mail fund-raising program, PTL's was devoted primarily to marketing PTL services and products, whereas Falwell's, Swaggart's, and Robertson's more often addressed social issues or relief efforts in the Third World.

The major distinguishing characteristics of the *PTL Club* were, however, Tammy and Jim themselves. To put it bluntly, Tammy did not dress or act in a way one might expect of a woman member of the "Holiness" or Pentecostal movement. She wore heavy makeup, a great deal of jewelry, and clothes that were more revealing than some viewers were comfortable with. And the Bakkers made no secret of their marital problems. Tammy had spent time in California "finding herself," Jim once said.[38] Tammy and Jim regularly ran the gamut of emotions on the air, and their spontaneity was an important attraction for some viewers. The *PTL Club* was thus probably the most atypical of all of the major electronic church programs. It resembled the *700 Club* in some ways, but stressed testimonies and music, where the latter program moved toward more of a "magazine" format in the early 1980s.

Other successful formats

The existence of the cable networks owned by CBN, PTL, and the Trinity Network in California spawned a number of experimental Christian television programs. There have been talk shows, children's shows, quiz shows, travel programs, and advice programs. None of these has achieved national prominence, however, and none has ever rivaled the "majors" in terms of weekly ratings. This market was dealt a blow by a series of policy changes at CBN in 1985-1986 that eliminated most such programs from its cable network, by the financial crises at PTL following the Bakkers' exit in 1987, and by the Swaggart scandal in 1988.

One new religious format is doing extremely well, however, and that is gospel music. The program "Gospel Singing Jubilee" is undoubtedly the highest-rated religious program of them all (if one chooses to classify it as such). It is commercially sponsored, and is very successful. Gospel music is a growth industry, and this program showcases it much as "bandstand" programs do for the pop music industry. Gospel music is an important feature of many religious programs, though officials at CBN have eliminated most music from the *700 Club* as a way of clearly differentiating that program from its past and from its competition.[39]

Myths and realities of the religious television audience

From its earliest days, a debate has raged over the actual size of the electronic church audience. Dr. Ben Armstrong of National Religious Broadcasters heralded the new age of religious broadcasting by claiming a total audience of over 100 million.[40] William F. Fore of the National Council of Churches, a leading critic of the genre, responded that the figure was probably nearer 10 million.[41] The popular press has contributed to confusion of the issue, often unquestioningly accepting either high or low estimates, including estimates as high as 130 million.

Empirical studies[42] suggest that a figure in the range of 10 to 20 million is probably reasonable. More precision in estimates of audience size is complicated by a number of methodological factors.[43] For instance, the largest estimates have come from national opinion polls where there is no independent check on whether the respondents actually view as they say they do. In a country where the vast majority of adults claim to be religious and to attend church regularly (although published attendance figures do not match poll data), there is "social desirability" in claiming to view or listen to religious broadcasts. There is also the problem of duplication of audience ratings (a technique sometimes employed to inflate the total audience artificially for the religious broadcasting genre), where a viewer is counted each time he or she tunes in to any religious program. Duplication leads to inaccurately large estimates of the total religious viewing audience because the majority of viewers (nearly three-quarters, according to the most reliable data[44]) view more than one program regularly. Counting such viewers each time they view massively overestimates the audience for the religious genre.

There is the further problem of what constitutes religious viewing in the first place. A person's self-classification as a "religious viewer" may differ widely from that of an observer of his or her behavior.[45] These issues have their basis in the wider meaning of the religious culture. It has been suggested that the controversy over the meaning of religious viewing thus relates to more far-reaching questions.

It is part of our common "received history" of revivalism and evangelicalism that the question of what constitutes "an adherent" or "a believer" or "a convert" has always been a matter of debate. William Martin notes that there is a fairly common suspicion among observers of broadcast and non-broadcast preachers that they sometimes ". . . count arms and legs instead of heads." It is part of the grand tradition of revivalism to take "on faith" each new profession of salvation by a participant in a rally, service, or meeting. Each such convert adds to the total fold of the saved, *and* to each evangelist's reputation, adding to his or her credibility and overall audience appeal and power to continue the good work of pursuing Christ's "Great Commission."[46]

The total size of the audience is therefore both difficult to measure accurately, and really not the only important issue in understanding the implications of religious viewing. While the audience is certainly not as large as is claimed by electronic church broadcasters, there is another claim that is equally important: the idea that the electronic church represents a radically new kind of religious broadcasting. Neoevangelicalism has its origins in moves to form a more moderate, "new" form of fundamentalism, one that is more broadly palatable. The self-conscious attempts of electronic church broadcasters to craft new programs and formats have the same intent. They believe themselves to be attracting a broader audience than was available to religious broadcasting in the past.[47]

This leads to claims that the electronic church is attracting a new type of audience: younger, less traditionally "religious," and better educated. There is a long research record that would predict the opposite. The landmark study done in the 1950s by Parker, Barry, and Smythe[48] charted the basic characteristics of the traditional, pre-electronic church audience. The audience was made up of older, female, already religious viewers. Other studies added that religious viewers were more likely to live in rural, southern, and western areas of the country. Subsequent studies have done little to dispel the notion that the audience for religious broadcasting, even into the 1980s, is made up of the "already churched," and of people of a rather narrow demographic range.[49]

More recently, major research undertaken by the Annenberg School of Communications and the Gallup Organization amplified what was known from this earlier work.[50] This study, which included both content and audience analyses, was significant for the quality of its sample. Earlier researchers had been cautious in their conclusions about the nature of the religious television audience because of the unreliably small numbers of viewers of religious television in most random surveys. While previous studies had provided a general picture of who religious viewers are, what they believe, and how they behave in aggregate, the Annenberg-Gallup data provided a more definitive description. They were not satisfied with relying on survey "self-reports" as their measure of religious viewing because of the likelihood that many people would claim to view when they do not. Instead, the Annenberg-Gallup team located a random sample of verified viewers of religious television through ratings archive data of the Arbitron Corporation.

Table 3.1 presents data[51] on the relationship between religious television viewing, conventional television viewing, and contributions to religious television and a variety of demographic, religious, and behavior variables in the Annenberg-Gallup regional survey.[52]

As can be seen in the table, this study's findings, from well into the electronic church era, indicate that the basic characteristics of the audience were not far different from earlier times. Viewing was found to be positively associated with church attendance, giving, and private religious behaviors like prayer and Bible reading. Heavier viewers of religious (and conventional) television tend to be lower in income, lower in education, and older than lighter viewers. Nonwhites are also more likely than whites to view. The Annenberg-Gallup findings thus tended to relieve the worst fears of the electronic church's critics: that it is drawing members away from conventional religious behaviors. At the same time, the finding that the audience is not radically different from the past undermines the cherished idea that the electronic church is something new and different in the history of religious broadcasting. Specifically, a more moderate, "upscale" audience seems not to be the dominant pattern.

The religious audience seems quite similar, in demographic terms, to the conventional television audience. The comparison in Table 3.1 between religious and conventional television viewing reveals some interesting, though not surprising, differences. Religious attitudes and behaviors are much more highly correlated with religious than with conventional television viewing. The strongest correlation of all is that between conservative attitudes and religious viewing, a finding consistent with the presumed content of most religious programs.

Because of the quality of the data, a number of additional conclusions can be drawn, based on more careful and detailed analysis. First, viewing of these programs is so heavily integrated into the religious lives of its viewers that it should be seen as an expression of conventional belief and behavior, not a substitute for them. The association between viewing and conventional behavior holds up even under statistical controls.[53]

Second, there seems to be no group or subgroup for whom this is not the case. Because of the quality of the sample available, this study was able, for the first time, to specify reliably different "levels" of religious viewing, and see if there were, in fact, a type of "heavy" viewer for whom viewing constituted a *substitute* for more conventional religious expression. It was found that those who view religious television the most do not differ in this way. In fact, they are more likely to be heavily involved in conventional

TABLE 3.1 *Correlations between viewing religious television, viewing conventional television, contributions to religious television, and demographic, belief, and behavior variables: Full regional sample*

	Religious Television Viewing	General Television Viewing	Contribution to Religious TV
Demographic variables:			
education	-.262***	-.251***	.032
	(2496)	(2505)	(317)
income	-.232***	-.250***	.126*
	(2233)	(2242)	(294)
age	.321***	.169	-.032
	(2518)	(2602)	(317)
sex	.064***	.112***	.049
	(2518)	(2602)	(317)
race	.187***	.129***	-.061
	(2244)	(2320)	(279)
Religiosity variables:			
conservatism	.495***	.049*	.120*
	(1843)	(1864)	(246)
evangelical	.291***	.057**	-.032
denomination	(2447)	(2457)	(311)
church	.284***	-.011	.144**
attendance	(2468)	(2501)	(310)
local church	.205***	-.093***	.220***
contribution	(2260)	(2336)	(301)
frequency of	.194***	-.099***	.036
prayer	(2559)	(2496)	(317)
importance of	.382***	.083***	.129*
religion	(2503)	(2521)	(316)

NOTE: Direction of codings are generally with higher values moving toward the labeled value—that is, prayer: high = frequent; contributions: larger; importance: very important; race: high = nonwhite; conservatism: high = conservative.
*p < .05; **p < .01; ***p < .001.

church behaviors than are others.[54]

Belief and behavior subgroups were also investigated. That is, are there groups, such as nonconservatives, or members of liberal denominations, for whom viewing of religious television might be substituting for (or otherwise negatively associated with) conventional religious behaviors? Tables 3.2 and 3.3 test this question.

As can be seen there, higher levels of church attendance and giving are reported along with more frequent viewing of religious television for all the denominational categories except Catholics.[55] Actual levels of attendance and giving for the heaviest viewers are very similar across these various

TABLE 3.2 *Percentage attending church once a week or more among categories of viewing of religious television by denomination and "conservatism" categories*

| | Religious Viewing | | | | | | |
	None %	Rare %	Some %	Frequent %	CD[a]	N	P (Tau)
Evangelical denomination:							
evangelicals	38.5	54.3	66.6	69.3	15.0	(905)	.001
mainline Protestants	38.9	43.9	62.3	65.9	22.0	(824)	.001
Catholics	54.8	77.3	64.0	74.5	–2.8	(521)	.001
other faiths	20.6	42.9	52.6	64.3	21.4	(154)	.001
Religious conservatism:							
high	61.3	64.9	74.3	78.7	13.8	(629)	.01
medium	50.9	66.1	58.7	60.5	–5.6	(450)	—
low	33.9	46.4	50.8	52.1	5.7	(736)	.001

a. See Table 3.3 note.

categories. Higher levels of attendance and giving are also reported by more frequent viewers among the *most* and *least* religiously "conservative" viewers, with an insignificant contrary pattern for the moderates there.

Third, the study confirmed the widely held assumption that viewers of these programs are much more conservative than nonviewers on a range of political and social issues. They are more likely to favor capital punishment and endorse "traditional" roles for women, for instance.[56]

Fourth, while heavy viewers of conventional television are less likely to vote, religious television's politically conservative heavier viewers are *more* likely to vote than are its lighter viewers.[57]

Fifth, there are some small differences between audience preferences for various religious programs. Probably due to factors such as leisure time availability and scheduling, more viewers report viewing Sunday morning programs than those shown on weekdays. The composition of the weekday audience also was different. The programs that most resemble conventional television (the weekday category, which includes the *700 Club* and the *PTL Club*) seemed to draw a theologically more conservative and slightly less upscale audience than the weekend programs.[58] This is significant to the question of how the electronic church audience is different from that of earlier eras of religious broadcasting. These weekday programs are the ones that have done the most, in scheduling and format terms, to attract a "new" or "different" audience. In fact, the opposite seems to be happening.

Sixth, to emphasize the obvious point here, there is no general tendency for nonreligious or non-Christian people to view religious programs. This suggests that a major function of the programs for their supporters—

TABLE 3.3 *Percentage making contributions to local church among categories of viewing of religious television, denominational, and "conservatism" categories*

| | Religious Viewing | | | | | | |
	None %	Rare %	Some %	Frequent %	CD^a	N	P (Tau)
Evangelical denomination:							
evangelicals	44.3	54.9	58.9	60.4	5.5	(830)	.01
mainline Protestants	41.0	51.0	60.6	63.9	12.9	(755)	.001
Catholics	43.0	53.1	57.5	49.0	−4.1	(486)	.01
other faiths	21.2	50.0	52.9	61.5	11.5	(141)	.001
Religious conservatism:							
high	55.9	70.6	65.8	66.0	−4.6	(580)	—
medium	44.5	52.8	48.5	50.0	−2.8	(425)	—
low	36.1	46.9	57.9	54.7	7.8	(682)	.001

a. The differential calculation compares "rare" with "frequent" viewers. For example, a negative CD shows that a lower percentage of frequent viewers in that subgroup report a given behavior than do those who "rarely" view religious television.

"converting the unbelievers"—is probably not being realized. It is not surprising that people who are less religious tend to watch conventional television. While religious television viewing is positively associated with religious involvement and belief, conventional television viewing has contrary associations. That is, higher levels of overall television viewing go with lower levels of various religious behaviors.[59]

Robert Wuthnow has given additional insight into the relative motivations for religious television viewing and conventional religious behaviors. He investigated claims that the "uses and gratifications" of these programs involve dissatisfaction with the conventional settings of religious life. He found marginal evidence to support the claim, but, overall, no evidence that this dissatisfaction is attracting large numbers of "nontraditional" viewers (viewers other than the demographic types traditionally drawn to religious broadcasting), nor defections from conventional churches.

> Of those polled . . . only 15 percent of the viewers and 14 percent of the nonviewers said they were dissatisfied with "the way things have been going in your local church or synagogue." . . . Despite whatever reservations people have about their churches they still overwhelmingly look to the churches instead of religious television for spiritual guidance.[60]

The "two-party" dynamic might lead to substitution for some viewers. The evangelicalism of the electronic church could prove to be an outlet for interests not being met in mainline churches. There was little or no evidence in the Annenberg-Gallup research that more conservative members of the mainline churches are being drawn to religious television as a substitute for church attendance. There is little or no difference in church attendance between evangelical and mainline members who are viewers of religious television.

The available data then suggest that, in spite of their much-touted new formats, new appeals, technological sophistication, and prominence in the "secular" world, the audience for religious television today is what it always has been—older, less educated, more rural, and more conventionally religious than its nonreligious-viewing cohort. There is little reason to believe that many outside of the traditional audience are actually viewing. Further, the new genres of religious programs that are specifically intended to increase the size of the audience seem to be ineffective at doing so.[61]

The meaning of the audience

The actual size and nature of the audience is only part of the story, however. Claims about audience size have a life and a function of their own. To religious broadcasters, anecdotes of viewers who have received blessings and salvation through their ministries are sufficient confirmations to them and their viewers of the power and importance of their work. The very unreliability of actual audience-size measures serves them well by leaving open the question of who is being reached, while allowing the anecdotal evidence to take precedence over statistics.

The electronic church thus derives its power and prominence from several directions. The image of religious broadcasting in the decades before the neoevangelical revival was one of insularity, controversy, and marginality. But after 1975, a new type of religious broadcasting emerged, available to more people, with modern, less insular appeals and formats. The claim that this new genre would move outside the traditional ghetto of religious broadcasting, while not supported by the best available evidence, nonetheless gave new credibility to these ministries. The new programs, they claimed, were unique in both their theological and their political potential.

But if the electronic church is not drawing large numbers into the neoevangelical tradition, then what is its significance? Is it only to, as Joel Carpenter put it earlier, "convince themselves—and many others, apparently—that they are a real presence in American public life"?[62] If the electronic church serves primarily a "publicity" function, then what role can it be playing in the wider revitalization sought by the evangelical movement?

There are a number of viewers (though not as many as is often claimed) who are loyal to these programs. There are contributors and members for whom, presumably, media religion is important. To understand the phenomenon better, we need to examine carefully the meaning of electronic church viewing in the lives of actual viewers.

To do so, we move next to a more extensive investigation of the most prominent of these ministries, Pat Robertson's *700 Club*. As we have said, this program in many ways is the quintessential electronic church. It was the first to experiment with a new format. It has been heavily involved in the sophisticated fund-raising and direct-contact work necessary for success. It has achieved a level of public awareness matched only by the scandal-ridden *PTL Club* and Jerry Falwell's aggressively political *Old Time Gospel Hour*. In the midst of the fray, it offers to be a more sober and refined vision of televangelism (in spite of Pat Robertson's own political ambitions). As we will see, its viewers and members see it precisely this way, and have developed an impressive loyalty to the *700 Club*.

Notes

1. Joel Carpenter, "Tuning in the Gospel: Fundamentalist Radio Broadcasting and the Revival of Mass Evangelism, 1930-1945" (Paper delivered to the Mid-America American Studies Association, University of Illinois, Urbana, 13 April 1985).

2. Carpenter, "Tuning in the Gospel," p. 15.

3. For detailed arguments of this view, see Ben Armstrong, *The Electric Church*, and Richard N. Ostling, "Evangelical Publishing and Broadcasting," in *Evangelicalism and Modern America*, ed. George Marsden (Grand Rapids, MI: Eerdmans, 1984).

4. Carpenter, "Tuning in the Gospel," p. 4.

5. Ibid., p. 10.

6. Ibid., p. 12.

7. Ibid., p. 13.

8. Ibid., p. 12.

9. For a complete discussion, see J. Harold Ellens, *Models of Religious Broadcasting* (Grand Rapids, MI: Eerdmans, 1974); William F. Fore, "A Short History of Religious Broadcasting" (Unpublished report, National Council of Churches, New York, 1967); Erik Barnouw, *The Golden Web*, vol. 2, *A History of Broadcasting in the United States, 1933-1953* (New York: Oxford University Press, 1968); and Ralph M. Jennings, "Policies and Practices of Selected National Bodies as Related to Broadcasting in the Public Interest, 1920-1950" (Ph.D. diss., New York University, 1973).

10. Will Herberg, *Protestant—Catholic—Jew* (New York: Doubleday, 1956), p. 274.

11. Jeffrey K. Hadden and Charles E. Swann, *Prime Time Preachers* (Reading, MA: Addison-Wesley, 1981); and Peter G. Horsfield, *Religious Television* (New York: Longman, 1984).

12. Ellens, *Models of Religious Broadcasting*; Armstrong, *The Electric Church*.

13. Ellens, *Models of Religious Broadcasting*, p. 24.

14. Ibid., p. 24.

15. Ibid., p. 27.

16. Ibid., p. 32.

17. For a complete discussion of this history, see Ellens, *Models of Religious Broadcasting*; and Horsfield, *Religious Television*.

18. Hadden and Swann, *Prime Time Preachers*, pp. 82-83.

19. Everett C. Parker, David W. Barry, and Dallas W. Smythe, *The Television-Radio Audience and Religion* (New York: Harper, 1955), pp. 390-91.

20. Ellens, *Models of Religious Broadcasting*, pp. 123-39.

21. Barnouw, *The Golden Web*, p. 137.

22. Michael F. Abrams, "The FCC and the Electric Church," Freedom of Information Center, Report No. 415 (Columbia: University of Missouri, School of Journalism, January 1980).

23. Linda Jo Lacey, "The Electric Church: An FCC-'Established' Institution?" *Federal Communications Law Journal* 31, no. 2 (1978): 235-75.

24. Horsfield, *Religious Television*, pp. 13-14.

25. One of the petitioners published a history of this controversy under a pen name. See A. W. Allworthy, *The Petition Against God* (Dallas: Christ the Light, 1976).

26. Lacey, "The Electric Church"; Allworthy, *The Petition Against God*; National Religious Broadcasters' mailing, 17 June 1975.

27. Armstrong, *The Electric Church*, pp. 103-6.

28. Charles Swann, "The Electric Church," *Presbyterian Survey* (May 1979): 9-16; Stewart M. Hoover, "Religious Group Use and Avoidance of Television: A Study of Reasons and Effects" (M.A. thesis, Annenberg School of Communications, University of Pennsylvania, 1982); Horsfield, *Religious Television*.

29. Armstrong, *The Electric Church*; Hadden and Swann, *Prime Time Preachers*.

30. Minutes of National Council of Churches Communication Commission (New York, September 1977). This had little practical effect, as the member groups of the NCC were not prepared to fund broadcast activities at a level that would prove to be a significantly prominent alternative to the electronic church.

31. See discussion in Chapter 2; George Marsden, "Preachers of Paradox," in *Religion and America*, ed. Mary Douglas and Steven Tipton (Boston: Beacon, 1982), p. 155.

32. Armstrong, *The Electric Church*, pp. 94-97.

33. See Carpenter, "Tuning in the Gospel," pp. 13 ff., for a description of how Graham emerged from the earlier movements and began to establish his own approach.

34. Both Armstrong, *The Electric Church*, and Hadden and Swann, *Prime Time Preachers*, reserve the mantle of the first electronic church syndicated program for Humbard, though both acknowledge that Graham preceded Humbard by several years. These two histories provide the basis of the capsule descriptions presented here.

35. Historian David Harrell reports in detail about the process Roberts went through to develop his new format and style. See David E. Harrell, Jr., *Oral Roberts* (Bloomington: Indiana University Press, 1985).

36. Hadden and Swann, *Prime Time Preachers*, pp. 30-32.

37. "Power, Glory—and Politics," *Time*, 17 February 1986, p. 65.

38. Reported by researcher in the monitoring of PTL. G. Gerbner, L. Gross, S. Hoover, M. Morgan, N. Signorielli, H. Cotugno, and R. Wuthnow, *Religion and Television*, technical report of the Annenberg-Gallup Study of Religious Broadcasting conducted by the Annenberg School of Communications and the Gallup Organization, Inc. (Philadelphia: Annenberg School of Communications, University of Pennsylvania, 1984). (All details of this study's findings and the tables presented in this chapter are taken from this technical report.)

39. Hoover, "Religious Group Use."

40. Armstrong, *The Electric Church*.

41. William F. Fore, "Religion on the Airwaves: In the Public Interest?" *Christian Century* 92 (17 September 1975).

42. See, in particular, William Martin, "The Birth of a Media Myth," *New Yorker*, June 1981; Hadden and Swann, *Prime Time Preachers*; and Gerbner et al., *Religion and Television*.

43. For a complete discussion, see Stewart M. Hoover, "The Religious Television Audience: A Matter of Significance, or Size?" *Review of Religious Research* 29, no. 2 (December 1987).

44. Gerbner et al., *Religion and Television*, p. 63.

45. Hoover, "The Religious Television Audience."

46. Ibid.

47. See David W. Clark and Paul H. Virts, "Religious Television Audience: A New Development in Measuring Audience Size" (Paper delivered to the Society for the Scientific Study of Religion, Savannah, Georgia, 25 October 1985).

48. Parker, Barry, and Smythe, *The Television-Radio Audience*.

49. See Judith M. Buddenbaum, "Characteristics and Media-Related Needs of the Audience for Religious TV," *Journalism Quarterly* 58 (Summer 1981): 266-72; Gary D. Gaddy and David Pritchard "When Watching TV Is Like Attending Church," *Journal of Communication* 35, no. 1 (Winter 1985): 123-31.

50. Gerbner et al., *Religion and Television*.

51. The Pearson correlation coefficient (the statistic in Table 3.1) is a measure of the strength and direction of the relationship between two factors. It varies from -1 to $+1$, with negative scores indicating an inverse relationship. The higher the score, the more direct the relationship. Aside from the obvious demographic measures here, certain others should be explained. The "conservatism" item is a factor-based index (Armour's theta = .64) of attitudes toward the conservative side of the "two-party" controversy (made up of items on charismatic experience, biblical literalism, the second coming of Christ, and respondent self-description as having been "born again"). Therefore, those who score on the "conservative" side of this measure would be those most involved in the neoevangelical, fundamentalist, and charismatic movements. "Evangelical denomination" divides respondents' church memberships into either classically "evangelical" or "nonevangelical" denominations.

52. See Gerbner et al., *Religion and Television*. The Annenberg-Gallup study included both a national survey of a probability sample, and regional surveys in ten northeastern and ten southeastern markets. These latter surveys were based on the higher-quality Arbitron sample.

53. Gerbner et al., *Religion and Television*, p. 111.

54. Ibid., Appendix, Table III.5.

55. Because Catholics report such a high level of attendance overall, the contrary pattern for heavy-viewing Catholics may be a "ceiling" effect, not an indication of a contrary pattern for them with regard to religious viewing.

56. Gerbner et al., *Religion and Television*, pp. 113-31.

57. Ibid., pp. 115-16.

58. See ibid., Appendix, Table IV.2.2; Chapter 5, Table 5.4.

59. Gerbner et al., *Religion and Television*, p. 139.

60. Robert Wuthnow, "The Social Significance of Religious Television" (Unpublished paper, Princeton, NJ: Princeton University, 1984), pp. 11-12.

61. Hoover, "The Religious Television Audience."

62. Carpenter, "Tuning in the Gospel," p. 15.

4

Pat Robertson and the
Prototype of the Electronic Church

Pat Robertson and the Christian Broadcasting Network (CBN)[1] have come to typify the electronic church for many observers. The life story of Robertson, CBN's founder and its president until 1987, is a model of modern spiritual testimony. After earning a law degree at Yale, he had begun a career in business when he had a life-changing conversion experience that led him to a seminary and the ministry.[2] After a two-month stint in an inner-city neighborhood in New York as an evangelist in 1959, he felt God's call to return to his home state of Virginia, and to take up a broadcast ministry.

Robertson started CBN as the country's first "Christian" television station, WYAH-TV in Virginia Beach, Virginia, in 1961. Early experimental programming gave way to the *700 Club* concept in 1966. This show, dominated by prayer, music, and testimonies, evolved into a format that more resembled a conventional television talk show, and, by 1975, it was syndicated in a daily 90-minute length to a large number of cities nationwide, appearing twice a day in some places.[3]

CBN's most important development occurred in 1977, when it became the first religious broadcasting organization to lease a satellite channel full-time, opening up hundreds of potential new cities to its programs through cable television. This satellite "network" gave CBN millions of potential new viewers, and 24 hours a day of airtime to program. Other religious broadcasters were quick to sign up for time, and CBN rapidly became nearly a full-time religious channel. Its own programs, including the *700 Club*, and later the first "Christian soap opera," *Another Life*, were joined by a wide variety of new forms and genres of religious programs, giving the CBN channel the ambiance of an alternative network devoted entirely to religion.

Cable distribution of religious programs had potential beyond just the number of additional households that might view. On such a channel, CBN's and others' programs could be shown at better times than on over-the-air broadcasting. The plethora of programs on CBN in the 1970s, and their presence in unconventional time slots on its channel, was largely responsible for the general perception of a "boom" in new formats of religious broadcasting in the late 1970s. CBN and the other major religious broadcasters continued to syndicate their programs directly to broadcast television as well. The cable channel gave them additional reach and flexibility.

Building on programming and fund-raising successes, CBN moved to extend its capital holdings in broadcasting. In its heyday in the early 1980s, it owned three additional television stations and five radio stations, as well as the satellite transmission and distribution facilities over which its channel was fed to over 250 television stations and hundreds of cable television systems with nearly 30 million potential subscribers nationwide.[4] Most of its broadcast holdings were sold by 1985 so that CBN could focus on programming and on operating the satellite channel, which by then carried no religious programming other than the *700 Club* itself.

From the beginning, Robertson acted independently. While establishing the first station in the tidewater area, he found his market among evangelical and charismatic Christians in the area, but he was "on his own" as far as established churches were concerned. It is worth noting, however, that according to his own accounts (and indeed those of other electronic church figures), Robertson was driven not by the neoevangelical or new religious consciousness movements, but by a simple vision and a process of trial and error.[5]

As his broadcast ministry developed, its sophistication in production, fund-raising, and theological controversy grew as well. Robertson was offered a defunct UHF-TV station by its then owner, who had gone broke trying to compete with the established VHF stations in the area. To succeed, Robertson had to obtain a license transfer, arrange financing, and perform many other "miracles." Robertson found striking early evidence that his mission was somehow "blessed" in a decision by the RCA corporation virtually to donate to CBN the television cameras it needed to begin broadcasts.[6] This episode and other stories of success with fund-raising, programming, and management have been woven by electronic church figures like Robertson into a larger justification for broadcast ministry. Thus the "history" of CBN (and other such ministries) becomes both a documentary and a mythic account.

The *700 Club* got its name from an early fund-raising experiment by Robertson and his staff. In the fall of 1963, Robertson began using telethons to raise money for his station. He then needed $7000 a month to stay on the air.

> I asked our viewers to believe with me that God would raise up 700 people who would trust him to supply $10 apiece each month for the coming year. We called the telethon "The 700 Club," and as the people called in, we recorded their pledges.[7]

Even though only half of the needed money was raised at that time, the telethon became the basis for all funding activity at CBN. According to former employees,[8] these early fund-raising efforts were "experimental," that is, undertaken without much idea as to whether they would work out. Robertson knew that the only way to get his audience to support CBN financially was by using airtime to do it. Fund-raising using a telethon format (where fund-raising telethons were concentrated in one-week periods four times a year) also freed more air time for other endeavors, and enabled the *700 Club* program normally to have no fund-raising appeals in it at all. These early experiments led Robertson fully to develop one technique that first distinguished CBN from other religious and secular television fund-raising operations: the use of telephone banks to receive and record easily donors who call in pledges.[9]

Robertson's efforts to find new ways to fund his television operation grew, in part, from the bitter experiences he had had with the "religious establishment" during CBN's beginnings. In his book, *Shout It from the Housetops*, and other writings, Robertson refers to a feeling of ostracism by both evangelical and mainline church leaders, a consequence of the "two-party" phenomenon discussed in Chapter 2. The pastor of one church Robertson attended asked him to leave because of his charismatic theological leanings and his interest in starting a television station. Robertson also was asked to leave his own job as a minister because of his involvement with the television ministry. He had approached that church with the idea of getting it into television, but he was rebuffed. He also approached the local mainline ministers' group for support, but found none there, so he undertook the project as an independent. There is some doubt about how cooperative or ecumenical Robertson would have been, but he now points to the feelings of alienation and rejection on the part of the institutional religious establishment, both evangelical and mainline, as a primary reason for his decision to make CBN an independent (and independently funded) ministry.[10]

CBN's use of phone banks for fund-raising soon evolved into another kind of use. After installing a battery of telephones to accept donor pledges and getting volunteers to operate them, Robertson found that the character of some of the calls began to change.

> The calls were coming in by the hundreds as people cried out, asking for spiritual help and requesting prayer. . . . God was performing miracles. One woman had been crippled in her legs for years, and as a young housewife prayed with her over the phone, the crippled legs were suddenly healed.[11]

Former staff report that the discovery of this method of interaction with the audience was as accidental as the idea of using the telethon for fund-raising.[12] They found it curious that many people watched the programs even though there was no "program" in the formal sense on the air, only ringing telephones and appeals for funds (a lesson that was not lost on Robertson or his staff). Robertson has observed:

> All of this was happening without any kind of programming—just the camera recording what was going on in the studio as people called in or as others came into the station to testify of what God was doing all over the city.[13]

Robertson has said that he is convinced that television viewing has less to do with the formal features of programs than with the ritual of interacting with the set:

> People don't watch the darn thing, anyway, it interacts with the alpha waves of the brain and sort of puts people into a kind of slumber . . . we turn that whole process over to God. We use that to get people involved.[14]

While the response of the CBN audience may seem curious given the lack of formal programming, the intensity of their response seems incredible. Robertson reports that pledges totaling $150,000 were received in one week during the first telethon, along with thousands of calls requesting help, prayer, and healing.[15]

The format of the original *700 Club* program was set after the 1966 telethon, according to Robertson. On the Monday following the end of the telethon, they began broadcasting a program with two hosts (in keeping with a biblical mandate) and musical and other guests. They also retained some of the phone banks from the telethon because calls for prayer and counseling were still coming in. Robertson says:

> Now we finally had God's program. There was a total involvement with our audience. The program was simulcast on radio and television. Those with spiritual, physical, or other needs could call in their requests, and as they did, the phones ringing in the background would be heard on the air. When the requests were shared with the audience, the people could pray for one another. When an answer to prayer was reported or someone was led to Christ on the telephone, the audience could rejoice together.
>
> We were completely free in the spirit. . . . If God said sing, we sang. If he said give an invitation, we gave it. If he said interview a guest, we interviewed the guest. . . . Since this was the last program of the day, we could stay on until three o'clock in the morning if God was touching people's lives. If nothing seemed to be happening we could sign the station off the air and go to bed.[16]

This basic format, that of a "Christian talk show," driven by "the movement of the spirit" characterized the *700 Club* to some extent until 1980, when the program changed to a "magazine format." The freedom and serendipity of the early days was first sacrificed when the show went into syndication in the 1970s. Commercial stations were more comfortable knowing roughly what was planned and, of course, they required that the show be a predictable length. Stations were a bit restive about "free-form" programming because of their own FCC license requirements.

Though the *700 Club* changed as its audience spread across the country, some of its traditions were maintained. As the program became more widely syndicated, for instance, the phone operation also expanded, so that by 1986 there were over sixty regional counseling centers nationwide.[17]

The program and its format

The genre known as the electronic church is striking in itself, primarily because these programs sharply differ from what most Americans have known as "religious broadcasting." The basic formula can be seen in programs like the *700 Club*. The program clearly intends to compete with commercial TV for viewers by adhering to the same production values. Using the latest in four-color video equipment and the most sophisticated staging, lighting, and production techniques, the *700 Club* looks very much like any talk or "magazine" format programs on American television.

What is different, of course, is the content. As they have come to be involved in the neoevangelical "new right," electronic church ministries are widely known for their political conservatism. The *700 Club* embeds politics in its program in a variety of ways. Pat Robertson and the other hosts often comment on issues of the day, typically focusing on news events related to the "social agenda" of the new right.[18] Content analyses of the program have revealed that many such issues appear in the program's news and documentary segments and typically are then commented upon by the hosts and their guests.

The program has opposed abortion, and has favored prayer in the schools, capital punishment, banking reform, a strong defense policy, censorship of "pornographic" and violent media, and has opposed the women's movement on some key issues including the Equal Rights Amendment, and urged a more isolationist foreign policy. These political messages are purveyed in an evangelical and fundamentalist context but within a video setting that is unashamedly secular. Robertson and his guests sit in a modern, well-appointed (if a bit overdone) set. The news reports and remote film and other video segments are interposed smoothly in ways consciously modeled on the commercial networks. Station breaks and other announcements interrupt the flow of the program, though they are most often produced by CBN itself to promote its own programs and other services. These "spots" also follow the form of commercial broadcasting and are technically sophisticated.

Most of the direct, exhortative political material emerges in comments made by the hosts[19] and the guests. A news item about controversy over public display of nativity scenes at Christmas is an occasion for commentary on the general loss of religious direction in the country at large. A film piece on arms policy leads to discussion of the need for a strong defense. Often, Robertson himself will present a brief talk on a matter that concerns him, most frequently on banking and economic policy.

Guests lend credibility to the program. Leading figures of the evangelical, charismatic, and fundamentalist movements are frequent guests. Also on the guest list are public figures (political and otherwise), who appear to share their faith, or discuss issues of concern to the movement. Guests of a purely "informational" sort also appear.

The *700 Club*'s telephone counselors are always available to viewers. Shown at the beginning of the program, the phone banks are referred to repeatedly throughout, with telephone numbers superimposed on the screen for nearly the entire program. During prayer or following particularly moving testimonies, the hosts will refer to the telephone facilities directly, suggesting that viewers call in for prayer or counseling. There is rarely, if ever, mention of money on the air. Aside from twice- or thrice-yearly telethons, there is no on-air fund-raising. Members and support are solicited primarily by the telephone counselors.

The program has a "feel" similar to that of a conventional talk show. Pat Robertson and his cohosts speak and manage the program with ease and professionalism. Aside from the occasional prayer and frequent testimonies by guests, the program does not appear to be excessively "religious." It lacks the earnestness of its major competitors, Jerry Falwell's and Jimmy Swaggart's programs (both of which are intensely critical of contemporary life and religion). At the same time, the *700 Club* is more sober and contained than the rival *PTL Club*, with its ecstatic Pentecostal music and overt emotionalism.

Robertson's efforts to present a program that can attract and hold a broad, national audience have produced a program that closely resembles the rest of television. Pat Robertson could be (for a particularly naive viewer) Johnny Carson's or Merv Griffin's replacement. Only with rather intent attention over a period of several minutes does the difference emerge.

The sociopolitical perspective of the program, as expressed by guests and in commentaries by the hosts, is broadly populist, but with a difference. Robertson's interest in the area of finance has lead him to frequent homilies on the ills of the U.S. and international banking industries. The conservative fundamentalist and evangelical roots of the program are the source of its strong opinions on abortion, prayer in the schools, even on apparently nontheological topics like bilingualism and the Panama Canal treaty of the late 1970s. The movement's millennialism also imbues the program with claims about the possible place of the United States in biblical prophecy. The lower-middle-class roots of the movement and the long tradition of jingoism and nationalism derived from fundamentalism give the program an ethnocentric air with regard to international affairs and domestic cultural pluralism.

The dimensions of CBN

CBN's *700 Club* presents three dimensions to its viewers. First is the program itself, the visible presentation that is sent out to syndicated stations and over the cable channel live each morning for 60 or 90 minutes (and repeated in the late evening in some markets). The second dimension of the *700 Club* is the prayer counseling division. The third dimension is a more recent development at CBN, the direct-mail operation. These primary parachurch activities are supplemented by a number of others. There are a variety of publications, newsletters, magazines, pamphlets, and other media produced and distributed from time to time, and a program of seminars, meetings, and other direct-contact opportunities available to interested people who visit the CBN headquarters in Virginia Beach. Each of these three aspects of CBN entails unique administrative and creative challenges. The objectives of each activity offer insight into the goals of CBN and its staff and into its programming.

Program production

The *700 Club* is crafted both to be similar to conventional TV and to be different from classic religious broadcasts featuring worship and preaching. Robertson's decision to replace CBN's original Christian talk show format with one that mimics the magazine style of secular broadcasting was, in part, a decision to exert more control over the production. The change grew out of his desire to break the traditional mold of religious broadcasting and appeal to a broader audience. According to a CBN associate producer:

> We take the program out of ecclesiastical trappings and use *production-oriented* settings so it's a *television* program instead of a church program on television.[20]

This change in format added elements to balance the long testimonial segments that had dominated the program.

> Surveys showed that Christian talk shows were the *least* watched of all religious programming. We felt that we were reaching only 1% of the national viewing audience in America. We only had 3% of the total Christians, only 30% of the Christian audience. We switched to a "segment" format where we present such things as cooking hints, time management, political stuff, exercise classes *and* testimonials.

This same producer felt that the new concentration on broader issues, outside the normal content of religious broadcasting, quickly set the *700*

Club apart from many other programs. This was largely responsible for the program's prominence, in his view:

> We've gotten heavily into politics and economics. Oral Roberts and Robert Schuller concentrate on salvation but not how salvation relates to the world.... Christians can't live in a state of suspended animation.

While Robertson himself tends to be rather pietistic in describing the success of the *700 Club*, laying it to the work of God, some of his staff are less circumspect.

> The Holy Spirit is involved in our ratings increase, but we've been presenting a greater variety of guests and ideas for the audience with the new format.

Religious broadcasters are sensitive to suggestions that "they are preaching to the choir"—to the already committed—instead of reaching out to the unchurched and the non-Christian. It is a potentially devastating criticism because it undermines support for their broadcast organizations, which allegedly exist only to extend the reach of community-based churches, not to compete with them—a claim that Robertson and others make constantly.

The electronic church audience can be said to have *two* potential segments: The "patrons," or contributors who pay the bills, analogous to art patrons; and the "audience," those who are actually watching for spiritual sustenance. But if their programs are not reaching the masses of spiritually needy they claim to reach, then the "patrons" and the "audience" are actually one and the same group, all of whom believe the program they support is really aimed for someone *else*—someone "out there" who "really needs it." The broadcasters' own perception of whether there are two distinct groups watching, of course, is crucial to their decision making.

How do Robertson and his staff know when they are succeeding in producing the desired "effects" on a "real audience"? One *700 Club* producer explained that their impressions of audience composition and audience tastes were shaped by feedback from the phone counselors, by anecdotal evidence obtained from unsolicited letters and phone calls directed specifically at program format issues, and by direct market research and audience surveys. Reports of audience reaction to the new magazine format in 1981-1982, for example, drew on these sources, representing feedback from the two audience groups. Traditional patrons of the program, the producer noted, called and wrote their disapproval of such things as music being dropped from the format. But, at the same time, over 5000 letters requested recipes after a new cooking segment. Analysis of data collected as part of the activity of the phone counselors revealed that many newer viewers seemed to be attracted by the new format. CBN focus group studies and surveys revealed broad satisfaction with the new approach.[21]

This evidence suggests that the producers of the *700 Club* aim their program at a "target" audience made up of people "who need to be reached" with a message of salvation. What is their impression of the audience, though? How easy is it to reach? What special challenges face them in this process? Overall, one CBN producer's impressions of the audience are that they are hard to reach ("people get to the show by passing it on the dial," he says), somewhat amorphous, and programmed by the experience of viewing conventional television:

People have been conditioned by television . . . people have been trained to stop listening after seven minutes. The human mind can grasp more than we can deliver, however, and the electronics of the industry allow us to make it exciting for the viewer. There is a hypnotic effect of the frame situation in television. On a conscious level people stop concentrating, but on a subconscious level the mind becomes focused . . . while they see television in general as a purveyor of garbage, we are able to bring Jesus Christ to them through their TV antennas.

Some people are seen as unreachable, though:

Now if I were to watch a Hindu or Buddhist program where the speaker would do what Pat does—look me in the eye and say, "Here it is."—I might be impressed, but I wouldn't be convinced. Pat can't reach everybody—some predisposition is necessary.

In spite of this apparent cynicism regarding the impact of the program, a great deal of time and attention goes into production. The production staff is large, and the production facilities are considered state of the art.[22]

A typical segment observed from the studio during production included news clips; a remote satellite question-and-answer interview about abortion with Robert Dornan, the leader of the "pro-life" forces in the U.S. House of Representatives; a taped interview with two musicians from the rock group Kansas, including one of their songs; a remote story about El Salvador's political problems; an interview with an ex-member of the Maryland film censorship board; an exercise feature; and a testimony from a woman in the studio audience who had been healed at one of Robertson's personal appearance services.[23]

Other production elements observed in the studio included teleprompters, four-camera color recording, full stage sets, and an audience warm-up. The program incorporated canned applause and canned telephone rings when the call-in number was flashed on the screen. The bank of phone counselors was visible to the studio audience and was shown on camera from time to time. In all, it was a tight and sophisticated production.

The prayer counselors

The telephone banks that were installed for the earliest CBN telethons to log in financial pledges are now used for many other purposes. CBN telephone operators provide daily prayer counseling services and record pledges during telethons. A staff of full- and part-time volunteer counselors operate the phones.

At CBN headquarters, where most of the phone work is centered, a staff of approximately 1500 volunteer counselors, 600 to 700 of whom are active at a given time, are used regularly. Aside from the headquarters phone center, there are regional centers where calls can be directed to a more "local" number. These regional centers are staffed by both paid and volunteer directors; the paid directors are in the largest cities, where the volume of calls justifies a center and adequate volunteer help might not be available. The total number of volunteer counselors nationwide is 5000, including those who are used for the peak telethon periods.[24]

Aside from telethons, phone counseling does not involve overt fundraising or membership solicitation. One of the staff in charge of the counseling center observed that

> phone counselors are there only to minister to needs. People who call in can ask counselors for information about membership in the "Club" or about contributing, but the purpose of the counselors is not to lead people to membership . . . we really have our fundraising down to a dull roar, and Pat never asks for money on the air, that is all done through direct mail.

One of the most controversial aspects of ministries like CBN (from the perspective of mainline churches) is the possible adverse impact that viewing of these programs might have on conventional church membership, attendance, and giving.[25] Robertson has said that CBN's own research indicates that local church involvement goes up for those who become heavy viewers.[26] The Annenberg-Gallup study and other recent data, particularly from opinion polls, tend to support his claim. The philosophy of CBN regarding church involvement is put strongly by Robertson:

> We believe that the local congregation is the true body of Christ. Television can't be church, it's just television. We avoid scheduling programs in direct competition with church services.[27]

A CBN producer:

> It is never our purpose to create programs that people attend instead of going to church . . . we do get blamed, however, for whatever people do after they watch our shows, and there are some people who do watch instead of attending regular churches.[28]

And a director of the phone counseling center:

Some of the other television ministries *are* "church on the air," but we aren't and we don't want to be. Churches are called upon to "feed my sheep" . . . *we* call the sheep to the fold in the first place.[29]

There is, then, some pressure for phone counselors to encourage callers to go to church. This is accomplished by referring to a list of 6000 churches nationwide that have been approved by CBN. Not just any church will do, however. The 6000 churches on the list have contacted CBN (or have been contacted in a few cases) and have been evaluated for suitability. A staff person comments, "They are evangelical, they support our doctrine . . . and are "full gospel."[30]

After a person has called in for prayer or counseling, they usually are connected with one of these local congregations for follow-up:

> Often, callers will say, "Why can't you spend more time with me?" or "I'm in the hospital and my pastor hasn't been to call on me." We can refer them to one of our cooperating local pastors. . . . We can have a pastor knocking on their door in three days. . . . The prayer requests are passed along to the regional center, which then refers it to a pastor.

This "switchboarding" of local congregations by CBN is fairly unique among religious broadcasters, but the general idea that only certain local congregations may benefit from the "flock gathering" of the electronic church has been supported elsewhere in the continuing debate. Armstrong has said:

> If, after someone has been attracted by the message of the Gospel presented by the electric church, and goes to a local congregation which does not carry the same life and vitality in the spirit that is seen on the screen, then he will naturally keep on looking [for such a congregation].[31]

Another broadcaster, Jerry Falwell, often exhorts his followers to attend church, but only "Bible-believing" churches.[32]

The terms *Bible-believing* and *full-gospel* have specific institutional meanings in the context of the "two-party" controversy of the neoevangelical revival, and they may well have the effect of directing mainline Protestants who are viewers of these programs not to avoid church altogether but to seek out a specific kind of church, or to attempt to bring about changes in their own congregations.

The format change of the *700 Club* provided an opportunity for CBN to evaluate the type of viewer who tends to be ministered to through the phone center. The format of the *700 Club* always was intended to attract curious, nonevangelical viewers.

> We come from the "full-gospel" church. . . . Conventional churches are not "full-gospel" . . . there has been too much concentration on controversy and

division there. . . . We present our message tastefully, tactfully, over the air. . . . CBN is an *exhorting* ministry, prophetic . . . not intended to *divide*.

This "nonconfrontational" style has been enhanced by the shift in format.

Our "prayer partners" [CBN's term for members] notice that the new format is more magazine, less "ministry." Before, we were ministering to a small audience of *believers*, of people who were already *saved*. Now we're not losing audience, its just shifting. We're adding people who are curious. This is reflected by calls, letters, by changes in giving, by the market response.

Thus the impression CBN receives of its target audience is that it has changed from the early days, from one that already agreed with CBN theology, to a broader one, one that needs more "tasteful," "tactful" content.

We've made a commitment to reach the *unsaved*—other programs talk to themselves. We're not reaching old viewers, we want to get *new* viewers.

Robertson seems to be convinced, then, that at some time in the past, they had been reaching an audience that was already "convinced," that watched and supported because it was *theologically* supportive of the program. By shifting to a new format with more diverse programming and scheduling, CBN has tried to enlarge its audience while holding onto its "natural constituency." The obvious implication for the program is that it should not "turn off" this new, "seeking" audience with "petty" controversies. CBN seems to have concluded that their mandate is to present a "prophetic call" in a way that will readily engage and convert a "curious" audience, an audience that is large and heterogeneous because it is being gathered through the mass medium of television.

The efforts to make CBN as broadly palatable as possible also are evident in the way the telephone counselors are selected and trained. Phone counseling staffers report that, aside from the high attrition commonly associated with volunteer labor, the biggest problem is the *theological* stance of phone counselors.

Phone counselors volunteer for their positions by filling out an application, giving their personal testimony, submitting a recommendation form from their local pastor, and attending CBN's eight-week training course. Aside from helping volunteers "straighten out their own lives" before they help others do so by phone, course instructors report that they must "shave off" certain theological rough edges that the counselors bring with them.

We are constantly having to say "don't do this" or "don't say that" to them. We don't want them to get on the phone and turn first-time callers off by preaching extreme beliefs to them.

Among the largely sectarian and particularist beliefs that have been encountered among counselors are that women should not cut their hair or wear makeup; that Christians shouldn't watch movies; that callers' problems are caused by demons; that ill callers are ill because they are "sinners"; that financial prosperity will follow salvation; that healing will always follow salvation; that Catholicism and/or Judaism are "sins"; that "speaking in tongues" is bad; and that immersion baptism is the only acceptable form of that sacrament. Some have been unable to deal with grief, the occult, or homosexuality. A counseling center staff person reflects on the implications of this particularism:

> I see now why the church has largely failed. We have let petty disagreements get in the way of leading people to the Lord. People tend to make a "god" out of "shepherding." CBN tries to be a balanced ministry.

Counselors get specific help in "ministering" from the Bible. Each counselor is given a blue card called "*700 Club* Scripture References for Counselors" that lists biblical passages for each of 37 issues or problems (from "Abortion" to "Wisdom"), subdivided so that various approaches to each can be taken by the counselors. Counselors may also refer to several brochures by Pat Robertson that outline his philosophy and theology.

CBN phone counselors offer prayer and guidance to callers, the majority of whom call for help with a specific problem. Counselors are instructed to provide that help without pushing callers to become members, but almost all forms of ministry CBN offers result in the taking of a caller's name, address, phone number, and vital statistics (age, sex, "special need," "spiritual life," and so on).

The usual reason a caller contacts CBN, for instance, is to ask for prayer. A yellow form in the phone counselor's packet, called the "*700 Club* Prayer Request," directs the phone counselor to write down the caller's address (or city of residence at least), along with his or her request for prayer. The yellow form also includes a checklist for recording demographic information on the caller and the nature of the prayer request. The needs prayed for are listed with boxes for the counselors to check. (Presumably, those listed on the form are the most frequently needed ones, primarily health related, with a category of "other.") Once the appropriate boxes are checked, the prayer counselor then prays with the caller and assures him or her that the request will be prayed over by the staff of CBN, following the close of the program. (This actually takes place with hundreds of yellow forms piled on the altar in the prayer chapel at the CBN Center.)

Once prayer has been said over the request forms in the chapel, they are taken to CBN's computer center where they are read into the data base. Along with them go the various other forms that counselors have filled out according to the type of call received. Counselors can request follow-up to a call by one of the cooperating local churches, or CBN "area coordinators" (the title of the professional staff persons at the regional phone counseling centers). These forms include the name, address, and so on of the person, and indicate whether the counselor "prayed for their salvation." Presumably, this form is filled out in addition to the prayer request form, but having both forms gives CBN additional information.

There also is a form for reporting "answers to prayer" by callers who have found help or healing through the program or through prayers. Again, the name, address, and the specific need met are recorded on the form (asking if they also wish to receive a free magazine). This form includes a space to record financial pledges to go along with the prayer pledges. There also is a form to record requests for the special needs of callers, or a request for a visit by a cooperating congregation pastor, again with the name and address space provided.

CBN counselors, of course, are happy to help callers interested in providing financial support for CBN or in membership. There also is a pledge form on which counselors can record pledges that come in either for initial support or for increased giving. These forms are the same ones that are used during telethons and, indeed, the training and all the forms used by the counselors are exactly the same during telethon periods as during regular programming. The volunteers who work the phones for telethons also are called prayer counselors, even though their goals are certainly more in the direction of enlisting financial support. Both activities, counseling and fund-raising enlistment, occur simultaneously under the processes set up by CBN.

The careful attention to detail in compiling mailing lists is crucial, according to staff of the counseling center.

> Our support until now has come from the telethons, but we're moving more to direct mail . . . though we'll always need one telethon at least. . . . Callers are encouraged to call the center or any one of the 71 regional centers to ask for help.

When calls come in, they are moved onto a track that results in the vast majority of callers being listed by name and address and cross-referenced by demographics, needs, and spiritual condition in CBN's master data base. Their needs *are* served to a certain extent (there is, of course, disagreement about the effectiveness of a media church ministering to human needs[33]) through follow-up by local pastors, telephone calls, letters, and literature from CBN. While CBN makes those initial referrals and follows up on them, it also challenges those on its mailing lists to ever higher levels of involvement and support of its own work.

CBN as an example of "long distance community"

The type of community created by CBN's organization is not really a "church," even a vicarious one. Rather, it relates to a wider reality, what we might call the *parachurch*: an extensive network of organizations, ministries, missions, revivals, broadcasts, recording companies, publishers, and clubs, which surround the more formal denominations and congregations of American Protestantism.

William Fore has suggested that the future of CBN and the other electronic church programs may be as formal denominations on their own.[34] The development of CBN's regional phone centers could serve such a function, as well as the more modest one of involvement in the parachurch community. While these centers might once have been primarily for the purpose of taking local calls and handling local referrals from CBN headquarters, their role has expanded.

"Operation Blessing," for instance, was launched by CBN in 1980. The program matches phoned-in needs with local resources. Phone counselors record needs including food, financial help, employment, and housing assistance on the CBN computer and match them with gifts donated to "Operation Blessing." Where needs match up with resources, CBN's local area directors take care of arrangements, thereby performing a very direct and conventional ministerial function.[35]

One staff member has said, "The trend is for our area directors to get into more financial planning work and to get into more and more work with local churches." When asked if this new visibility on the part of the regional centers and area directors would result in them eventually becoming local congregations of a CBN "denomination," he responded:

> No, that is in opposition to what CBN is about—we're here to communicate the Gospel via the airwaves. We work *with* local churches in communities so we unify and get them involved in the needs of the local community.

It is clear that CBN's local activities relate—in a way almost independent of the program—to viewers on the local level and, from their perspective, could become an important part of the program.

The direct-mail center

CBN began direct-mail work in 1963 in conjunction with its first TV broadcasts. In 1980, state-of-the-art direct-mail packaging equipment, complete with computer-generated letter capacity, was installed.[36] It allows a high degree of direct-mail personalization so that a recipient is not only addressed by name but the problem about which they called can be mentioned as well.

There is very little doubt that CBN's direct-mail center is primarily a fund-raising operation. CBN needs millions of dollars a year to maintain its operations, and direct mail is central to providing this money. While firm figures are hard to obtain, Internal Revenue Service filings by CBN indicate that, in fiscal 1984, total income was $159 million, of which $129 million came from gifts (the balance was earnings from satellite syndication and other program services). Of that figure, $17 million was spent on program production, $36 million on the purchase of airtime, $26 million on satellite operations, $31 million to provide the phone counseling and direct-contact ministries, and the balance for the general operating expenses of the organization.[37] Raising such amounts is a daunting task for any organization.

A staff person responsible for direct mail reports that CBN's approach to fund-raising is to challenge as many people as possible to begin regular, monthly giving to CBN. Major emphasis is placed on "tending" the mailing list to reduce membership attrition:

> You only have to decrease attrition by 2-3% to increase revenue by 20-30%. . . .
> We try to educate them [CBN members] through the mail. The *Perspective* [an opinion piece written regularly by Robertson at the time of this interview] is the most important thing we send. We've even cut the *Flame* [a more general interest magazine] to bi-monthly from monthly, and have made it more of a news piece. For our funding appeals we have to have a credible *reason* to ask for money, so we acquaint them with an aspect of our ministry.

Telethons were CBN's original fund-raising method—through the enlistment of pledges—but a mix of on-air and direct-mail fund-raising has proven more effective. Telethons provide valuable income and new names.

> We've found that, rather than feeling guilty about the telethons, we bring people in that way . . . our research indicates that people don't object to the telethons . . . but, while PBS has had quite a bit of success with just telethons, we find that our supporters need more regular tending.

The relationship between the program and the direct-mail operation is a curious one. In a sense, the program's purpose is to gather names for the CBN mailing list.

> Except for PTL, I don't know of any other ministry that has television like we do . . . I'm nothing but the offering plate for a television ministry. We're not using TV as well as we are using direct mail and support systems. We have distribution of product every day in just about every market . . . that makes it easier to be a direct mail person . . . telethons help perpetuate the cycle for us—they get new viewers that become new members.

Research with new callers in CBN telethons indicates that, on average, they have been watching for two and one-half years before calling in to offer a pledge. CBN staff think, then, that their average prospect is someone who has been a viewer for some time, who watches two or more times a week for 30 to 50 minutes. Once prospects call for counseling, or during a telethon, they may become contributors. They will continue to receive solicitations and other mailings. Along the way, they will be challenged to become members (CBN calls its members "partners") as well as givers, and eventually, they may become "special givers," or prospects who give large sums to the support of CBN.

> The sophistication of modern fundraising requires "fine segmentation" . . . now we're doing more with tactical and constituency segmentation . . . we're looking up what and how they give. We look at history—we segment them into groups where we ask them for gifts within their reach . . . they are asked for gifts in keeping with their status . . . then, we go for "stretch gifts" . . . asking prospects to move up a bit in their giving.

It seems, however, that the ideal CBN contributor is a regular one, not a major one.

> Our average partner is a woman in her mid 40s—though they're getting younger—a member who makes a monthly commitment. That's our strongest base. There are some spontaneous non-member donors, but I'll take a member with a $15 a month gift rather than a non-member with $200 any day. Members work out well if they are tended.

While most regular donors are enlisted by the direct-mail operation, special or major donors (4% of all donors) contribute 50% of CBN's yearly budget.[38] In 1987, CBN's income was reported to have reached nearly $200 million.[39] These donors naturally are given special attention by the direct-mail division, which has a staff of "special counselors" who periodically call major donors and offer to pray with them. This special treatment is accorded some lesser donors as well under a program called "operation appreciation" that selects donors at random, calls them, and offers prayer. While this may sound quite mercenary, CBN staff point out that giving is part of the biblical mandate (a claim not unknown to religious organizations of all kinds).

> We make sure that they support their local church first, even though there are a lot of church people among our members . . . we work with the local church. . . . The first thing we try to get a new believer to do is to go to church. . . . We can't offer the Bible teaching that a church can, we can't compete with a church.

Hadden and Swann presented the following philosophy of stewardship of one of the electronic church ministers.

> There is no higher worship expression than giving. . . . I don't believe in solicitation. I don't like the word. We don't solicit. That's begging. We feel religious giving is the Christian frame, which is a sacrificial expression of worship and is axiomatic.[40]

The fund-raising philosophy of CBN, and indeed, most Christian churches, is similar. Stewardship of personal resources as a Christian involves giving to the church. Few, if any religious organizations feel embarrassed about their fund-raising activities. Many, like CBN, talk freely about them. To them, it is as important a part of their "ministry" as anything else, and one that has clear theological justification.

CBN and its viewers

The *700 Club* provides many opportunities for viewer involvement. They can, of course, just watch, though they are encouraged to do more than that. Eventually, many make themselves known to CBN by calling to pledge a donation during a telethon, by calling to ask for prayer or to request a publication or other offer, by writing in, or by visiting the CBN center (as the audience is often invited to do). Once they are known to CBN, they often become involved in the work of CBN.

It is clear that CBN is more than "just" a "television ministry." Viewers become involved in a personal way with the program, if they call for prayer or counseling. They may even meet a CBN representative, in the form of a local pastor registered with CBN, or a representative of the local counseling center. They may become a member of CBN. If so, they may find that CBN calls *them* from time to time, thanking them for support, asking if they want prayer, and asking for additional financial support.

CBN also regularly holds development banquets throughout the country, where viewers might be invited to meet Pat Robertson or other CBN figures in person. They can read CBN publications, including a magazine, a newsletter, brochures, and books. They can travel to the CBN center itself, attend the program as a member of the studio audience, or attend one of CBN's periodic seminars or ministry workshops, where they might meet other people like themselves in addition to leading stars of the evangelical and fundamentalist world.

Through the guests, publications, and contacts, CBN puts its viewers and partners in touch with a wider reality, that of the informal (but highly organized) transdenominational parachurch. This parachurch exists in an amazing variety of services and organizations identified generally with the conservative side of the two-party dimension and largely independent of formal, denominational religion. There are recording companies and Christian record labels, book publishers, bookstore chains, magazines, newsletters, tract publishers, manufacturers and distributors of "Christian kitsch" artifacts, film producers and distributors, broadcasters, advertising agencies, consulting firms, radio and TV format syndicators, and a plethora of specialized and general ministries. These latter include both classic revival ministries, where the stress is on evangelism, and specialized ministries, such as Chuck Colson's "prison ministry" movement, and the Teen Challenge organization. Over time, representatives of the full range of this parachurch network appear on programs like the *700 Club*, in CBN publications, and in CBN projects.

Who are the viewers?

The CBN staff believes that the *700 Club* attracts an audience broader than thought to be typical of most religious broadcasting. We know something about whether they have been successful in this. The Annenberg-Gallup study[41] suggests that *700 Club* audiences differ from others in *some* respects.

Weekday religious programs, of which the *700 Club* is the most prominent, attract a fairly distinct but small audience. A minority of viewers of religious television, and a minority of viewers of weekend religion, watch weekday programs in addition to the others. The weekend programs clearly were more popular.[42] Even the most conservative viewers seemed to prefer weekend programs.

Weekday programs, like the *700 Club*, however, are more attractive to the members of traditionally Pentecostal or charismatic denominations than are the weekend programs.[43] Conservatives, members of evangelical denominations, women, and minorities seemed to prefer weekday religious programs over weekend programs.

This suggested to the Annenberg-Gallup team that the weekend programs are more attuned to those associated with traditional denominations (Baptist, Catholic, Presbyterian, and so on) and with relatively more upscale and professional classes. Weekday religious programs attract, on the other hand, larger proportions of institutionally independent and lower-class respondents.

Table 4.1 presents data for all religious viewers and viewers of weekday programs for the northeast region in the Annenberg-Gallup study. These are presented as frequency distributions because there are no mutually exclusive categories, that is, a given respondent may watch more than one type of program.[44]

As can be seen in Table 4.1, the demographic characteristics of weekday viewers in the Northeast are a reasonable approximation of those of all religious television viewers. There are also some interesting differences among the religiosity items. Weekday viewers appear to be more frequent in their church attendance than religious viewers in general, with nearly twice as many of them reporting that they attend more than once a week. Weekday viewers overall also appear to be theologically more conservative

TABLE 4.1 *Northeastern subsample: Frequency distribution of various characteristics among categories of religious viewing*

	All Religious Viewers	All Weekday Viewers	Total Subsample
Percentage among			
Denomination:			
evangelicals	24.2	28.2	17.0
nonevangelicals	41.3	43.1	35.8
Catholics	29.8	23.1	38.0
others	4.7	4.6	9.2
total N	(620)	(216)	(1221)
Age:			
18-29	13.2	9.9	19.7
30-40	33.5	39.6	38.0
50-65	34.5	36.5	28.9
over 65	18.8	14.0	13.4
total N	(638)	(222)	(1258)
Education:			
LT high school	24.1	19.1	19.7
high school graduate	44.0	50.9	42.0
college and more	31.9	30.0	38.4
total N	(634)	(220)	(1249)
Race:			
white	77.1	76.1	84.3
nonwhite	22.9	23.9	15.7
total N	(582)	(201)	(1134)
Family Income:			
< 15,000	41.7	41.3	34.1
15,000-24,999	29.4	29.6	29.1
25,000-35,000	14.1	14.8	17.3
> 35,000	14.8	14.3	19.6
total N	(561)	(196)	(1107)
Church Attendance:			
> 1/week	15.0	25.2	10.5
1/week	45.9	42.7	40.4
2-3/month	10.7	6.9	10.2
1/month	8.0	8.3	7.9
several/year	9.1	6.4	10.2
1/year	6.4	5.0	10.5
never	5.1	5.5	10.2
total N	(628)	(218)	(1234)

(continued)

TABLE 4.1 (continued)

Religious conservatism:			
high	40.7	62.4	23.9
medium	25.4	15.0	23.8
low	34.0	22.5	52.3
total N	(477)	(173)	(924)
Call program:			
no	81.0	64.4	
yes	19.0	35.6	N/A
	(638)	(222)	
Contribute to program:			
yes	30.6	51.4	
no	69.4	48.6	N/A
	(631)	(631)	
Television viewing:			
low	25.4	26.1	34.4
medium	32.6	28.4	31.2
high	42.0	45.5	34.3
	(638)	(222)	(1258)

than their weekend-viewing cohorts.

The relationship of these viewers to the institutions behind the programs they view differs as well. Weekday viewers report calling the programs they view in higher percentages than do religious viewers in general, and they contribute in higher proportions as well. Both of these latter findings are probably related to the institutional characteristics of the *700 Club* as we have described it. All of the weekday programs, but not all of those on weekends, have telephone counselors available. The weekend programs include many that operate on a shoestring, or do no fund-raising other than on-air solicitation.

Weekday viewers may also be looked at, as a class, in comparison with all respondents in the Annenberg-Gallup regional sample along the demographic, belief, and behavior dimensions described in Chapter 3 for that larger sample. Table 4.2 presents the same data as in Table 3.1 (Chapter 3), this time for the weekday, northeastern viewers only.

In comparing these two tables (Tables 3.1 and 4.2), some interesting, though slight, differences emerge. For the northeastern weekday audience, viewing of religious television is associated with slightly higher educational and income levels. Religious viewing seems to be slightly more common among men in this group than is the case in general. All of these relationships should have been expected, based on the earlier demographic

TABLE 4.2 *Correlations between viewing religious television, viewing conventional television, contributions to religious television, and demographic, belief, and behavior variables for northeast sample weekday viewers*

	Religious Television	General Television	Contribution to Religious TV
Demographic variables:			
education	−.185**	−.147*	−.001
	(218)	(220)	(93)
income	−.036	−.175**	.127
	(194)	(196)	(86)
age	−.172**	.070	−.087
	(220)	(222)	(93)
sex	−1.33*	.098	.159
	(220)	(222)	(93)
race	.055	.080	.019
	(200)	(201)	(82)
Religiosity variables:			
conservatism	−.270***	.093	−.133
	(172)	(173)	(74)
evangelical denomination	−.069	−.118*	−.166
	(214)	(216)	(91)
church attendance	−.176**	.019	−.199*
	(216)	(218)	(92)
local church contribution	.237***	−.138*	.223*
	(204)	(205)	(92)
frequency of prayer	−.159**	−.062	−.119
	(220)	(222)	(93)
importance of religion	−.235***	.034	−.175*
	(218)	(220)	(92)

NOTE: Direction of codings are generally with higher values moving toward the labeled value—that is, prayer: high = frequent; contributions: larger; importance: very important; race: high = nonwhite; conservatism: high = conservative.
*$p < .05$; **$p < .01$; ***$p < .001$.

analysis. What is more obvious here, however, is that these weekday viewers present a different relationship between media and religiosity measures than does the general sample. They appear to be less conservative than the sample as a whole, and less likely to report that religion is "very important" in their lives, though these differences are slight.

It appears, then, that the self-perception of the *700 Club*—that it is unique in format and appeal—has yet to be realized in success with its audience. The claim of its power and appeal serves important functions for its viewers, however, regardless of its basis in hard data. The self-consciousness of producers in seeking to reach beyond their natural constituency is both an important motivation *and* an important policy determinant for them as well.

The myth of "atypicality" is important to viewers and critics alike, particularly with regard to the potential *political* impact of the program. It is clear from the Annenberg-Gallup data that viewers of religious programs, including the *700 Club*, are more politically conservative (and more politically active) than cohorts who do not view. If the *700 Club* does mobilize previously uninvolved people and enlist them in either political or theological causes, concern about its significance would seem justified.

A new type of research needed

Previous researchers have not talked directly to viewers of these programs. What is their perception of their involvement in it? Why do they view? How did they start viewing? What do they get out of viewing? Previous research has done little to answer the question of *causal direction*, that is, what came first, their viewing, or their evangelicalism? Their viewing or their political conservatism? More important, and more profound, where does viewing fit into the fabric of their lives, their faith, their developing consciousness? If the electronic church is related to revitalization, or to an evolving "new religious consciousness" in America, the experiences of these viewers could provide invaluable insights into that process. Their personal, community, and social-cultural experience of the program could tell us much about its impact.

In the next chapter we will consider, in some depth, the experiences of some *700 Club* viewers. The method we are pursuing might be called "elaboration." We have analyzed quantitative and demographic data for the audience, and have a number of questions still remaining. We intend to elaborate the quantitative findings through direct interviews with a sample of viewers.

We take a number of questions about the meaning of the *700 Club* to its viewers (beyond those we have raised in previous chapters) into our analysis of the viewers we will meet in later chapters. What is the central message or meaning of the program for them? Do they agree with the manifest intentions of the producers of the program? How important is the wider institution of CBN to them? Do they care about it, or use it, or is viewing of the program alone the major gratification for them? What is their degree of involvement in the *700 Club*, the wider CBN organization, and the wider parachurch to which it is related? The program clearly is lodged in the neoevangelical movement, and proposes to bring a "new consciousness" to its audience. What is the evidence, in their lives and experiences, that this is taking place? What about the conflict between neoevangelicalism and modernism? Does this underlie the program for any of its viewers?

We know what the *700 Club* represents in the sociocultural and religious context of its time. What we want to know now is how it is used and what meanings are engendered by its use. The institution that has evolved around the *700 Club* is an extensive one. We want to know how viewers find their way into this extensive network of relations and obligations, and what difference it has made in their lives.

Notes

1. The term *network* usually applies to one of the commercial television networks, which are financed and organized far differently from such "networks" as CBN, PTL, or even the Cable News Network. The major difference is that, in true networks, the local affiliates are paid directly by the network for the airtime they give to network fare. In these ersatz networks, the programming is essentially free to the affiliates.

2. Pat Robertson, *Shout It from the Housetops* (South Plainfield, NJ: Bridge, 1972). Robertson's own story is a curious parallel to the testimonies of many of his guests and many of his viewers. While he was a New York lawyer, he was not unacquainted with southern evangelicalism, having grown up in Virginia as the son of a Republican U.S. Senator.

3. Ben Armstrong, *The Electric Church* (Nashville: Thomas Nelson, 1979), pp. 106-7.

4. Armstrong, *The Electric Church*. In early 1986, CBN underwent a major change in organization, selling all of its television and radio stations and concentrating on operations of its cable network, renamed CBN Continental Broadcasting Co.

5. Robertson, *Shout It from the Housetops*.

6. Ibid.

7. Ibid., p. 178.

8. Unless otherwise cited, all subsequent staff interviews are quoted from Stewart M. Hoover, "Religious Group Use and Avoidance of Television: A Study of Reasons and Effects" (M.A. thesis, Annenberg School of Communications, University of Pennsylvania, 1982).

9. Robertson, *Shout It from the Housetops*.

10. Pat Robertson, Presentation to the Electronic Church Consultation, New York University, 6-7 February 1980.

11. Robertson, *Shout It from the Housetops*, p. 191.

12. Hoover, "Religious Group Use," p. 64.

13. Robertson, *Shout It from the Housetops*, p. 192.

14. Robertson, Electronic Church Consultation.

15. Robertson, *Shout It from the Housetops*, p. 203.

16. Ibid., p. 204.

17. "Power, Glory—and Politics," *Time*, 17 February 1986, p. 62.

18. The political implications of simply *being* on television were illustrated in 1986 when Robertson withdrew as host of the program and as president of CBN while he pursued a bid for the Republican nomination for the U.S. presidency.

19. Aside from Robertson, a number of hosts and cohosts have appeared on the program. Ben Kinchlow, the longtime cohost of the program, is black, and, more recently, a woman, Terri Meuwsen, was added, though they have both left now.

20. Unless otherwise cited, all quotations about *700 Club* production and institutional activities are from Hoover, "Religious Group Use." See note 8.

21. Ibid., p. 71.

22. *Time*, "Power, Glory—and Politics," pp. 62-63.

23. Hoover, "Religious Group Use," pp. 72-73.

24. Ibid., p. 74.

25. For a complete discussion of these issues, see G. Gerbner, L. Gross, S. Hoover, M. Morgan, N. Signorielli, H. Cotugno, and R. Wuthnow, *Religion and Television*, technical report of the Annenberg-Gallup Study of Religious Broadcasting conducted by the Annenberg School of Communications and the Gallup Organization (Philadelphia: Annenberg School of Communications, University of Pennsylvania, 1984). See also Gary D. Gaddy and David Pritchard, "When Watching TV Is Like Attending Church," *Journal of Communication* 35, no. 1 (Winter 1985): 123-31.

26. Robertson, Electronic Church Consultation.

27. Ibid.

28. Hoover, "Religious Group Use," p. 77.

29. Ibid., p. 77.

30. Ibid., pp. 77-78.

31. Ben Armstrong, "Electronic Church—Pro and Con" (Unpublished colloquium presentation, Annenberg School of Communications, University of Pennsylvania, 1981).

32. Armstrong, *The Electric Church*, p. 155.

33. Ben Armstrong and William F. Fore, "Electronic Church—Pro and Con" (Unpublished colloquium presentation, Annenberg School of Communications, University of Pennsylvania, 1981).

34. Fore, "Electronic Church—Pro and Con."

35. Hoover, "Religious Group Use," pp. 88-89.

36. Ibid., p. 90.

37. U.S. Internal Revenue Service.

38. Hoover, "Religious Group Use," p. 93.

39. *The Philadelphia Inquirer*, 20 September 1987, p. 5-A. By this time, CBN had diversified operations, and was running its satellite service as a commercial entity. As a result, presumably somewhat less than the total income can now be attributed to donations.

40. Jeffrey K. Hadden and Charles E. Swann, *Prime Time Preachers* (Reading, MA: Addison-Wesley, 1981), p. 113.

41. All analyses reported here were conducted on the raw data from the northeastern regional database of the Annenberg-Gallup study, *Religion and Television*. These data were derived as described in Chapter 3, from samples taken from Arbitron ratings diary archives. As the interviews to be presented in later chapters are from a northeastern city, it was decided to present only the northeastern data here. There were, however, no systematic differences between northeastern and southeastern samples in the terms of this analysis, so these frequencies fairly well represent the entire Arbitron sample from the Annenberg-Gallup study.

42. Gerbner et al., *Religion and Television*, p. 71. See also Stewart M. Hoover, "The Religious Television Audience: A Matter of Significance, or Size?" *Review of Religious Research* 29, no. 2 (December 1987), for a discussion of relative audience size.

43. The weekday programs, in most markets the *PTL Club*, the *700 Club*, and Jimmy Swaggart's program, share in common that they represent the charismatic wing of evangelicalism, at least in terms of their founders' backgrounds. David E. Harrell, Jr., a historian who specializes in contemporary revivalism, argues that the most successful of the electronic church programs are from Pentecostal roots, though some of them would deny this. (Interview with David Harrell, July 1986.)

44. The purpose of the table is to compare the frequency percentages. It should be noted that the actual numbers (Ns) in parentheses should not be compared across the columns. The two "religious viewing" columns represent an intentional oversampling for religious viewers within the northeast population. The "total subsample" column has been statistically weighted to account for this oversampling. Therefore, it is *not* the case that 20% of the population in the northeast views weekday religion, as it would appear if one were to divide the weekday column N by the total N. It should also be noted that, because these must be presented as frequency distributions here, statistical tests of the significance of the differences are not available.

5

What Attracts People
to the Televangelists

Research on religious television audiences has found, not surprisingly, that viewers of the electronic church are unusually religious people. The data in Chapters 3 and 4, for instance, document that typical viewers are avid churchgoers and also are heavily involved in nonchurch religious activities.

The "prehistories" of viewers influence how they interpret the message of an evangelist like Pat Robertson and which elements they will pick up and integrate into their own religious worldviews. If they have been "born-again" evangelicals since childhood, for example, they are likely to have very different reactions to the program than if they come from a mainline Protestant or Catholic background. The social class and education of viewers also affect how they view programs. In the case of television ministers like Robertson, who have such a strong political identity, viewers' political attitudes directly affect how they perceive him.

Personal crises often lead people to seek out religious broadcasting. These programs have multifaceted ministries that are geared to both spiritual and temporal needs. Testimonies about salvation and healing are powerful dimensions of the evangelical and fundamentalist worldview, and provide an important justification for religious broadcasting. If a viewer has been "born again" and/or healed, clearly it would affect his or her perception of the electronic church.

It is not clear from the evidence how many viewers initially tune in to the *700 Club* because of spiritual or physical needs. Most probably watch it because of long-standing involvement with evangelicalism or fundamentalism. But both types of viewers—the "needy" and the "evangelicals"—are part of a larger movement. That movement has pretensions beyond ministering to individual souls.

We want to look beyond the most obvious aspects of religious broadcasting to its role in the development of the neoevangelical religious consciousness in our era. If religious broadcasting is integral to a movement of revitalization, it should be obvious in the lives of its viewers, regardless of how or why they first became involved with the program.

We will investigate viewers' experiences with religious broadcasting within the contexts of their religious consciousness. The electronic church is, first of all, experienced within the context of *individual* cognitive and religious development. Theories of cognitive faith development can provide an analytic structure for this context. How does religious viewing relate to individual processes of faith development and maintenance? Second, we will look at electronic church viewing as it relates to wider contexts of *community*. The studies of Victor Turner suggest important linkages to ritual processes of meaning in community, particularly as those processes are based in important catalytic experiences such as rites of passage. What is the relationship of the electronic church to other communities within which its viewers live? Can it ever be a community of any kind? Finally, the electronic church is experienced in the context of a *wider society*. William McLoughlin's work on revitalization movements has found that such movements have specific implications for the societies where they occur, often having reform of those societies as their goal. How does viewing support or undermine a relationship to the broader society for individuals in the electronic church audience?

We will look at how religious television, specifically the *700 Club*, addresses viewers' religious and social concerns. What are the structures of identity and consciousness related to their experience with it? What catalytic events of crisis or consciousness have they experienced that have led them to search for certainty in an age of dissonance and dissolution? How do these viewers come to terms with new symbols and systems of belief, identity, and practice? Finally, and most important, what evidence can we find of a true reorientation in their lives?

Individual growth as a cognitive process

All the rituals of daily life—including television viewing (and other forms of entertainment), work, social activities, church, and parachurch activities—contribute symbols and values to our individual identities and beliefs.[1] In contemporary America, religious symbols and values often are conveyed outside the confines of traditional church and family groups. Structures and rituals that lead to changes in religious consciousness are thus in place around the phenomenon of the electronic church.

Such changes in consciousness grow out of individual *cognitive* processes of development. James Fowler has described such developments as "stages of faith," moving from the individual and insular to the more communitarian and universalistic. Based on the earlier work of Jean Piaget, Erik Erikson, and Lawrence Kohlberg, Fowler's seven faith stages parallel generally accepted psychological and cognitive stages of individual development. These stages are not dependent on the *content* of the beliefs developed so much as on "the styles, the operations of knowing and valuing, that constitute the action, the way of being that is faith."[2]

There are, typically, three stages of development through preadolescence, based on individual cognitive growth toward better mastery of abstract thinking. In terms of belief, Fowler notes, the adolescent must begin to account for the fact that "either God is powerless . . . or God is asleep." Through experience, adolescents learn that the structures of reciprocity upon which they have organized their beliefs ultimately do not prevail (they cannot depend on God always to reward the good and punish the bad), and they must revise their faith to account for this.[3]

Further development of religious consciousness in adolescence requires that the individual take account of the perspectives of others in a new, dynamic way. Fowler calls this fourth stage synthetic because it entails a synthesis (for the first time) of personal beliefs and experiences with those symbols, values, and ideals presented by the wider community. One constructs "a supportive and orienting unity . . . a 'story of my stories'—a sense of meaning of life generally and of the meaning and purpose of his or her life in particular."[4] The point of orientation is *interpersonal*. The testing of belief that accompanies development is brought about by personal encounters with new beliefs and practices.

Fowler has found that many people "equilibrate" (that is, stay) at this *synthetic/conventional* stage. The synthesis results in an internalization of authoritative and powerful guides for life—a structure that if left unexamined can continue effectively to guide individual consciousness—provided no crises undermine its legitimacy. The most important transition of adulthood is the transition from this stable structure to one where the individual critically *reflects* on the faith structure itself. At the synthetic/conventional stage, religious consciousness is *tacit*. At the later stage, it is examined and refined more consciously.

Critical examination of one's beliefs leads to the stage Fowler calls *individuative-reflective faith*. Once there, the individual must make choices about the definition and boundaries of his or her beliefs. Instead of depending on standards set by "others" in the community and culture, the individual strives to unify his or her beliefs and to take responsibility for them.

The individuative stage gives way later in life (midadulthood, Fowler says) to a *conjunctive* stage, where the self-reflective belief structure adapts once again to take into account other traditions. "Truth must be approached from at least two or more angles of vision simultaneously," says Fowler.[5]

This "conjunctive faith" is particularly open to symbols and myths from outside the dependable structures through which consciousness has developed. The stage of conjunctive faith never quite integrates these polarities, however. It is possible for individuals to know that other systems of belief are as valid as their own, without learning from them.

At the seventh stage, *universalizing*, there is an expansion in "perspective taking," Fowler says, so that individual consciousness draws on both the traditions of one's "home" faith *and* those of an ever-widening circle of belief systems. At this stage, the individual bases his or her consciousness both on an awareness and appreciation of other traditions *and* on a process of "valuation" in which the concerns of others, "*their* fears and anxieties about worth, significance and survival,"[6] come to define consciousness.

Fowler's "stages of faith" carry important implications for our understanding of the electronic church. As cognitive development continues, individuals consciously choose their belief systems, rather than uncritically accepting "givens." Symbolic input, such as that from television and the popular arts, can have a particular impact here. Finally, individuals learn how to hold in tension and harmonize their beliefs and those of others. Fowler attributes these qualities to a growing ability to take the perspectives of others.

> Each new stage brings a qualitative expansion in *perspective taking*. With each later stage, the circle of "those who count" in one's way of finding or giving meaning to life expands. From primal relations in intimate family, we gradually widen our circle of awareness and regard to extended family and friends, to those who share our political and/or religious identifications, and finally beyond those to humankind or Being, in an inclusive sense.[7]

Religious consciousness thus develops as an ever-widening circle of beliefs are encountered through which our personal religious *identities* are shaped. Rather than an egocentric sense of identity, though, mature beliefs take into account a range of contexts and communities. A fully developed religious consciousness merges personal beliefs with an ultimate, more universal reality.

Religious broadcasting has the potential to foster this process of development. It is a rich source of symbolic input. For viewers who do come from belief backgrounds that contrast with the evangelical values espoused in a program like the *700 Club*, it could provide a contrasting perspective that might lead to the broadening and universalizing of belief that Fowler proposes. We will look for evidence of such growth and development.

The modern ritual contexts of religious consciousness and identity

The most basic business of a culture or subculture is the celebration and testing of cultural symbols and the integration of new symbols as conditions of life change. A cultural or anthropological approach (as introduced by Carey in Chapter 1) would help in understanding the mechanisms we encounter. Victor Turner[8] has contributed much to our understanding of these processes through his concepts of *liminality, communitas,* and *societas.*

Turner's concept of liminality arose from his observations of community-based kingship and initiation rituals. These rites of passage entail an elaborate ritual suspension of the structures of everyday life (kinship, social practice, daily routines, and so on). This creates a moment of freedom in which individuals can question old relationships, values, and routines, and reorganize them in new ways. Through ritual, these structures are suspended and new ones tested. As a result of this "threshold" state (which he called "the liminal"), individuals recognize new possibilities in their lives. The result is an awareness of an ideal universal community (Turner's "communitas") that imbues subsequent life with new meaning and possibilities. Individuals emerge with a sense that such an ideal community is possible and desirable. The contrast between the ideal of communitas and the profane, structured, secular world (which he calls "societas") produces a constant tension that motivates individuals to reform their real communities to more nearly approximate the ideal.[9] This tension is made more profound by the realization that the wider society and its structures, societas, are hostile, even dangerous to the new consciousness achieved through communitas.

The traditional setting of cultural meaning and cultural transformation is thus striking, epochal, unique, once in a lifetime. Even in more modern settings, the powerful rituals of "social drama," or of *pilgrimage* (such as the Moslem *Hajj*), identified by Turner as parallel to these more "traditional" ones, are not everyday, or even common experiences.[10] In the industrialized societies of the Western world, however, the myths and symbols through which we know and learn and shape our culture come to us not in unique rites of passage or in "once in a lifetime" pilgrimages, but through the multifaceted symbolic environments within which we live our lives. Liminality in modern life, say Turner and others, is the constant flow of cultural "possibility" that we encounter through our rich cultural environments.[11]

Modern myths of deep cultural meaning are thus expressed in such places as social gatherings and popular entertainment. As the sources of such cultural meaning, these liminal aspects are thus highly attractive, salient, and even pleasurable episodes in contemporary life. Bernice Martin[12] has suggested that a "framed liminality" (a liminality that is limited to discrete "frames" within life experience rather than being allowed to exist constantly) is the basis of contemporary leisure activity. Holidays, weekends, theater, and television provide regular, ongoing liminal spaces within the routines of day-to-day life. Rituals of social interaction in church, community, and club are thus supplemented by (and more recently replaced by) liminality experienced through the popular arts. Martin and others[13] assert that, far from being a time when nothing of importance is done, leisure becomes crucially important because it is the context (one of the few such contexts) in which these symbolic processes occur. Martin argues that most societies find the need to limit liminality in this way, due to the fact that "pure" liminality cannot be sustained. Films, newspapers, theater, sporting events, political involvements, and other leisure activities therefore are particularly significant because they offer access to new myths and symbols.

All mass media, including the electronic church, are potential sources of liminality. Individual consciousness, based in experience with ever-widening contexts of input and belief, should find within such media symbols and values that are relevant to the search for meaning.[14] Viewers of such programs should find within them "codes" that help focus their efforts toward "revitalization."

Liminality and communitas are lenses through which we see the development of contemporary religious consciousness. Liminality helps individuals understand and accept new cultural possibilities. The profound motivations of cultural revitalization and individual cognitive growth are given their form by the desire for true, universal communitas.

The role of neoevangelicalism and the electronic church in "revitalization"

In Chapter 1, we noted that the resurgence of evangelicalism and fundamentalism in recent years has been cited by William McLoughlin[15] as evidence that a new Great Awakening may be under way in American religious culture. Peter Berger and Wade Clark Roof have proposed, as we saw, that religious mass media have been central to this resurgence.

In the electronic church, we see many of the elements of revitalization that we have discussed. These ministries have self-consciously lodged themselves at the center of individuals' experiences of dissonance, frustration, and need in the cultural crisis of recent decades. They see a role for themselves in addressing the tensions between traditional cultural symbols and a wider culture now "out of control."

They have done this by developing a total, universal explanation of life, a *weltanschauung* that proposes to resolve the dissonances felt in contemporary life (a "code," to use Wallace's[16] terminology). Programs such as the *700 Club* present leaders, like Pat Robertson, who come to embody the process of change that must ensue if true revitalization is to occur—to take up the role of "prophecy" in McLoughlin's model. There is at least anecdotal evidence that viewers of these programs feel profoundly, even ecstatically, involved in this "mission."

Is it a true revitalization, though, or is it merely a reaction, a particularly prominent articulation of reactionary fundamentalism that ultimately rejects instead of embracing change? We will evaluate these and other questions by looking for dynamics of revitalization in the lives of viewers. We expect to find stress, dislocation, and change at the center of their faith and life histories, and will look for evidence that they have found, in the electronic church and elsewhere, new forms and symbols through which this dislocation yields new meaning and a broader religious consciousness.

Individuals develop their faith, Fowler tells us, when they encounter and incorporate worldviews outside their own, when they develop a sense of the universalism of faith. They respond to cultural dissonance, says McLoughlin, by searching for new cultural symbols that can give meaning to situations that their native beliefs do not. In both dimensions, they need to find for themselves a sense of wider possibility, of communitas, and space for reorganization of meaning, in order to move along their life trajectories. This sense of possibility is made real, even transcendent, for them when it emerges from a ritualized experience, the liminal, where they are able to see beyond the restrictive structures and meanings of the past.

Through the experiences of viewers

Individual experience is central to our understanding of cultural development. People are notoriously unreliable informants about their own behaviors, however. There has been much comment about how opinion surveys are imperfect indicators of individual belief and action, particularly for issues beyond the most basic and unequivocal ones. Viewers are the only ones, though, who can give us qualitative insight into the questions we have asked. In the following chapters, we will begin to hear from some members of the *700 Club*. They are representative of the membership in one metropolitan area and were chosen to represent diversity in social, educational, and ethnic background.[17]

The research methodology employed was what we might call "elaboration." The Annenberg-Gallup study discussed in Chapters 2 and 3 involved a refined survey questionnaire from which most of the data reported there were derived. It included a variety of questions having to do with religious and social attitudes as well as religious media and nonmedia behaviors. Each interview began with the Annenberg-Gallup questionnaire, with viewers encouraged to reflect on and expand on questions and answers as they went along. A less-structured interview followed. Our purpose, in the present inquiry, is to elaborate the findings of that survey, by investigating key questions and dimensions in greater depth than is possible with a large sample of viewers. What is lost in statistical representativeness (and we should not underplay the implications of this loss) is gained in depth of understanding of meanings and relationships that are not obvious from quantified data.

Viewers were asked simply to recount their "faith histories." They were aware that they had been sought out because of their participation in religious television, but they were not asked to described how their viewing was or was not central to their faith. In most cases, they described religious television as simply one component of their religious background or experience, along with other major components.

Faith has a personal *background of experience and belief*, and most of these histories began there. For evangelicals (and for the nonevangelicals we hear from here), their faith also developed around personal *catalytic experiences* of social or religious crisis, loss, or transformation. Such catalytic experiences are characteristic of the evangelical worldview, and most of these viewers report having had a major catalytic *religious* experience (such as being "born again") at some point in their lives, though not necessarily, or even commonly, in any way connected with their viewing of religious television. Faith also develops out of interactions with wider *communities of reference*, as we have said, and for these viewers, external forces including the broader neoevangelical movement, and their feelings of dissonance with the postindustrial society and culture, also interact in their religious consciousness.

The dimensions of faith histories
surrounding the *700 Club*:
Viewing/involvement trajectories

Individual faith histories should reflect the influences of background, behavior, community of reference, and social context. To clarify these relationships, we have devised a schematic matrix[18] to represent these influences graphically. Through these "Viewing/Involvement Trajectories," we hope to see patterns of developing religious consciousness.

It should be noted that these diagrams violate one basic criterion for the presentation of data—that the data be of parallel and comparable levels of measurement and elaboration. These diagrams are pictures of the influence of dimensions that are not directly parallel or measurable. They are "subjective" data, not evidence (in and of themselves), but they are intended honestly to show how faith develops in response to influences that range from the tangible (the sociocultural context) to the intangible (catalytic religious experiences).

Religious consciousness develops over the course of a lifetime. What we are interested in here is the particular contribution that one area of influence—the *700 Club*—has made in individual lives. We are looking at one "slice" of a lengthy life trajectory, a slice that we hope accurately represents the interaction of their involvement in religious television with the other dimensions.

The influences we have discussed fall into four broad categories of analysis, with two subcategories each. These categories provide a framework for our discussion, *and* are visually represented as the major dimensions of the Viewing/Involvement Trajectories we present.

Religious orientation

The first major category is *religious orientation*. We will classify each viewer according to a *prehistory of belief* and a *prehistory of behavior*. Social research has used a number of measures of involvement in traditional church "community," including church attendance, financial contributions, and self-designation as a "religious" person—and much research on the electronic church makes use of them.

Peter Berger points out that merely "functional" descriptions of religiosity (such as measurable behaviors) mask a wide range of "substantive" elements of religious experience (beliefs) that are more important than these more easily measurable ones.[19] There is the further problem of seeing religious practice as located only in formal church institutions. Fundamentalism and neoevangelicalism have had an extensive history of nonchurch or parachurch institutions and involvements. Religious self-identification is highly desirable for the vast majority of Americans, even those who do not attend church regularly or belong to a particular denomination.[20]

Every person has a history of belief, behavior, and social participation that has formed the basis of his or her vision of life. Family, church, community, and the broader social environment all contribute to his or her awareness and involvement in religious experience. Individual consciousness evolves within specific structures of society and culture—in the case of most of the viewers here, within the structure of American Protestantism, with its various sects and "parties." American Protestants grow up in a specific congregation, in a specific denomination, and within a specific family. They may develop values that congruent with all three, with any one, or values that are entirely unique.

An individual's piety and beliefs are not necessarily the same as those of the larger faith community, and they may be starkly aware of this. The two-party controversy becomes most critical in settings where the faithful and their church leaders disagree about "the basics." If survey data are to be believed, there are many such "stranded" Protestants.[21] People do not necessarily leave a church community because they do not feel at home, however. Assuming that the majority of such disaffected Protestants are evangelical, fundamentalist, or charismatic Christians caught in religious institutions hostile to those beliefs, it is possible that the electronic church serves as a valuable outlet for them. In our trajectories, such stranded Protestants would be evident in that they would have evangelical beliefs, but would show nonevangelical membership (behavior).

The Viewing/Involvement Trajectories separate dimensions of *belief* (basic or substantive consciousness) and *behavior* (formal church participation) in the lives of these viewers. Realizing that these two concepts are not neatly separable, we nonetheless want to know whether a given viewer is, at heart, an evangelical or fundamentalist, or comes from a nonconservative background, and whether he or she is now involved in a conservative or an establishment church community. These distinctions are essential to establishing how successful religious broadcasting can be in attracting "atypical" viewers. They are also essential to establishing the role that religious broadcasting plays in the broader process of evangelical revitalization or reaction. These dimensions, and change in them, can also give us insight into the role that broadcasting plays in individual faith development.

The catalytic personal experience

The second trajectory category is the *catalytic personal experience*. Most evangelicals, and many nonevangelicals, can describe a point in their lives when they had a striking faith experience. For many, it was their baptism. For others, it was an insight or awakening outside formal ritual. These viewers also report other, less significant experiences as well, however, in some cases in conjunction with their viewing of the *700 Club*. We are particularly interested in the latter, more situational experiences. These seem to be of two types. Some viewers have had substantively religious experiences that they connect with their viewing. Others have had more social or personal (nonspiritual) crises, such as health or financial difficulties.

The major catalytic "religious experiences" that mark a change of life (being "born again" for a neoevangelical, for instance) are the backdrop against which we see most of these viewers. We are more interested in how viewing of the *700 Club* relates to such experiences, and at what depth. Do viewers credit their viewing with stimulating such focused life-changing experiences? We chart on each trajectory the nature of these catalytic experiences, and whether they were more substantively *religious* or more in the nature of a *personal* or *social crisis*. We further attempt to show how personal or social crises may or may not have led to *focus* on the religious or spiritual level.

Sociopolitical and cultural orientation

The third category of analysis presented in the trajectories is *sociopolitical* or *cultural orientation*. The wider social context is integral to understanding how involvement in these programs might relate to revitalization in the present "age of uncertainty." Social and political attitudes form a major dimension of the concern about the electronic church phenomenon, and social class and sociocultural orientation are important determinants of religious behaviors and religiosity. The trajectories present two major dimensions of this category, *social class* and *sociopolitical attitudes* (derived from responses to the survey instrument and subsequent discussion). We want to understand how viewing of the program relates to viewers' local communities, and their social class is central to such networks.

It is widely assumed that these programs have major political impact, and we want to see how viewers' politics relate, if at all, to viewing. If viewing is, as we have suggested, an expression of a desire for renewal in an age dominated by social and political developments that make these viewers uncomfortable, then this should be revealed in their self-consciousness of class, and their political beliefs. If viewing of religious broadcasting involves a more universalistic, "modern" fundamentalism, now called "neoevangelicalism" (as described by George Marsden in Chapter 2), then we should expect to see evidence that this explains viewers' attraction to, and interpretation of, the *700 Club*.

In the modern era, religious consciousness develops within a society that is itself an important dimension of that consciousness. It is not possible to be as insular as it was before the industrial and communication revolutions. Not only does the individual need to recognize the existence of a wider society that surrounds his or her "local" communities of reference (Robert Redfield's sense of "communities within communities"[2]), wider society bears a *qualitative* relationship to the community of reference, providing challenges to it.

Using Turner's terms for the ritual evolution of consciousness, these processes depend on the recognition of the *differences* between communitas as the "ideal community" and the profane, even dangerous societas that surrounds real communities of reference. This operates on three levels. First, the wider society provides a social context that fosters the development and maintenance of community identity. Evangelicals, fundamentalists, charismatics, and Shiite Moslems, as "revitalization movements," all articulate their personal and community identities by reference to how they differ from profane society. Second, the wider society's symbols and values provide the "foil" for the specific social issues, norms, and values that are the *content* (codes) of the cultural critique of these movements. The evangelical new right, for instance, develops its "witness" to the world out of the specific challenge laid down by contemporary American social practice in such things as sexual mores and abortion. Third, society is the *natural field of witness* for evangelism. There is a "need to turn outward," to speak to society while condemning it. This is a point of stress for many sectarian communities. "Being in the world but not 'of' it" is a difficult task, and a constant source of tension and temptation.[23]

Orientation toward the neoevangelical movement
Finally, we will look at orientation toward the *neoevangelical movement*. This movement exists within congregations (and is thus expressed through the "prehistory of behavior" dimension of the trajectories) and in the broader parachurch of which religious broadcasting is an important part. We are interested in seeing how the two dimensions of this category, *religious television* and *parachurch involvements* relate to one another and to other aspects of faith histories.

We have seen how the "voluntary society" movement was important in the Great Awakening of the mid-nineteenth century, and how such organizations have become important foundations for the fundamentalist and neoevangelical movements in the twentieth.[24] David Noord[25] has described the extensive influence that nondenominational Bible societies had on American publishing in the last century. McLoughlin, Marsden, and others hold that the various waves of American Protestant evangelization, institutionalization, and schism have had an antiestablishment bias, and that its Awakenings have been metadenominational events. The revivalist movements of the second and third Awakenings were part of this nondenominational, noninstitutional, parachurch reality.

A great number of contemporary organizations and institutions have inherited this legacy. Campus Crusade for Christ International, Jews for Jesus, The Way International, the Slavic Gospel Association, and the Full Gospel Businessmen's Fellowship International are all examples of religious organizations that work outside denominational circles, but that hold services, provide counseling, develop local social networks, and organize evangelistic activity. Other parachurch agencies exist that are less conventionally "churchlike," however. ABC (the commercial broadcasting company) publishes religious periodicals, and has produced religious record albums under the *WORD* label.

These parachurch institutions rely on communication technology to a greater extent than do conventional churches. The newsletters, magazines, mailing lists, recordings, motion pictures, and cassettes marketed by these organizations far outstrip, in volume and in sophistication, the combined output of the conventional churches.[26] Even "person-to-person" ministries, such as traveling revivalists and musical groups, rely heavily on modern marketing and public relations techniques. Parachurch involvements may also result in more than just the purchase of records or reading of pamphlets. There are ministries devoted to counseling and self-help. There are missions that deal with prisons, drug and alcohol abusers, family violence, and foreign relief work, all offering opportunities for people to devote both time and money to them.

The parachurch today is dominated by neoevangelicals and funda-mentalists. It is not a foregone conclusion that religious conservatives will readily adopt devices of modern communication, as historian Joel Carpenter makes clear.[27] That they have done so, however, helps explain the power and ascendancy of conservative Christianity. The parachurch introduces the individual to another community besides the formal, institutional communities of church congregation and social group. The parachurch and its key spokespersons may be coming to serve the "prophecy" role anticipated by McLoughlin. If this is so, then modern communication technology offers us an entirely new forum for the working out of religious and cultural change.

For the viewer, a number of questions emerge when we consider the role of the agencies of the parachurch, including the *700 Club*. Did religious television predate their overall involvement in the parachurch or vice versa? How do each of these relate to their beliefs and behavior? What wants or needs do these involvements satisfy that are not satisfied by their more conventional activities? Are political views a major aspect of their interest in these areas? Have the symbols and values of the parachurch infused their faith with new meaning, and otherwise stimulated growth and development?

The dynamics of development

Viewing/Involvement Trajectories outline these dimensions and the interactions between them. We will use these trajectories as a framework to analyze the life histories of individual viewers of the *700 Club*. These processes are dynamic ones. Viewers' backgrounds of belief and behavior set an agenda through which they seek out new visions of life. In the trajectories, these dynamics are represented by arrows. Where a viewer's experience includes a relationship between these dimensions, the direction of that relationship is indicated by an arrow.

The basic dimension of the trajectories is time, moving from left to right (though it is obviously not an interval scale). The simplest relationship we will see is *temporal order*. Certain experiences precede others, and we are particularly interested in the progression of their involvement in the *700 Club* vis-à-vis other traditional and nontraditional religious-institutional contexts. Arrows indicate this order.

We will see *movement of affinity*. As these viewers search for meaning, their loyalties shift. Fowler and Turner would both predict a gradual widening of the circles of "community" through which they draw meaning, from insular, structured, and immature, to a broader, universalist, voluntary, and mature level. In the process, they come to identify with different communities of reference.

The third dynamic is the *focus of religious experience*. As consciousness develops, within reform movements, the central quest for new meaning forces an immediacy of interest and focus on those involved. Simply put, priority is given to resolving contradictions between personal beliefs and wider societal and community values and practices. The process of "writing a culture," described by McLoughlin, becomes a near obsession. Therefore, we expect to see our informants moving from diffuse interests and concerns to ones focused on their religious quests.

We expect that these viewers will have been involved in the two-party controversy, and so we will be looking for movement toward or away from the conservative side in that struggle. We expect to see an alternative vision of modern life, one that stresses the particular piety of neoevangelicalism. This *movement toward neoevangelicalism* should be most clear among those whose histories of belief and behavior change most drastically (for instance, Catholics, Jews, liberal Protestants).

We will also look for *movement in social and political attitudes*. Does the electronic church engender social and political conservatism, or does this conservatism stem from the social and belief backgrounds of its viewers? Does viewing of these programs and/or involvement in the parachurch lead to new attitudes about social and political matters?

Finally, we will look for changes in viewers' *relationships to the wider parachurch*. Is religious television the major focus of their informal religious activity, or are they engaged in this larger parachurch area? Which of these involvements came first?

An analytic typology

The experiences of 20 viewers and viewing families follow. They fall into three general types in terms of their motivations for, and satisfactions from, their involvement. For some, their histories reveal that their backgrounds, or "prehistories," are most important in explaining their attraction to the *700 Club*. For others, viewing has been primarily related to catalytic experiences of faith, crisis, or loss. For still others, viewing is dynamically related to the larger sociopolitical or cultural sphere.

In Chapter 6, we focus on "prehistory," and find, not surprisingly, that for many of these viewers, a background of evangelical or fundamentalist belief is an important component of their current beliefs, and an important explanation for their interest in the *700 Club*. Some of these viewers are evangelical in *belief,* but not in *membership* ("behavior"). We will consider the impact of such "divided loyalties." We will also see how such a background of conservative, traditional religiosity responds to a ministry that uses the most sophisticated communication tools of the media age.

Chapter 7 presents the experiences of viewers for whom catalytic experiences (either social or religious) have been important in interesting them in religious broadcasting. All evangelicals can probably relate a catalytic "turning point" in their lives—such an experience is basic to this community. What we are interested in here, though, is the extent to which viewers identify the *700 Club* program or other religious television with such experiences. Some of the stories we will hear are striking stories of religious conversion, others powerful experiences of crisis and loss. All of them relate in one way or another to experience with religious television.

In Chapter 8, we will consider the stories of those for whom the sociopolitical or cultural dimension seems to be most important. We will see that religious television has a particular characteristic that gives it a unique role in this regard. Electronic media have a way of violating traditional structures and creating new ones, and of finding new ways to bring "community" and "culture" to individuals. The producers of the *700 Club* understand it to be present in the lives of a wide range of people in heterogeneous society. Its viewers understand it to have emanated from cultural contexts far different from their own.

Each chapter begins with a representative case that fits the overall theme of the chapter. Additional cases are presented in somewhat less detail and with the purpose of "fleshing out" the concepts evident in the first. People have complex histories of religious consciousness. No one case fits only one of the chapters, obviously, so some of our informants will appear in more than one place, as more than one dimension could obviously have exerted an influence over any one of them.

Some of these stories are inspiring. Others are tragic. All are highly personal glimpses into the lives of people who are willing to share details of transitions in their lives that are important to them. We will attempt to present them clearly and forcefully, obscuring as little as possible about their experiences. We have changed some essential features of their lives in order to protect their anonymity. Each narrative documents the lives of people searching for meaning in a contemporary world that they see as potentially hostile—intellectually, socially, and spiritually—to them.

Notes

1. For discussion of the extent to which leisure activities, such as television, can be *liminal* experiences essential to the development of consciousness, in the sense used by Victor Turner, *The Ritual Process* (New York: Cornell University Press, 1982), see Bernice Martin, *The Sociology of Contemporary Cultural Change* (Oxford: Basil Blackwell, 1981); Roger Silverstone, "Television, Rhetoric and Everyday Life" (Paper delivered to the symposium, "Rethinking the Audience: New Tendencies in Television Research," Blaubeuren, West Germany, February 1987); and Robert A. White, "The Mass Media and the Religious Imagination" (Unpublished paper, London: The Centre for the Study of Communication and Culture, 1986).

2. James Fowler, *Becoming Adult, Becoming Christian* (New York: Harper & Row, 1984), p. 52.

3. Fowler, *Becoming Adult*, p. 58.

4. Ibid., p. 60.

5. Ibid., p. 65.

6. Ibid., p. 69.

7. Ibid., p. 68.

8. Turner, *The Ritual Process*; and *Dramas, Fields, and Metaphors* (Ithaca: Cornell University Press, 1974), pp. 23-59.

9. Turner, *The Ritual Process*.

10. Turner, *Dramas, Fields, and Metaphors*; and "The Center Out There: Pilgrim's Goal," *History of Religions* 12, no. 4 (1972): 191-230.

11. Turner, *Dramas, Fields, and Metaphors*.

12. Martin, *Sociology of Contemporary Cultural Change*.

13. See ibid.; Silverstone, "Television, Rhetoric and Everyday Life"; and White, "Mass Media and the Religious Imagination."

14. There is a significant developing school of thought that holds that all of television is a uniquely liminal element of contemporary life. Horace Newcomb, for instance, argues that television is a major ritualized context for the exploration of new identities and cultural meanings in modern life. Our considerations here are focused on self-consciously "religious" (and thus "meaning-oriented") programming. The possibility is very real that all of television, religious and commercial, serves such profound functions. See Horace Newcomb and Robert S. Alley, *Television: The Producer's Medium* (New York: Oxford University Press, 1983).

15. William G. McLoughlin, *Revivals, Awakenings, and Reform* (Chicago: University of Chicago Press, 1978).

16. See discussion in Chapter 1 of Anthony F.C. Wallace, *Culture and Personality*, 2d ed. (New York: Random House, 1970).

17. For a complete discussion of the sampling process used, see Stewart M. Hoover, "The 700 Club as Religion and as Television" (Ph.D. diss., Annenberg School of Communications, University of Pennsylvania, 1985). In brief, an interval selection was made from the total membership list of the *700 Club* in a major northeastern metropolitan area, resulting in 500 names. From that list, names were divided into four "pools" or strata, representing rural, suburban, urban-affluent, and urban-less-affluent areas, based on zip codes. Respondents were randomly called from each pool and administered the formal survey instrument used in

the Annenberg-Gallup regional studies. Interviewees who actually represented their intended "pools," and who agreed to do so, were interviewed, in person. These personal interviews ranged from two to four hours, involving a maximum of two visits per respondent. This resulted in a total sample of 20 viewers or families of viewers involved in the study. Analysis of the demographics and other characteristics of this sample revealed it to be reasonably consistent in profile with the northeastern sample weekday viewers of the Annenberg-Gallup study.

18. Hoover, "The 700 Club as Religion." The first trajectory is in Chapter 6. In cases where interviews were conducted with couples, a single Viewing/Involvement Trajectory is presented, representing them as a unit. It happens that there were no cases where this lost significant information about either of the spouses.

19. Peter L. Berger, "Some Second Thoughts on Substantive Versus Functional Definitions of Religion," *Journal for the Scientific Study of Religion* 13, no. 2 (June 1974): 125-33.

20. Opinion surveys consistently reveal a much higher incidence of both membership and attendance than actual statistics kept by the churches themselves would support. A large percentage believe in the Bible, pray regularly, and anticipate the second coming of Christ as well. (General Social Survey of the National Opinion Research Center, 1986.)

21. Dean R. Hoge, Everett L. Perry, and Gerald L. Klever, "Theology as a Source of Disagreement About Protestant Church Goals and Priorities," *Review of Religious Research* 19, no. 2 (Winter 1978): 116-38.

22. Robert Redfield, *The Little Community* (Chicago: University of Chicago Press, 1956).

23. For a discussion of these issues from the perspective of the mainline church, see H. Richard Niebuhr, *Christ and Culture* (New York: Harper, 1951).

24. See discussions in Chapters 1 and 2.

25. David Paul Noord, *The Evangelical Origins of Mass Media in America, 1815-1835*, Journalism Monograph No. 88 (Columbia, SC: Association for Education in Journalism and Mass Communication, 1984).

26. Jeffrey K. Hadden and Charles E. Swann, *Prime Time Preachers* (Reading, MA: Addison-Wesley, 1981).

27. For a discussion of evangelical adoption of modern technologies, see Joel A. Carpenter, "Tuning in the Gospel: Fundamentalist Radio Broadcasting and the Revival of Mass Evangelism, 1930-1945" (Paper delivered to the Mid-America American Studies Association, Urbana, Illinois, April 1985).

6

Recovering Evangelical Roots

Harry and Mabel Baldwin, now in their late 50s, have reason to feel that God has rewarded them with a good life. Harry's career with a prominent firm in the financial industry has advanced over the years. The Baldwins now live in an elegant rambling house on a wooded lot in a wealthy suburb of the city. There is a quiet sophisticated charm about their home. The swimming pool that was custom built into a sculptured garden overlooks a well-kept lawn. Mabel has never felt the need to work outside the home. Their daughter, Julie, in her 30s, unmarried and a teacher, lives with them.

In spite of their relative wealth, the Baldwins have also experienced family tragedy—the death of a son—that brought deep depression to the family circle to the point that another child attempted suicide soon after. The Baldwins feel that it was their deep trust in God that pulled them through. Indeed, the son's death was one event that took them deeper into their evangelical religion and into close association with Pat Robertson's *700 Club*.

Like many "born-again" Christians, Harry enjoys talking about his religious background. "My mother was an active Christian at home," he begins. "She had been going to a very modern church, a Methodist church or something, and one day switched to the Christian Missionary Alliance [a denomination known for its charismatic expression as well as its suspicion of intellectual, modernist dogma and legalism—important code words for the evangelical and fundamentalist traditions]. Harry's mother and father broke up over her change in religious allegiance, but Harry and his brother stayed with their mother and were active in her new church. During his military service, Harry "fell away" from religion a bit, but after his marriage to Mabel, he joined her Methodist church and became active again.

Mabel had been a Methodist all her life and attended church regularly. A religious turning point came when both Harry and Mabel "accepted Jesus" at a major Presbyterian church downtown, left the Methodist church, and joined the Presbyterian one. After they moved to the suburbs, they transferred to a Presbyterian church there.

It is a church well known for its neoevangelical leanings, its charismatic prayer groups, and especially for its social outreach. "Everyone there is involved in making the world better," comments Mabel. Although the church belongs to the mainline Presbyterian denomination, about half of its rapidly growing congregation is charismatic. The church runs a large number of outreach programs, such as counseling for alcoholics, guidance for teenage drug abusers, help for unwed mothers, and prison work.

Soon after he "accepted Jesus" at the downtown Presbyterian church, Harry began to be active on the boards of many religious organizations including Bible societies, missionary fellowships, and other ministries. The move to the suburban Presbyterian church involved the family even more in social outreach of this kind.

Today, the center of Harry and Mabel's religious faith is their prison ministry work. "We support our local church financially," Mabel explained, "and we go to many events there, especially prayer meetings, but we are out at prison every Sunday. So I don't think we've been to Sunday services in our church for over a year." They began prison work at the invitation of born-again Christian Chuck Colson, a Nixon administration official who served time in prison for his involvement in the Watergate scandals. They count Colson as a personal friend. He has been a guest in their home. The Baldwins hold church services on Sunday at the prison, where they deal largely with Christian prisoners. They also do "follow-through" work with many prisoners, including phone calls, letters, gifts, advice, and other help. For a time, they sheltered a parolee in their home, but this got too intense for Mabel, and they backed off from such direct help.

The Baldwins are emphatic in seeing their work with prisoners as not just religious in the sense of seeking their salvation, but as social uplift as well. The Baldwins reflect, to an extent, an important pragmatic tradition in American religion: the affirmation of religious faith through social reform and personal efforts to help the less fortunate. From this perspective, Christianity should help improve the conditions of life in this world, not just help people to attain eternal life in the next one. The Baldwins have been politically and ideologically affected by their prison work. They have come to oppose capital punishment and are now advocates of prison reform, including opposition to new prison construction. "There is no reason why non-violent criminals should be imprisoned. Prison reform is a necessity for economic if for no other reasons," argues Harry. They qualify their support for this seemingly liberal ideal, however, by suggesting that the "private sector" should be involved in prison reform.

Finding an intellectual Christianity through Pat Robertson

Like many other followers of the *700 Club*, the Baldwins began following Pat Robertson's TV program almost by happenstance. "About ten years ago, I started watching," Mabel recalls. "I had read Pat's book [*Shout It from the Housetops*]. One day I was watching something else and Pat came on and I said 'Oh, there is the man who wrote the book.'"

Very quickly, however, the Baldwins became deeply involved in Pat Robertson's evangelical movement and have become personally acquainted with Robertson and Ben Kinchlow, the cohost of the program. They became involved when they were struggling through the period of grief following their son's death, a topic that they still prefer not to discuss too openly.

"It was right after our son's death [when] we were invited to a seminar [at CBN] and Julie thought it would be a good idea for us to get away, to be away during his birthday," Harry explains.

> So we went down to Williamsburg and we wrote for tickets to be in the studio audience. And from there we were invited to seminars. Then we got to meet Ben Kinchlow through a friend . . . and we kept going to seminars. We've been to four, including the dedication of the new building and we'll be going down again this year for the dedication of the library.

Harry, Mabel, and Julie Baldwin all affirm that CBN is important to their faith. "It has opened up vistas we didn't know existed," says Harry. "It has shown us possibilities for our faith and put us in touch with people we never would have known about." The Baldwins now make monthly contributions of over $1200 to Pat Robertson.

From the beginning, Robertson strongly appealed to their more intellectual, cultured style of evangelical Christianity and shared their commitment to social outreach work. But above all, the *700 Club* fits their social-class identity. The Baldwins clearly see themselves as different from those who watch the *PTL Club*, in their view, a lower-class group of people. In describing his interest in Robertson, Harry comments: "I don't know whether this was right from the beginning, but I like what Pat has between his ears. If you want to put us down as 'spiritual snobs,' OK. . . . As intellectual snobs in the spiritual arena, we would not be so taken with PTL."

For their daughter, Julie,

> It's the cultural thing more than anything else. It's cultural *and* intellectual. I'm a musician, so for me some of the music on the PTL would not be what I would choose to listen to. The message [of PTL] might be what I want, but I'm lover of Bach. So that puts me in a different place from a lot of other people. . . . Culturally I'm in a different place.

The Baldwins identify with a cosmopolitan class of people and with broad interests in politics, world affairs, literature, and high culture. Pat Robertson preaches a form of Christianity that is close to traditional evangelicalism, but is also culturally uplifting and stimulating to the Baldwins. Robertson clearly also reinforces the political leanings of the Baldwins. For Harry,

Pat presents a perspective on things, including politics. He brings out things you don't usually hear. The Russians pulled out of the Olympics and he said, "What do they know that we don't know?" He really is on target with most things, and he's on live [and] it's much better because he can have up to the minute reports and interviews.

In Julie's opinion,

CBN and Public Television are alternatives for the same group, the more intellectually motivated group. Pat deals with things that are consciously religious. He talks about *issues*. A truly religious program should make you care about things, . . . care about prison reform, care about the poor, care about pain and hurt. I think you could tell the *700 Club* is religious by looking at its values.

Mabel Baldwin initially was attracted to the *700 Club* because Robertson brought her insight into evangelical religion.

I was fascinated, for instance, by what they call "the Baptism of the Holy Spirit" [a code-phrase for having a charismatic experience—such as speaking in tongues], and I think that's what brought me to the program. . . . I had heard about that before . . ., but I didn't understand what it meant really. I knew I was going to tune in the next day. . . . I was very attracted to him because he presented it [religion] in a way that didn't turn me off.

Mabel also was attracted to the *700 Club* by its intellectual and political format. "Not only in the area of spiritual messages, but I think that politically he is on top of things," Mabel says. "For awhile, he even had a newsletter that was . . . better than most of your news analysis or columnists as far as right, correct interpretation goes." Mabel would never separate the spiritual and temporal realms. "Oh no. I certainly would not be critical because the gospel is political, and the more well-rounded a program is, the better."

Julie, too, prefers that the gospel message have a fairly explicit political orientation. "It depends on what you mean by political, but if you mean that . . . God's world is everything, including the political, I approve of that." Mabel agrees. "I wasn't raised in a *narrow* Christian home. I learned that God and Christ are in and work in the world."

The Baldwins are typical of a growing religious phenomenon in contemporary American Protestantism—a loosening of ties with the routine of Sunday services in institutional churches. This has been accompanied, in mainline churches, with a movement toward parachurch activities more closely linked with social outreach or with intense spiritual experiences associated with the human potential movement. In Julie's opinion, "Most other churches aren't preaching the message Jesus taught us to teach. Most of them are personalistic, individualistic, or so secularized that they are irrelevant."

Harry feels that the institutional church still has a place and that his support of Pat Robertson does the church no harm.

> Our level of giving [to CBN] seems quite high, I'm sure. But we also give to our local church, as much, if not more, than we did before. CBN put us in touch with the prison work we now do. That has taken us out of church on Sundays, but we still think the church is vital. It is the body of Christ and cannot be shunted aside. ... I am sure that whatever money is going to the religious broadcasters is money that would not have gone to the local church anyway. It is extra and can't be seen by local churches as competition.

The Baldwins say they have grown spiritually and in social consciousness because of Pat Robertson's ministry. As Julie observed to her mother, "You have changed a lot, spiritually, in ten years." But they are skeptical about any true religious revival brought about by the televangelists or the evangelical movement. "No, there hasn't been any great evangelical revival or religious turn-around in America," says Harry. "Too much religiosity is just egocentric, just narcissistic. There would have to have been real social and political change in America, based on religious consciousness, and there has been none. This 'evangelical revival,' I see as nothing more than personalism without social conscience."

Harry and Mabel's trajectory[1] is presented as Figure 6.1[2], and Julie's as Figure 6.2. The center of the Baldwins' religious life currently lies in the parachurch, especially in their prison work. Their criterion for religious growth is the pragmatic improvement in the lives of people and in social institutions, not just the institutional growth of churches. They are attuned to the utilitarian Christianity of Chuck Colson and Pat Robertson, not so much for the personal religious comfort it brings, but for concrete changes in the actions of people. The Baldwins reflect the pragmatism that is a basic tenet of most American religious belief systems and American culture in general.

The *700 Club* as a confirmation of evangelical faith

John and Martha Hand are very different from the Baldwins. While they live comfortably, they are not wealthy, and where the Baldwins are somewhat cosmopolitan, the Hands are more closed and inward-looking. This is particularly true in their attitudes toward politics and social reform. While they are registered voters, they resist any political labels. When asked about his political positions, John answers, "That's a question that's impossible to answer. . . . Name tags don't mean a lot in today's world." Their positions on political and social issues are decidedly conservative, however.

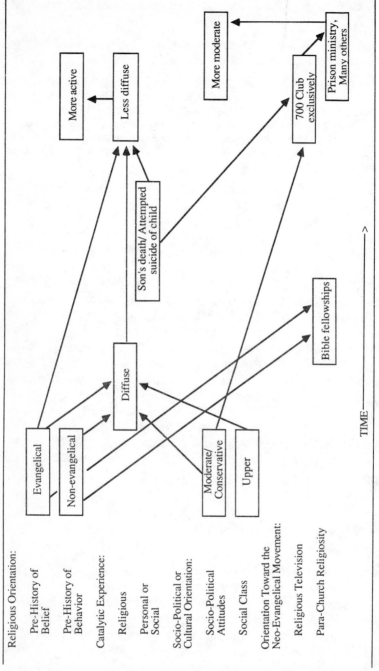

Figure 6.1. Viewing/involvement trajectory for Harry and Mabel Baldwin

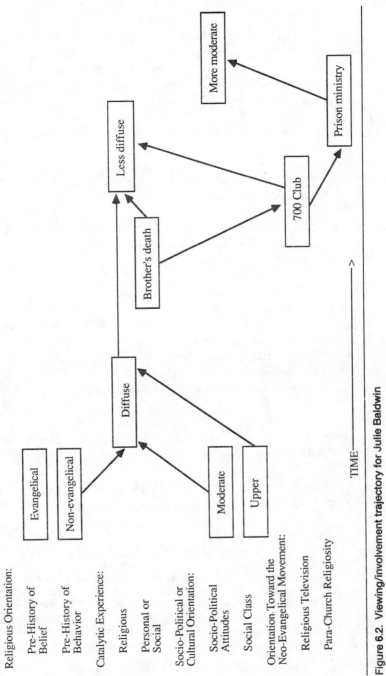

Religious Orientation:

Pre-History of
Belief

Pre-History of
Behavior

Catalytic Experience:
Religious

Personal or
Social

Socio-Political or
Cultural Orientation:

Socio-Political
Attitudes

Social Class

Orientation Toward the
Neo-Evangelical Movement:

Religious Television

Para-Church Religiosity

TIME————————>

Figure 6.2. Viewing/involvement trajectory for Julie Baldwin

121

In contrast to the Baldwins' social openness, the Hands seem distrustful of other people. "Our house was broken into three times recently," John notes. At the same time, John and Martha are positive, even buoyant, in describing a religious faith that is clearly fundamentalist. Asked about her belief in the second coming of Christ, Martha exclaims, "Amen, and I can hardly wait." Her faith is intensely personal. "Realizing that Jesus loved us enough to die for us is, you know, the greatest. That he has given us eternal life, what could be better, what could be greater?"

The Hands currently do not belong to a local church, but they do attend services weekly. Lack of membership in a congregation does not mean though that they are outside the sphere of conventional religious activity. They regularly contribute to the churches they attend, and to others whose ministries they believe in. They also have specific ideas about current controversies within local churches. For instance, as fundamentalists, they are opponents of the charismatic movement.

Their financial support of churches and religious activities has remained the same over the past three years, but they say they also give to the *700 Club* and Jews for Jesus. Just as they resist being labeled politically and socially, they resist being categorized by their religious beliefs, contending that the labels associated with the various controversies in Protestantism and other aspects of institutionalized religion hide the essential core of Christian faith. John asserts this point forcefully:

> Religion involves a kind of concept and philosophical projection. We believe you have a *personal* relationship with Jesus Christ, and so, to focus on the question of "what our religion is" is rather difficult because religion in some contexts could mean "all or nothing." But our relationship to Jesus Christ means *everything* to us.

Their involvement with the *700 Club* grew out of their openness to religious insights that transcend institutional labels and began with a personal recommendation.

Martha recalls that her mother first mentioned religious television to her.

> It was probably twelve years ago or so that my mother would write and tell me about this fantastic Christian programming that they were getting, and we couldn't get it here. And all of a sudden, I don't know how we started, but all of a sudden one day we were aware that the *700 Club* was on the air and we started watching, and I felt "one upsman" with my mother because I thought it was a little bit better than PTL, which was what she was watching.

John and Martha Hand agree with the Baldwins' assessment of the difference between the *PTL Club* and the *700 Club*. "I think the *700 Club* is more intellectual, with its news and up-to-date content," says Martha. John adds,

> I think it's that they represent *Bible*-oriented opinions. They do present news, but it is oriented again, when it can be, to Bible prophecy. They have a fine, edifying program. The PTL is more entertainment. It's like the difference between a Christian Johnny Carson show and a Christian *Good Morning America*. . . . The *700 Club* is simply more informative.

Just because the *700 Club* expresses itself in more "intellectual" or "informative" ways does not mean that it is any less spiritual than the *PTL Club*, say John and Martha. In fact, it is the power of the *700 Club* to bring a "Bible-centered" witness to areas that have not traditionally been a focus of evangelical or fundamentalist preaching that gives the program some of its spiritual value for them. It advances the idea that conservative Christianity should no longer confine itself to the "spiritual"—or individual faith—alone.

Martha sees the more traditional "spiritual" entertainment offered by the *PTL Club* as serving different needs for the same body of religious consciousness and beliefs. "I think their goals are the same, to bring honor and glory to God," Martha says.

> I think PTL—I've been down there, too—I think they're wild. My goodness, this guy [Jim Bakker] is a ball of fire. [But] I don't support them. I don't send them a penny, whereas I support "700" because it seems deeper. But I can't really say that PTL isn't. I mean, they're working on the same body. You know, it's [like] the arm and the leg; they don't do the same job.

John adds, "You really have to sit and listen to the *700 Club*."

Both the *PTL Club* and the *700 Club* are more than mere "news" or entertainment, though. They address basic issues of faith and controversy within the conservative Christian movements. As do most traditional fundamentalists, the Hands express reservations about the charismatic movement. While both the former hosts of the *PTL Club*, Jim and Tammy Bakker, and the *700 Club*'s Pat Robertson are charismatics, the Hands note that each program deals with this issue differently. They find the *PTL Club* far more aggressive and self-conscious about this issue than the *700 Club*. "Tammy and Jim are more demonstrative," John says. "I think it's equally obvious with Pat, even though he's not so demonstrative. It's a personal thing, essentially."

The Hands' own faith histories are not heavily grounded in traditional churches or church denominations (see Figure 6.3[3]). Martha describes her home as "basically Christian" with a Christian mother and a non-Christian stepfather. Her conversion experience came in a church other than the one

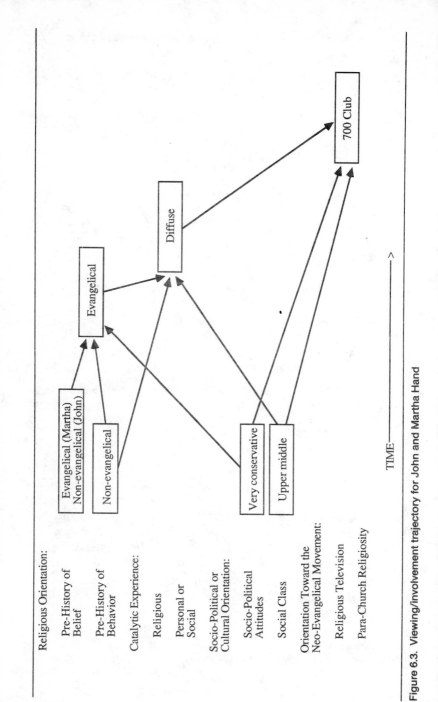

Figure 6.3. Viewing/involvement trajectory for John and Martha Hand

she had attended up to that time. "It was at a little Pentecostal church. . . . We went there to laugh and ridicule and watch them roll on the floor, but one night my mother was saved. A few years later, I was. I was just a kid then." John was not raised in a "Christian" home, but found the faith after marriage and children.

They are now active parachurch Christians, and are supportive of local churches, although they are not members of one. They are aware of concerns that programs like the *700 Club* adversely affect individual churches, but they contend that such fears miss the point of religious broadcasting. John is adamant. "It isn't intended to relate to regular churches in any way. . . . Even the staff people tell you there is no intention to compete with local churches." Martha argues that "to grow spiritually, you have to be involved, you have to be *doing*, not just sitting home, watching. Of course you can always pray and send money, but you have to be involved in a church or something, if you call yourself a Christian." But the issue of fund-raising by television preachers, and its potential impact on the local church, is something John has thought about a good deal. "I don't think money is even connected . . . there should be no 'self' involved, you should be willing to help others, and they to help you. If someone needed help, I'd help, regardless of CBN."

The Hands share with the Baldwins a deep appreciation of the *700 Club* and its founder, Pat Robertson. They have reservations about other television ministries, like the *PTL Club*, which emphasizes the "spiritual" and personal, as opposed to the public, more politically sophisticated approach of Pat Robertson and Jerry Falwell. Obviously they have thought about how to reconcile this activist political orientation with the fundamentalist tradition of quietism. They are particularly concerned that television evangelists may to be tainted by the heady egoism of the media spotlight. They are sensitive to allegations that televangelists might be more interested in personal gain than saving souls.

John acknowledges these dangers, but he is not worried that Falwell and Robertson might be tainted.

> For anyone to be faithful, you have to be humble, and destroy your self-image. When you find a holy man who has a direction that is essentially biblically oriented, Christ centered, without self, you can believe in him. There may be another man who is in it for the money or the power, who says, "I'm involved in politics" for his own self-interest. He should get out of it. But if one of them really believes—as I think Jerry Falwell believes—that if we don't [put] more godly men in control of this country, it's not going to be the kind of country we like to live in, then I would support him.

For John, godliness manifests itself in giving and service. "For instance, without godly men in control, how are we to know that we need to send money to help the poor down in Haiti? If you don't *apply* what you know, it doesn't do you any good to know it."

The Hands, like the Baldwins, seem to have readily accepted the politicization of their beliefs evident in the social content of religious broadcasting. For the Baldwins, this fit quite naturally with their more intellectual and urbane approach to life and religion. But the politicization of John and Martha Hand's faith came in reaction to social changes they find challenging to their values. "Because homosexuality, abortion, adultery, all of this is becoming a political issue . . . you have to be involved because they are biblical issues first," says Martha.

Still, they clearly do not think that mixing religion with politics is always a good thing. The traditional fundamentalist mistrust of politics has been overcome for them by a feeling that the times are so desperate that there must be a Christian political revival. They do not approve, however, of the kind of political involvements taken up by the more liberal, "social gospel" denominations.

John maintains that liberal churches have been involved in the "wrong kind" of politics, even supporting Communist causes. Political power and prestige must be tempered by religious convictions, he feels, because the danger of subversion is always there.

> I think it's awfully easy to find yourself into the [Communist] "networks." Some of it's apathy. How did Whittaker Chambers get involved? Look at what they did to Oppenheimer. . . . There was a man who was so involved with people of his own academic and peer level, academically, ethnically, who were Communist, that the brush painted him so pink that McCarthy nearly got him. It is so easy to drift in through the doors. . . . I believe you'll find that the KGB solicits people like that and they look for them and they do enough favors for them . . . that they can say "Hey, you owe me one." These churches, most of them that I know of, preach the "social gospel" as opposed to a real gospel. . . . They believe that man . . . can make himself good, . . . that this can happen without being born again. . . . Man doesn't control, God controls.

Overall, the Hands' worldview requires separation, even isolation, from a debased, secularized society. Religious television is an antidote, they feel, though it is not vital for them to know that it is reaching masses of people. The few they know of who have been "led to Christ" justify the whole endeavor. Referring to the broadcasts of radio evangelist Charles Fuller that he heard as a youth, John says, "They didn't have the money to put it in everyone's home like they can today."

The Hands' awareness that theirs is a minority worldview only reinforces the sense of community involvement they gain from the *700 Club*. The "secular" media constantly remind them of their insularity but the *700 Club* and other religious media offer an alternative for them that is "safe." Martha says that motion pictures no longer attract them because their content is so salacious. "We don't know too much about movies anymore because we don't go," Martha says.

> We went to *The Natural*, and the one about the runner [*Chariots of Fire*], and I went to see *Yentl*, because of the Jewish thing. I liked it, the history sense was good, [but because of] the nudity and everything else, I just feel dirty. I want to shower when I come out. . . . So we don't go, seldom.

John adds,

> I stopped a subscription to an otherwise good magazine, *National Geographic*, because I got fed up with the fact that I never saw any indication that there was anything but the humanistic view of evolution. It really makes me ill, because they can't prove their position. . . . Why, if they can't prove their position, are they giving it so much prominence? *Time*, we canceled that, and I wrote to *Life*, saying I didn't want it coming into the house, with my young daughters. We know it exists, but you don't have to feed on it. You don't deny it, but it doesn't have to be there all the time.

The Hands are unsure how the media became dominated by values they question. "It amazes me, because most of the people we know don't embrace [such values]," Martha says. "I look at people and say, 'They don't embrace that,' and all I can think is that there must be a lot of people out there who do." John adds: "It's covetousness—most businessmen get ahead by making money, and more power, and they get to the place where they know if they get ten percent more readership by doing this, then they get more money and power. . . . It's covetousness."

The Hands speak for a new kind of activist fundamentalism, one that combines a clear rejection of the values of secular culture with support for political action to change that culture. They share with the Baldwins a desire to see a new, "Christian" era in American politics, but their motivation is primarily reactionary. They see the world as increasingly hostile to their beliefs; even its religious institutions have been corrupted by secular values. While they are supportive of the local church, they find their faith better expressed by the parachurch, and generously support those ministries that they see as revitalizing society. Such ministries deserve support, they believe, because they serve the critical needs of faith and salvation without the hidebound trappings of conventional religious institutions. As a "bonus," Pat Robertson and Jerry Falwell represent, for the Hands, a decisive, prominent critique of contemporary America—an alternative vision that can and does stand alongside other centers of American social and political power.

The *700 Club* and Christian leadership

Joe and Doris Parker are even more involved in church activities than are the Hands. They are retired. Joe had been a minister in a mainline denomination, and Doris a bookkeeper. This is the second marriage for each of them; both were widowed. They describe themselves as having been evangelicals all of their lives, and they are generally as conservative as John and Martha Hand (see Figure 6.4[4]).

The Parkers have been members of the *700 Club* for several years and have visited CBN headquarters several times, including one time when Joe had his first experience "speaking in tongues." They agree with the Baldwins and the Hands that the *700 Club* is a program that satisfies their "intellectual" side, as much as the spiritual. They watch, in all, eight of the electronic church programs on a regular, though not necessarily weekly, basis.

Joe recalls how they first encountered the program.

> I first began watching it accidentally, on a Saturday. I just turned on the television and here was this fellow talking about Israel going through its agony in the Six-Day War. And this fellow was "aflame" . . . I thought he was a [conventional] announcer or something, and I said, "This fellow must be a Christian." It was Pat, you know. He was pleasant, and he enunciated, and he was for Israel, and I began listening, and took down his name, and made sure of the number and time.

Like John and Martha Hand, Joe and Doris Parker do not see their interest in the *700 Club* as any kind of a challenge to traditional Christianity. Conventional church discomfort with the conservatism of evangelicalism and the electronic church is unfounded, they say. There has been too much division, institutional preoccupation, and self-interest involved in denominational religion, as they see it. Joe observes:

> It's getting bad, I think, with organized religion, when the conservatives are criticized for their fundamentalism. I think it's good when we can get doctrines that are similar, but the Roman Catholic Church, they're very selfish, and they want things always for their benefit and you can't blame them, in a way. . . . The National Council of Churches, for example, I have practically no respect for at all—they're giving out monies to help these revolutionaries in Africa and different parts of the world. This is what our conservative magazines tell us.

Joe Parker was the child of Eastern European immigrant parents, and was "saved" in an ethnic evangelical congregation. Perhaps because of his background, he is extremely sensitive to the social-class-oriented aspects of traditional American evangelicalism, particularly the tendency for evangelicalism to be associated with less education and less social sophistication. In

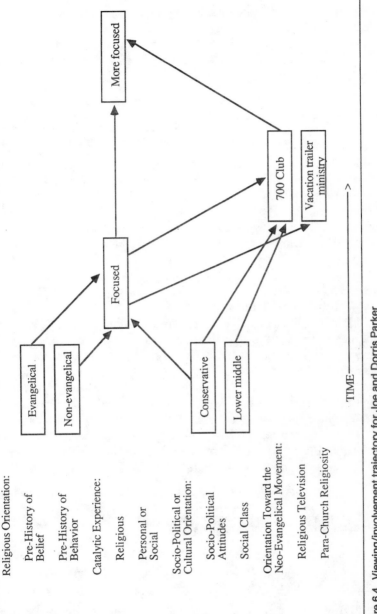

Religious Orientation:

Pre-History of
Belief

Pre-History of
Behavior

Catalytic Experience:

Religious

Personal or
Social

Socio-Political or
Cultural Orientation:

Socio-Political
Attitudes

Social Class

Orientation Toward the
Neo-Evangelical Movement:

Religious Television

Para-Church Religiosity

Evangelical

Non-evangelical

Conservative

Lower middle

Focused

More focused

700 Club

Vacation trailer
ministry

TIME———>

Figure 6.4. Viewing/involvement trajectory for Joe and Dorris Parker

129

his own case, his ethnic and class background put him at a disadvantage in expressing himself.

Joe's conversion came, he recalls, when he "asked the Lord for one thing . . . , to be able to speak clearly for him and make a witness." Since then, his life has been full of such "speaking."

> And now I've been able to speak to governors and those running for governor, personally, and politicians, and getting to the subject quickly, and professors from colleges around here, and other places, coming to the point, not just a mere evangelical witness, but it's on creation versus evolution, or something specific.

This outcome of his conversion clearly is very important to Joe. In retirement, he and Doris continue informal mission work. "We've been appointed to be in charge of the mission-education program at our local church. That involves being sponsors of young missionaries and 'missionettes.' We teach how to do presentations, and all," says Doris. They also run a trailer ministry at a campground near the seashore all summer, something they do on their own without any institutional support. The Parkers share with the Baldwins and the Hands the sense that faith can lead to authentic expression and involvement outside, as well as within, conventional church settings.

Joe sees some contrasts between religious broadcasting and conventional local churches. The *700 Club* puts him in touch with powerful preaching and other communication, more effective than that available at most local churches. "You see, inspiration, even spiritual inspiration, comes from information," Joe says. "So when your spirit senses that this man is preaching and it comes from his heart, with facts, with humility, and with power, you sit there with your tongue sticking out and your jaw drops."

Joe's attraction to the high-tone sophistication of the major religious ministries is obvious in his response to a comment from Doris that they think that there should be more *local* religious programs. He breaks in,

> No, I don't think we'd watch them anyway. We have our good men who are "top" men. The other men are men of God, but when you get a man like Charles Stanley [a minister from Dallas who appears on a Sunday morning syndicated religious program], he's the man for me.

Joe and Doris share the Baldwins' and the Hands' perception that the *700 Club* is the intellectual's electronic church. Doris compares the *700 Club* with the *PTL Club*:

> PTL would be more on an emotional level. I don't mean they base their decisions on emotions, I mean it's a talk show, but they discuss issues, personal problems, more so than the *700 Club*. Of course they've built this big ministry complex at PTL, so he's [Jim Bakker] always been talking a lot about that, talking about the

"needs." Pat Robinson [sic], may be more apt to tell something about someone who is not *saved* because he covers news, issues, "man-on-the-street" interviews. With PTL, I think the Christians who are watching are getting more spiritual material, more *entertainment*, and the average Christian, I think, would respond to that more quickly than to Pat.

Joe adds, "Pat Robertson appeals more, I think, to the *leadership* that is found in the different churches, people who may be experienced, and people who want information."

Doris seems to differ from Joe on the subject of what is more important about the various programs they watch: the appeal to intellect that he is attracted to versus the spiritual content that attracts her. She has always had a highly spiritual, expressive faith, and feels that programs that stress such faith are to be preferred. For example, she is well aware of the widespread criticism of the former cohost of the *PTL Club*, Tammy Bakker, but thinks she had a valuable ministry in spite of the Bakkers' extravagant life-style.

"At one time I didn't care much for Bakker's wife, Tammy. But now, nobody can say anything," Doris says.

> I *really, really,* believe she's a woman of God and a child of God, and gets the leadership from God. I've never *sensed* that she's out of the spirit in anything she's had to say, never, never. If she had, I would have sensed it. Now at one time I would have said, "She has no right to put on these wigs, and everything like that," . . . but now, no one can talk to me about her. I say, "God's told her to be that way." She's winning souls, and sure, it's a glamorous appeal, but what does it matter, more Christians are coming closer to Christ. "So what," I say, "she's not out there in the world." People's hearts are touched, and people want to go down there and pay a thousand dollars a year to go to their vacation center.

How Joe and Doris Parker know that Pat Robertson and the Bakkers are worthy of their support is not clear. "You just know, you feel it in your heart," Doris says. It is related in part to the question that concerned the Hands as well: How can the potentially dangerous and seductive medium of television, with all of its power and potential for ego gratification, be turned toward good? Doris speaks of the "sophistication" of some of the religious programs: "As long as it's not their *motive* to be sophisticated, like the rest of television, then they are all right. Behind it has to be that God told them to do it that way, otherwise they're just adopting the world's methods."

As do the Baldwins and the Hands, the Parkers profess a faith that has long been evangelical. Far from being a major cause of their faith, the *700 Club* fits well into a faith history that is oriented toward a world outside the traditional realms of local churches and revival meetings. For Joe and

Doris, retirement has opened up new vistas for witnessing about their faith, and the *700 Club* offers moral support for their witness. It has been something more for Joe, as we will see in the next chapter.

Overcoming isolation

Where we might have called the Baldwins intellectual, even liberal rationalists, the Hands closed, rather narrow religionists, and the Parkers class-conscious viewers, Helen Purton seems cool and distant from the whole enterprise. While she has been a supporter of the *700 Club* for years, Helen does not view the program regularly and knows little about it, concentrating her energies instead on a wide range of parachurch agencies and ministries.

Helen is 76, a widow who lives comfortably in an older suburb of the city. A watershed for her came with retirement, when she and her husband left the city for the suburbs. In her retirement, she left behind her full-time volunteer work at a large mainline congregation in the city. Over the years, she had felt that her church was growing away from her strongly held fundamentalist positions, and once she left, she did not look back. It is surprising, for someone who was long involved in her church, that Helen cares little where her church membership now resides.

Helen has endured tragedy and personal crisis. She was driving the car the night she and her husband were in an auto accident in which he was killed. She had a vision and a visitation immediately following the accident, she says, but sees these as milestones that strengthened her faith, rather than as turning points for her. Her fundamentalist faith remains a great comfort and inspiration to her, and her parachurch activities and the ministries she supports are expressions of her faith more than things she does for herself.

She is personally involved in evangelism, including a summer-long Bible school she runs for a church near her vacation home, and a Sunday school program she runs for a black church also near her summer home.

Helen's remarkable disinterest in viewing the *700 Club* program sharply contrasts with the intensity with which she views the state of American religion in general. She has watched the conflict grow between evangelicalism and modernism with some alarm. "I feel that all churches are truly trying to carry out the commission that Jesus gave us . . . , each in a different way. I also feel each group should present it in the way they see it but should *not* criticize the others." Helen shares with others a distaste for religious factionalism, holding that such things as which biblical translation to use [a long-standing controversy between fundamentalism and modernism] and specific doctrinal issues pale in comparison with the overall "great commission" of Jesus. "Jesus said 'Anyone who's not against us, is for us,' so when you criticize other groups, you turn off people who do not listen to what *you* have to say."

Helen has always been a fundamentalist. Her faith history since her retirement has moved to a new stage, one emphasizing her personal testimony and away from traditional churches. This is a remarkable change, considering the level of involvement she had had in the church she and her husband attended before retirement. Helen had directed that congregation's Sunday school program for years.

But retirement gave her an opportunity to act on a faith that was not well served by that mainline congregation, she says. For example, many of its ministers were too liberal and intellectual, not expressive enough. "We had some ministers who were sincere, . . . but some ministers don't really have enough love for people. They know their subject, and would probably be much better as theologians, teaching in a theological college. . . . If you aren't sincere, people aren't going to hear what you have to say."

Retirement (and her husband's death) brought with them opportunities to move from her former position of dissatisfaction within a denomination, to active involvement in the parachurch.

> After we moved away from [the city] to here, I began to be very much involved in the organizations that were trying to reach people with the Bible . . . and my support went heavily in that direction—toward the Slavic Gospel Association, Underground Evangelism, Christian Truth Cinema, Billy Graham, Vigilance, *700 Club*, Campus Crusade for Christ, . . . it's a long list. I just became involved in serving and witnessing in the world, but I didn't go to any church here, where I live now.

Instead she has taken up a personal ministry. She delivers for Meals on Wheels. She teaches Sunday school. She bakes cookies and uses them to witness about her faith by giving them to people she meets.

As with the Baldwins, Helen's religious activism runs counter to the stereotype of the electronic church viewer as someone who uses the program only for vicarious religiosity, but never practices what's preached. Helen not only acts on her beliefs, she also seeks enlightenment on her own. "At this point, I write a great many letters and read a great many books and do a lot of studying, especially about prophecy and send out Xeroxes of these things to my friends. I mean, you can have a witness of your own of many kinds."

Helen's active life-style contradicts the image of an uninvolved, conservative traditionalist caught in the past.

> During the Depression, we went without an awful lot of things . . . we just didn't buy them. . . . But, then again, we didn't have to have a car; we didn't have to have a phone; we didn't have to put our trash out in bags. There are a lot of things that we didn't have to do in those days, but we really do today. So, this is

why you can't compare. . . . Our generation keeps saying, "In the old days," but you really can't compare. You can't compare the minds of these young people with our minds. They've been raised in an entirely different environment, subjected to entirely different influences.

Helen's apparent open-mindedness is reflected in her religious activities. She is active in picking and choosing among the options presented to her by the parachurch. At the same time, however, the range of her choices is circumscribed by the evangelical world.

"I really do not look at many religious programs," Helen says.

I do see the Billy Graham Crusades because my daughter likes to look at those, and I have been a contributor to the *700 Club* for years, and to Christian Cinema, which is on, I think that's on TV, too. The reason I don't watch much religious TV is that I like to read the books that are available, written today, and they're all by preachers, and most of them come from Texas. Texas theological schools must be wonderful. I read all of them—Francis Schaeffer, etc.—and the parts I like I can write down, or Xerox. That seems to be the valuable thing about the television programs because occasionally they'll offer a book, or a pamphlet you can write for, and then they have something concrete, which you don't get after most sermons. Some pastors do Xerox their sermons so people can take them home. Sometimes I look in on Jimmy Swaggart, and I think he's awfully good, and Dr. Estep, *The King Is Coming*. But as I say, I don't make a practice of viewing any of them.

Prophecy is important to Helen, particularly prophecy involving Israel, and she cites this as a major reason she has increased her contribution to the *700 Club*.

I raised it when he [Pat Robertson] went to the Middle East, and Mike Evans, I send him money because he's trying to get the president to recognize Jerusalem as the capital of Israel. I don't know, I have a feeling that the United States will not support Israel. In Ezekiel, where it's describing the attack of Russia [on Israel], with all the many allies she has today, there are two people who watch this attack: one group is the merchant princes of Tarsus. Now Tarsus was a seaport that the Phoenicians built, and from there they colonized Great Britain, the United States and the rest of the world. So the merchant princes of Tarsus stand by. They give very weak criticism but nothing backing it up.

Religious broadcasting and these other parachurch ministries offer Helen an opportunity to articulate her beliefs in concrete ways not open to her through conventional churches. As do John and Martha Hand, Helen believes that there need be no division between the work of churches and of parachurch agencies. Religious television and conventional churches should serve the same ends, she says.

I feel that the gospel has to be offered in hundreds of different ways. We are all individuals, and we all have to get it in different ways. Eventually the church will be the apostolic church that's in prophecy, but I don't think it will be because television has supplanted it. Many people will turn on the TV, they're bewildered, they're hurt, they don't know what the answer is. I think that we feel that just because the church is there or that maybe even the children will have gone to Sunday school for years that that is enough, but they didn't get the message.... Now I'm not blaming the church either, if someone needs to get the message from television, they've really never heard it in a way that they could listen to.

Helen sees religious broadcasting as one tool of religious expression and believes that most viewers, unlike herself, are people "who really need it."

Most people involved in religious broadcasting are not Christian. I mean most of the *viewers*. Now [televangelist] Robert Schuller once said that you can't have communion, etc., with these people who are not church members. But he said, "Don't ever forget that you are preaching to unchurched people" and [are] trying to "... make them comfortable." I think that is very true.... If you are going to antagonize people, and use language that goes against their grain, they'll turn you off.

Helen feels that conventional churches typically are insular and too closed off to attract needy, "unchurched" people. What she likes the best about the parachurch is its commitment to meeting people "where they are."

I guess I think you have to say something in the beginning that will appeal to their need. They have problems. The successful books are about personal experiences, just like I talk about my own experiences in what I'm trying to tell everyone else. If you tell them about the troubles you have had, and how you've been helped.... I don't think the preacher ever does that. He's up there and he's afraid to let on that he's the same as you "down there."

Helen is one of the "stranded" Protestants mentioned in Chapter 5. The Presbyterian church, in which she had spent most of her adult life, no longer has her loyalty. She sees this as a process of the church "growing away from its roots," more than one of her rejecting *it*.

My church didn't used to be what it has become. It has *changed*. Suddenly the new church school curriculum wasn't Bible stories, it was just "God loves you," and I would supplement it. When my husband and I first began to go there everything was fine, but then in the '30s, we began to say, "What's going on?" Francis Schaeffer said in his book, *The Church and the Watching World*, that the moderator, the fundamentalist moderator, had been put out and a liberal one put in, and then the other churches kind of followed suit. I think that all of this ecumenism and the World Council of Churches is the Babylon church, the false church of prophecy. I don't think there is any doubt about it. But I think there are still some very fine churches. When we started [going to that church] it was fine.

The Baldwins, the Hands, the Parkers, and Helen Purton would agree that conventional churches often lack the authenticity of ministries like the

700 Club. One way conventional churches have failed, they believe, is by concentrating too much on secular issues and on doctrines that divide them. The electronic church is important and valuable for the universalism it represents in the face of the rampant particularism and insularity of traditional fundamentalism. Despite their fundamentalist backgrounds, all of them feel that it is essential for Christianity to understand and accept a certain amount of diversity in order not to "turn people off" too quickly.

From a closed to an open witness

Jeff Wilson is a full-time military chaplain, and Joan Wilson a pastor's wife and homemaker. Both come from the same conservative, Pentecostal "holiness" denomination. Joan was raised in it, Jeff joined after they met and after he completed his military service. Jeff has a graduate degree in theology from a conservative seminary, and Joan has a college degree. As with others from such conservative backgrounds, they are sensitive to the common prejudice that people from such roots are necessarily less intelligent and less sophisticated. Jeff shares with Joe Parker a strong interest in Christian leaders who can make themselves heard at centers of secular power.

Jeff and Joan both look back somewhat wistfully on the closed, conservative churches from which they came, but this sentiment is tempered by their experience in the "real world" outside those closed, rural communities.

Both have personal experiences of religious healing. Jeff nearly died of cancer, and Joan was seriously injured in an automobile accident. Both say that their faith helped pull them through these crises, but they do not describe these experiences as watersheds in the development of their beliefs as much as confirmations of those beliefs. Because their crises were ministered to by a community church, they both feel strongly about the power of conventional churches to help in this way. Unlike some others, they make no particular connection between their health crises and their viewing of religious television. Instead, they consider religious broadcasting an intellectual activity, one they support because it puts a Christian opinion alongside others in the national media.

Jeff and Joan are clearly mass media "information seekers" in the standard sense of that term. They watch a great deal of news programming on broadcast and cable television, and consider such information an important aspect of the *700 Club*.

Because Jeff is a professional minister, he takes an analytical approach in his evaluation of the electronic church. His taxonomy of program types runs from those to the left of the *700 Club* like Robert Schuller ("It's too show-biz, that's all it is"), to those on the right, including the *PTL Club*. He particularly dislikes Schuller and his Crystal Cathedral. "I don't like to see people building up kingdoms for themselves on earth," he explains, adding that Oral Roberts also fits that mold.

The *PTL Club*, on the other hand, holds a certain fascination for the Wilsons, a fascination with a culture that reflects their past in a way. Tammy Bakker embodies the contradictions of their "holiness" past for them. "Tammy comes from a very closed, holiness background. It's a sociological fact that when people grow up in these holiness churches, they can overdo it when they come out," Jeff says. "Like Dolly Parton says, 'When you're dirt poor all your life, you promise yourself you'll never do without again.'"

The Wilsons clearly feel that there are more limitations than advantages to such a closed background when it comes to acting on their beliefs in their present situation. "We started out more conservative than Tammy, more legalistic," Jeff says.

> I think one reason I'm in the military is to be able to preach the word without having to pay attention to petty legalisms like I would have to in my home denomination. I can just witness to Christ without worrying so much about dogma.... We aren't like Tammy now because we read scripture differently than she does. She takes grace to be *license*, we don't.

The Wilsons trace their religious roots from a conservative, Pentecostal past to their present comparatively liberal universalism. Jeff came from a home that was not particularly religious.

> I was packed up by my parents and taken to the neighbors to be taken to a church, that was Church of God, Anderson [Anderson, Indiana, the more moderate of the fundamentalist Church of God denominations]. My other exposure was to an EUB church [Evangelical United Brethren, a moderate "modernist" group now part of the United Methodist Denomination] occasionally, and then to summer Bible camp occasionally.

Joan had a more consistent upbringing in the Pentecostal Church of God, Cleveland [Cleveland, Tennessee, the more conservative of the Church of God Denominations]. Both continue nominally to be members of this latter group. Joan says that she was born again at the same time as Jeff, after his military service. Both had "life-changing" conversion experiences, and both have experienced the "Baptism of the Holy Spirit" (have had charismatic experiences).

Jeff felt called to the ministry and went to college and graduate school to prepare for this career. Both Jeff and Joan ascribe their relative liberalism to their college educations. As a result, the *700 Club* fits their religious consciousness today, unlike the *PTL Club*, which represents their past. "I think that the PTL is shallower," Jeff says. It doesn't have the content that the *700 Club* has; it's not as informative."

There are, however, limits to the Wilsons' tolerance of the *700 Club*'s relative liberalism. Jeff asserts,

> Some of the people they choose to have on there we have some real questions about where they're at because of the lifestyle they live in the world. Singer Marilyn McCoo is on that Solid Gold show and comes on the *700 Club* and talks about how much she loves God, and yet I think that's a ribald show, *Solid Gold*—people up there half nude going through all kinds of contortions.

> They need to be more selective, and anyone who marches through claiming to be a Christian, well, our definition and view of Christianity is not as broad as a lot of peopies'. One time they had some kind of religious dance they were supposedly doing on there. Ballet, it was supposed to be an expression of religion of some kind. We don't approve or disapprove of dancing, but in the tenets of our church it is not to be done, and I think that if a guy's gonna dance he ought to dance with his own wife, not with somebody else's. . . . I don't want anyone dancing with mine. . . . I think that's just plain sinful.

Joan adds, "In a class I took in sociology in college, they said that dancing and drinking are the two worst things you can add to a marriage."

Helen Purton expressed deep concerns about the direction of the mainline church, but made no particular distinction between the effects of the *700 Club* on mainline and fundamentalist denominations. The Wilsons share her opposition to the mainline church, but think that there is a very real potential effect of the electronic church on certain churches. Jeff is aware of the criticism that the electronic church might hurt local churches in some way.

"I think religious television helps the local church," he says. "You've gotta divide that up though between the mainline denominations that were grasping at straws and dying anyway and the strong evangelical movement. Now those people are losing, but they were losing to start with." Joan describes the difference as a matter of style within local congregations. "You walk into some of the mainline churches and people will sit there and fall asleep; they're bored. I mean, they'll give you a movie review and give you this and give you that instead of the gospel."

Like others we have spoken to, the Wilsons see the world and the *700 Club*'s place in it in a particular way based on both their theological and their sociopolitical backgrounds. For all of these people, the mainline, or liberal church has failed to address their vision of Christianity. This failure is profound, in their view, because churches should be spreading born-again religious consciousness. On the personal level, the establishment churches have failed to provide meaningful and consistent teaching and preaching, and have failed to encourage evangelical witnessing. On the community and cultural level, they have failed to affirm the conservative values of fundamentalist Christianity, and ignored, and even encouraged, the degeneration of values and morality, they would argue. From the perspective of the Baldwins, the Hands, the Parkers, Helen Purton, and the Wilsons, evangelical Christianity offers alternatives to this "establishment." These alternatives include the many independent evangelical churches around the country, which they see as "growing," and the institutions of the parachurch, of which the electronic church is a prominent component.

Evangelical religion and politics

The *cultural* witness of the evangelical and fundamentalist consciousness is only one part of the story. How this all plays in the broader *social* context is also important. Society provides a context in which these people form and reaffirm their individual and community identities. The rise of conservative Christian consciousness also has clear political implications. Jeff and Joan Wilson, for instance, endorse Pat Robertson's efforts to speak to "centers of power." Ross and Ruth Jackson, in contrast, express overtly *political* motivations for their participation.

The Jacksons have always been politically conservative evangelicals, but have generally attended liberal, mainline churches (Figure 6.5[5]). Their youngest child was born with a serious birth defect, and has since developed serious psychological problems. This has kept them from having a normal religious life, and Ruth began watching religious television partly to supplement what they were missing. She has called the *700 Club* several times for prayer for her problems and for their son, and she feels that those prayers have helped her and him.

The Jacksons are a comfortable upper-middle-class couple in their 50s who both work. They are disappointed that they are not tied more closely to a conventional church, though the pastor of their church has been helpful to them and to their son. Unlike Helen Purton, who had also spent most of her life in a liberal denomination, they do not have specific complaints about their church, even though it is more liberal than they would like. It has not failed them in their times of need.

The *700 Club* has helped too, though. Ruth recently was in a traffic accident that kept her away from work for several months, and she has required plastic surgery. She feels that prayers by the *700 Club* prayer counselors have helped her through this crisis.

But more important, the Jacksons insist that the *700 Club*, and other religious television ministries, serve an important *political* function. The

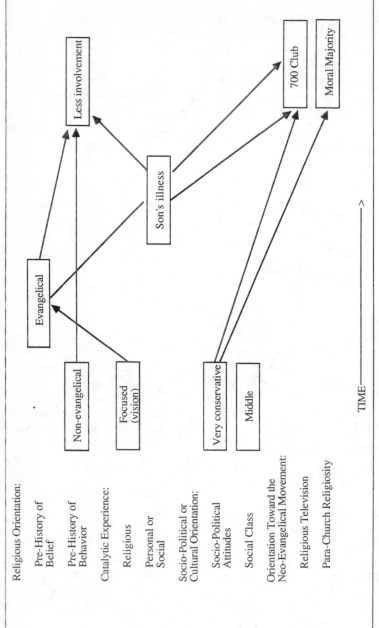

Religious Orientation:

Pre-History of
Belief

Pre-History of
Behavior

Catalytic Experience:

Religious

Personal or
Social

**Socio-Political or
Cultural Orientation:**

Socio-Political
Attitudes

Social Class

Orientation Toward the
Neo-Evangelical Movement:

Religious Television

Para-Church Religiosity

TIME ———————————————>

Figure 6.5. Viewing/Involvement trajectory for Ross and Ruth Jackson

700 Club is "putting forward the Christian aspect on world affairs," Ruth asserts. This is a crucial part of the program for her and (she assumes) for others.

"CBN is more rounded, bringing in all the news from around the world, conflicts, economics," she explains. "Pat Robertson even has a way of making these things understandable to me. Economics has never been easy for me, but he gets out his charts and he combines the religion in very nicely. He brings in personal experiences, too—people who've had healings." Ruth sees a clear distinction between the *700 Club* and most other religious broadcasts because CBN presents topical information about politics and social issues.

> For instance, I think a fundamentalist would be attracted to PTL. To CBN it would be people who like to keep up with what's going on in the world, with the Christian aspect of the things that are happening all around, and how to deal with them. You get much better education in that way with CBN.

The Jacksons stress the importance of the program as a social and political witness, one that transcends the traditional boundaries of conservative Christian churches. CBN represents a powerful new public expression of their religious and political beliefs that can compete with the secular media.

Reconciling faith through the *700 Club*

Esther Garnet shares Ruth Jackson's interest in the political significance of evangelicalism. She has been an evangelical most of her life (as has her husband, George). In fact, she proudly declares herself to be "a fundamentalist," a self-designation not used by others we interviewed. She has been dissatisfied with most of the churches she has attended. The Garnets are "stranded fundamentalists"—they would prefer to belong to a more fundamentalist church, but somehow have always managed to get into nonevangelical congregations (see Figure 6.6[6]). Although she and George have "shopped around" for fundamentalist ministers, they find they often are replaced by liberals.

"We're more at home in a fundamentalist church, and always have been," Esther says. "Ministers make the difference, you see. We have one now. . . . He's a wonderful person, but it's never clear where he stands on the Bible."

Esther's fundamentalism has been tested by viewing religious television. Once she accepted these programs as good and valuable, she gained through them some insights into her own belief system. One example she offered has to do with biblical inerrancy, a cornerstone of fundamentalism.

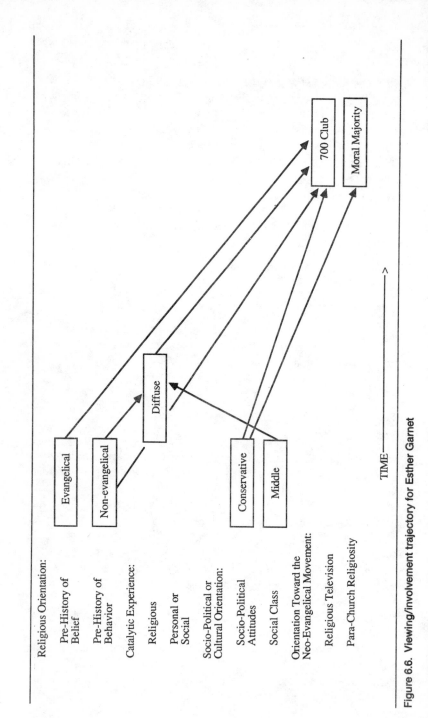

Figure 6.6. Viewing/Involvement trajectory for Esther Garnet

"Now I see, because of the Swaggart and Robertson programs, I think, that the Bible does have some contradictions in it," she says. "Like the most recent time I wrote to the *700 Club* was about the fact that there are two different creation stories in Genesis. . . . I haven't heard back from them on that."

Just as the *700 Club* opened a new path to social witnessing for the Baldwins, and has broadened the scope of evangelism for others, it has given Esther grounds for questioning one of the basic tenets of her faith. At the same time, the program has confirmed for her the validity of a fundamentalist critique of modern society. She has not had any dramatic religious or social experience related to her viewing of the program—no healings or personal crises. But the program gives her opportunities to share her faith.

> I talk to other people who I know are viewers of the program. I also suggest it to strangers, say people who are talking about current events in the check-out line or at the hairdresser's. I say, "If you want to see the news from an inspiring perspective, to see a *worldwide* picture of things, then you should watch."

It thus does not seem to be as much the spiritual content of the *700 Club* which draws her to the program as it is its universalist, "religious" perspective on world events.

The program also convinces her that the religious climate in America is changing, that it is easier to talk to people about religion than it used to be.

> I find that fundamentalist churches are growing. Those that are fundamental, that tell the whole gospel, are growing. I also find that it is much easier to talk about religion than it was 25 years ago, when I was looking for a church. Fundamentalists are more outgoing than they used to be.

Religious broadcasting and the local church

Bill Duncan is unemployed. He and Ethel have no children, and are in their early 40s. Ethel holds a job as a customer service representative with a manufacturing firm. Bill was a trucking dispatcher until he was laid off about a year ago. Bill is an evangelical who has consistently held his beliefs since childhood (Figure 6.7[7]). The Duncans belong to an evangelical church, and describe their viewing of religious broadcasting as an adjunct to churchgoing.

The Duncans' interest in religious broadcasting is related less to "social" issues than was the case for others we have heard from. Bill describes the differences between religious programs in terms of their spiritual value, with Charles Stanley getting top marks because "he helps Christians grow."

Bill sees the *700 Club* in universalistic terms. "The society is very

144

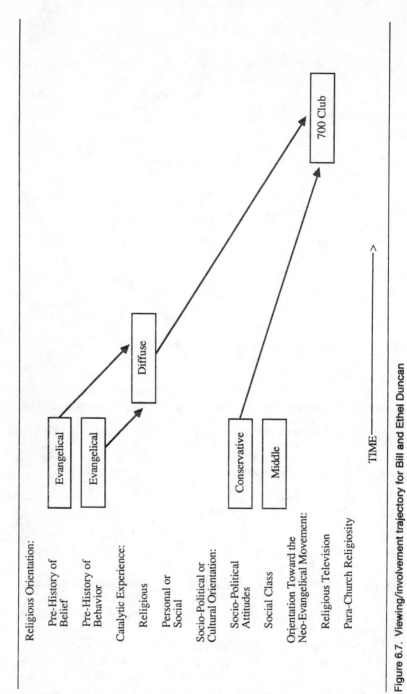

Figure 6.7. Viewing/involvement trajectory for Bill and Ethel Duncan

pluralistic and diversified, there's a need for a variety of evangelistic approaches." A program like Charles Stanley's, on the other hand, is "focused to people who accept his teachings." The *700 Club*, Bill says, presents an alternative to secular television, but it will never really directly affect conventional television (as some viewers seem to expect it to).

The relative openness of the *700 Club* can cause problems, Bill believes, because guests can confuse viewers by giving conflicting accounts of things. Programs that just preach and exhort, he believes, are less troublesome because they don't lose control over what is said. Interestingly, Bill believes that both the electronic church and the local churches may convey incorrect doctrine.

Bill says,

> I've seen people come on the *700 Club* who had revelations that they've been to heaven, or that they've seen angels, or that they've been to hell, and there are discrepancies between their stories and those of others who report similar experiences and that just adds confusion for the unbelievers, it just adds confusion. . . . Some doctrinal things bother me, too. I don't disagree with speaking in tongues, I don't do it, but don't condemn it. . . . But to say that to receive the Holy Spirit one has to speak in tongues is misleading.

Bill lays some of this trouble with the *700 Club* to its being self-consciously "fashionable." "It tries to deal with a wide variety of issues, and bring a wide variety of guests [to] let you know what's going on right now, while others deal with the viewers' spiritual lives."

Like the others we have heard, Bill does not relate his viewing of the *700 Club* to any revelations or crises in his own faith history. Even his choice of a local church was uninspired. "We chose the Presbyterian Church because it was more convenient, that's all," he says. He feels, however, that the value of religious broadcasting lies entirely in its service to local churches.

> I'm sure broadcasting helps the local church. It helps get them new converts because it allows the general population to be exposed to religious concepts and to accept Christ as their savior and then encourages them to attend church and that enhances local churches. People can't get fellowship and support except from a local body. The local church is the body of Christ.

Black evangelicals

Black evangelicals and white evangelicals may differ on social and political issues, but they have much in common in terms of their style of faith expression.

Alice Long is 76. She was raised in an independent black Baptist church, but has gone through several periods of soul searching, including an interval as a Roman Catholic. She has now rejoined an independent black

Baptist church. In spite of her obvious interest in developing her faith, Alice is free and almost offhanded in describing her faith history and the mystical experiences she has had, including a faith healing.

Most stories dealing with faith healing involve serious illnesses. Alice, by contrast, tells a story of how, through a vision, she was healed of the flu. This experience has done little to extend or focus her faith, rather she took it as a more or less expected outcome of her faith (Figure 6.8[8]).

Alice feels that the *700 Club* has helped strengthen her faith more than that it has given her new faith or theological insights. She credits it with encouraging her to express her beliefs more openly.

> The Christian Broadcasting Network has given so much to me, as a Christian, because I had a beginning, but I learned so much from CBN. . . . I've gotten a different impression of heaven and hell, of being a good Christian. I used to think that if you loved the Lord you did what you were supposed to do, and that was it. I've come to realize that doing things to help other people is actually part of Christianity, that your walk with the Lord is giving of yourself. You know . . . I've also learned to express myself better.

Alice agrees with the others we have spoken to that the electronic church "fills in" gaps often left by conventional churches. Her pastor, she says, may "love the Lord," but that is not enough.

> Our people need to get out and spread the word, and he's not doing that. I think I should tell him about the *700 Club* because that might help him see. I know of churches that are just *bubbling* over because of the movement of the spirit in getting people out to spread the gospel.

Her one criticism of the *700 Club* is its political bent. "People should be encouraged to get out and vote," she says, "but for who *they* support. The pastor should not tell them who that is."

Overall, Alice presents a profile and a set of experiences and reflections similar to that of the others we have heard from. Rita Payne differs from Alice Long and the others in that she is a member of a mainline church and has been actively involved in ecumenical church women's projects for a number of years. Where Alice is from a working-class family, Rita is upper middle class. Her husband is a doctor, and she has a college degree.

Perhaps because of her class and race, Rita is moderate on political issues, opposing capital punishment and favoring the "pro-choice" position on abortion, for instance, and (it is not surprising) indicating that she is a lifelong Democrat.

She is well aware that many religious programs take positions with which she disagrees on theological and social issues, but she watches them anyway. She is particularly attracted to the *PTL Club* because it is so energetic and enthusiastic, but she also likes the education and outreach of

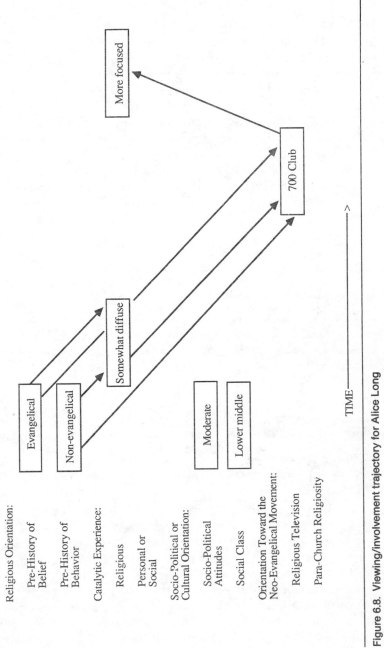

Figure 6.8. Viewing/Involvement trajectory for Alice Long

147

the *700 Club*. Because the *700 Club* addresses social as well as spiritual issues, however, Rita sometimes disagrees with the program. "He's [Pat Robertson] sincere, and deep but some of his interpretations are troubling for me. He favors capital punishment. It's hard to ignore it, to know what to do [but] you can't judge a person by that one issue. You're going to disagree with him, but I enjoy his teaching."

Rita agrees with others that religious broadcasting probably does not harm local churches. A few people may use the programs as "an excuse" for not going to church, she suggests, but not many. There is no way a television program can replace a real church in visiting the sick and serving the needy in local communities, she says, but churches have failed in an area where the electronic church is succeeding in serving the needs of lonely people.

> Most of us just do little things within our own little group and do not do a lot of helping, extending a hand like we should. We turn people away. You go to church and everybody's all dressed up, and there's no encouragement. They don't encourage people who are not dressed to come. . . . They make outsiders feel uncomfortable and out of place.

She echoes others in observing that religious television has another major advantage over local churches—the sophistication of its communication and its willingness to address social issues. Where others spoke of the political power of the program in its concern for social issues, Rita speaks in terms of "teaching" (see Figure 6.9[9]).

> I think that their *teaching* is the thing. Our churches don't teach a lot. Young married couples need to be taught and young parents, too. There ought to be some way in the church that they could have support. The church doesn't do that, and the programs do. Our young people don't get enough guidance in the church. They get a little, but not enough. When I was young, I would've appreciated having something like this [the program] to help me, but it just wasn't available.

Alice Long's and Rita Payne's perspectives on the *700 Club* differ slightly. The more conservative and Pentecostal of the two, Alice, finds religious broadcasting a liberalizing source of information about the outside world. The Pentecostalism of the program is comfortable to her, but political aspects are less so. Rita, more liberal herself, finds the programs valuable for their attention to the social needs of young people.

Both of them seem to be strongly attracted to the programs of the electronic church as a sort of "entertainment" rather than for social or political enlightenment. All the viewers we have heard from share this attitude that the program is somehow more for someone else than for themselves—that they and the programs' producers are colleagues, rather than that they are clients of a ministry.

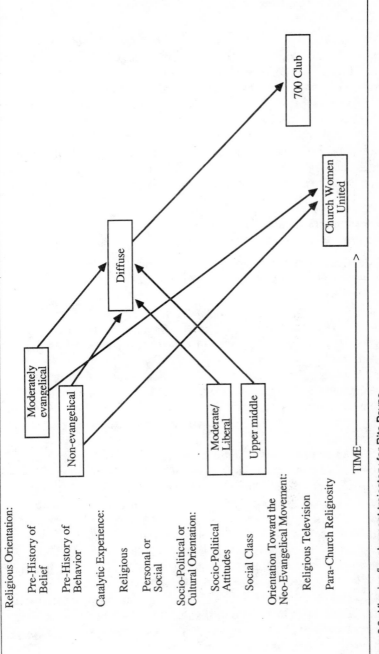

Religious Orientation:

Pre-History of Belief

Pre-History of Behavior

Catalytic Experience:

Religious

Personal or Social

Socio-Political or Cultural Orientation:

Socio-Political Attitudes

Social Class

Orientation Toward the Neo-Evangelical Movement:

Religious Television

Para-Church Religiosity

TIME ————>

Figure 6.9. Viewing/Involvement trajectory for Rita Payne

149

Alice and Rita both see the electronic church as an addition to, not a replacement for, conventional churches. Like all the evangelicals considered here, they view the *700 Club* as an adjunct to their religious activities unrelated to any great consciousness or change for them personally.

In the next chapter, we will meet people for whom the program seems to have been more closely related to their evolving religiosity. Among the viewers with whom we spoke, there were a number who have had striking personal experiences of religious awakening or physical or spiritual loss. Nearly all of these identified the *700 Club* as serving, in one way or another, to make these experiences meaningful and bearable.

The evangelical viewer: The *700 Club* as advocate for an alternate worldview

These viewers share in common a sense that the *700 Club* is an important part of a new religious alignment. The values and commitments of conservative Christianity are at last in a place of prominence on the national scene, and religious broadcasting has helped to put them there. The program has not served as a major factor in the evolution of their faiths, so much as it has been an expression of a faith already well established.

The trajectories outlining the faith histories of the Hands, the Parkers, the Garnets, the Duncans, Rita Payne, and Alice Long are similar. All of them come from backgrounds within evangelicalism or fundamentalism. All of them share a commitment to a faith that is personal and emotionally expressive.

For all of them, the *700 Club* has opened or broadened their traditional modes of religious activity. This broadening has taken two forms for most of them. First, they see religious broadcasting as a phenomenon that speaks to society in new ways. Jeff Wilson was not the only one who described the *700 Club* as an opportunity for a new and sophisticated radical witness to the wider society. Most of them also saw this social witness as unique because the program has "broken the mold" of traditional fundamentalism, showing that thinking, intellectual people can be conservative Christians.

The second aspect of this broadening has been the program's tendency to broaden *them* as individuals. Alice Long describes how the program has inspired her to be more bold in sharing her faith. The Baldwins, Helen Purton, and Ruth Jackson report that they also have been inspired by the program to speak openly about their faith.

All of them seem to recognize that this openness, this universalism, is a significant break from the traditions of fundamentalism, and that the program, and their experience of it, draws momentum from this discontinuity. Jeff and Joan Wilson recognize, quite unabashedly, that their theological roots are typified by insularity. Their faith has evolved away from particularism, and the *700 Club* has fit neatly into this evolution.

It is clear from what we have heard and from the faith histories we have diagrammed that, for most of these viewers, the *700 Club* has been valuable to their faith development, but not essential. The program is seen simply as consistent with their religious consciousness, but it is valuable to them for its divergence from the traditional evangelical or fundamentalist worldview. For all of them, the program's appeal to a broader, outside world in terms of class and theology is its major attraction. It deserves support not so much because *they themselves* are the objects of its ministries, but because of what it does for, and represents to, the rest of the world. With few exceptions, these viewers see the *700 Club* as there for "someone else."

These "someones" include several different communities. Believers in conventional churches may enjoy the program's intensity and sophisticated approach to Christian witness. Individual "unbelievers" can be helped through times of crisis, and can be reached and evangelized by the program's message that is not so intimidating that it turns them off. The wider public and political environment can benefit from the involvement of a sophisticated and articulate voice of conservative Christianity.

For the Baldwins, the Hands, and others, this latter value of the program is entirely novel in their understanding of American fundamentalism and evangelicalism. The *700 Club* represents for them just the sort of major revitalization movement predicted by William McLoughlin. Recent decades have been typified, for them, by a growing dissonance between traditional norms and values, and a society and world going out of control. Strong measures have been needed, and a revitalized, parachurch evangelicalism has been the result. The *700 Club* has found its place in the forefront of that movement. We will consider this in more detail in a later chapter.

The faith histories of these viewers have also revealed a role for the program in their *individual religious consciousness*. While the program has not been associated, for them, with a major reconfirmation of faith, or with experiences of faith healing or other crisis, it has brought all of them new perspectives on their beliefs, and new avenues for acting on them. The Baldwins credit the *700 Club* with involving them in the variety of social ministries that have dominated their recent lives. Helen Purton was been inspired by guests on the *700 Club* to increase her interest in and support of other parachurch ministries. Jeff and Joan Wilson and Esther Garnet have found that the program has challenged and broadened their beliefs, bringing them (and presumably others) new, more tolerant consciousnesses.

The program's role in promoting "translocalism" (the sense that it transcends "local" cultures, experiences, and beliefs) suggests a place for it in faith development consistent with James Fowler's developmental theory. The development, in later stages, of new consciousness is typified by an ever-widening circle of contacts and inputs, and an ever more open and universal understanding of the grounds of faith. For these viewers, the "*700 Club*" serves just such a function. As a program from outside their local frames of reference, it brings home the point that their worldviews must expand to include other people who also call themselves "Christian," "fundamentalist," or "evangelical."

On the individual level, then, the *700 Club* serves these evangelicals in a dynamic way, somewhat secondarily to their original development of a conservative Christian faith. Coming as they do from the "right bank" of mainstream American Protestantism and American culture, even so seemingly (to the mainstream) closed and conservative a witness as the *700 Club* serves to open, even liberalize their view of the world, and their faith.

In succeeding chapters, we will see that the program's appeal lies in two additional areas. It seems particularly important to viewers in personal crisis and stress. Its universalism and openness are also vital to some viewers, forming its major gratification for them.

Notes

1. Viewing/Involvement Trajectories will be explicated in notes for each figure. For a more complete description, see Stewart M. Hoover, "The *700 Club* as Religion and as Television: A Study of Reasons and Effects" (Ph.D. diss., the University of Pennsylvania, 1985).

2. Harry and Mabel's, and Julie Baldwin's (Figure 6.2), trajectories will be described here together. They record the wide range of involvements and experiences the Baldwins report. Harry and Mabel were both raised in evangelical churches, and continue to hold such beliefs, as does Julie. All of them now belong to a mainline congregation, though it is one that is decidedly evangelical in belief. None of them describes striking, focused personal experiences of either a religious or a social nature, at least up until the crisis brought on by the death of Harry and Mabel's son. The social class from which they come makes it difficult for them to talk about their faith among associates (though the difficulty does not necessarily stop them from doing so). Their political conservatism resonates with the *700 Club* program, though that is more the case for Harry than for his wife or daughter. They have all had a variety of involvements in the parachurch. Their major current involvement, that of prison ministry work, was actually stimulated by their viewing of the program. Their son's death was a major focusing event for them, and led to them becoming more involved in the *700 Club* program and in the parachurch.

3. John and Martha Hand come from belief backgrounds that were decidedly fundamentalist, and have been involved in church communities that are not necessarily as conservative as they are. They have moved toward viewing the *700 Club* as a supplement to an active interest in religion. Their lives have not been focused toward a major "religious experience," at least in recent times, possibly because they now find themselves in social contexts that they see to be hostile to fundamentalism. Even their experiences of conversion have faded. No major religious experience has coincided with their beginning to view the *700 Club*. Their social and political attitudes are quite conservative, and this, along with their

fundamentalism, have rung true with the content of the *700 Club*.

4. Joe and Doris Parker's pattern differs from others' mainly in that Joe reports having had a major religious experience—he spoke in tongues for the first time—at a meeting at CBN's headquarters (about which we will hear more in Chapter 8). Viewing of the program itself has been less important than direct contacts with CBN and its leadership, though. As with the others, the Parkers say they support the program because it has given evangelicalism a new force and prominence. Social class has an important affect on the Parkers' experience of the *700 Club*. Joe is very conscious of the traditional class associations with conservative Christianity, and is particularly attracted to the program because it represents "top-notch leadership" in an age where such leadership is needed if the wider world is to be changed by the Christian faith. Joe's religious experience at a *700 Club*-sponsored event has led to an increasing involvement in the program and its ministries. They are both longtime evangelicals, even though they have mostly attended mainline churches. Their evangelical background encouraged their focus on religious experience, but this dimension of their lives has become even more intense because of their experiences with the *700 Club*.

5. Ross and Ruth Jackson express some frustration with their religious lives, for two reasons. Both of them have always been conservative or evangelical in belief, but they have found themselves in congregations somewhat hostile to those beliefs, or at least where a more liberal agenda was the rule. Second, their son has had health problems that have made it difficult for them to engage in the normal range of social activities, such as church attendance. Ruth's faith was shaped by an early experience where she had a vision as a result of involvement in a charismatic prayer group. Political factors account for some of the interest and involvement in the *700 Club* and other religious programs, especially Jerry Falwell's. They contribute to Falwell's Moral Majority organization.

6. As with others, no particular experience of focused religious conversion has gone along with Esther Garnet's participation in the *700 Club*. Rather, her involvement with the program is based very much in her evangelical consciousness. She continues to be involved in nonevangelical churches, and looks to programs like the *700 Club*, and other parachurch organizations like the Moral Majority, to articulate an agenda with which she is more comfortable. Her political and religious conservatism finds powerful support in the *700 Club* and in these other parachurch agencies.

7. Bill and Ethel Duncan's trajectory is remarkably similar to Esther Garnet's. Evangelical faith and political conservatism form the basis of their worldview, and the *700 Club* speaks to these concerns for them. They report no dramatic religious or social experience in conjunction with their viewing of the *700 Club*, and have had no major crises, Bill's temporary unemployment aside.

8. Alice Long is the only one of the people we have heard from so far who clearly articulates the feeling that the program itself has been involved in focusing or refining *her* faith. Others tend to describe the program almost dispassionately, in terms of what it can do to witness to others. Alice has found the program useful, personally. It has inspired her to a more focused and refined expression of her faith. She did have a dramatic religious experience when she was healed of the flu several years ago. Her rather moderate sociopolitical attitudes (she supports prison reform and opposes capital punishment) and her social class seem to have little to do with her viewing of the program.

9. For Rita Payne, evangelicalism expressed in a mainline church is combined with being politically comparatively moderate to liberal. The *700 Club*, for her, is an example of the sort of effective and sophisticated *educational* enterprise in which conventional churches should be involved. Rita is the only one of our viewers who has been involved in parachurch activities that are not evangelical or fundamentalist at their base. Her work in Church Women United, a mainline Protestant ecumenical organization, predates her *700 Club* viewing. Her ecumenical work, and her political beliefs, are at odds with the program; something she acknowledges.

7

Seeking Solutions to
Personal and Spiritual Crisis

Proponents, critics, and observers alike share many myths and preconceptions about evangelists and religious broadcasting. Sinclair Lewis's mythical evangelist of the 1920s, "Elmer Gantry," is an icon of hypocrisy. Similarly, the electronic church preacher of today, whose political ambitions may outweigh his spiritual ones, is considered by some to be a demagogue. There is, however, a "substantive" (in Berger's[1] sense of the term) dimension to these programs. They are, after all, mainly about spiritual matters. No myth, or set of them, is as powerful as that of being "born again," a life-altering conversion that may even befall unbelievers who encounter these programs by "accident."

June Mason is a viewer, a member, and a volunteer telephone counselor for the *700 Club*. She became involved in the program, for many reasons, after the death of her son, including her loneliness and isolation after moving to a new city. She is convinced that the *700 Club* and its ministries are worth supporting for reasons beyond loyalty born of her own experience with it. The notion that it can change the lives of people who are not even seeking help is especially exciting to her.

"You have heard of Efrem Zimbalist, Jr., haven't you?" she asks.

> I heard him speak, and he said he had everything in the world [but] that he had a real emptiness inside. So one night he just flipped the dial until he saw the *700 Club*.... He couldn't sleep [and] he said he laughed his head off. He thought this was funny, these Christians and all. And he watched the next night and said "Just listen to this guy, I can't believe what he is saying!" and so became addicted and said he had to know more, and gradually he became aware that Pat Robertson was speaking to him.

This image of a lonely individual, often in a hotel room, or alone at home, seeking something undefined (often without realizing it) is a powerful one. Television can relieve loneliness and isolation with its potent message of individual salvation. As in June Mason's account of Efrem Zimbalist's experience, religious television often is felt to have an almost mystical power, even over people who are not really searching for anything. The fact that this happened to someone famous, of course, lends great credibility to the story.

There are many such stories of religious conversion sparked by personal crises of faith and crises of a more immediate nature. For many viewers, the

700 Club confirms these stories. For others, it does not. Still, the remarkable range of personal, medical, and spiritual crises reported by *700 Club* viewers is amazing. There are suicides, accidental deaths of spouses, serious illnesses, unemployment due to disability, business failures, annulments, divorces, and the deaths of children. The Viewing/Involvement Trajectories[2] that follow outline the range of these events and the ways they relate to faith, religious expression, and involvement in the *700 Club*.

The conversion experience

Ed Horne is currently on disability leave because of an accident at work. He has had his share of troubles. Ed is divorced and the father of a young daughter who lives with his ex-wife. He lives simply in a modest house in the suburbs and has tried to fill his time usefully during the months that he could not work. This proved to be difficult for a man in his 30s who was used to filling his days with work. He was saddened by his circumstances, but a newfound involvement in religion has been a comfort to him.

Ed traces his new interest in religion to the *700 Club*, and he traces his involvement with the *700 Club* to a personal religious experience he had when watching television on Christmas Eve.

> I was watching it on Christmas Eve and I had an experience, and then I just started watching it all the time. . . . I had seen it before, but I had never really followed it. My hand had just hit the [remote control] button and they were there saying the "sinner's prayer." It was a mistake, really, I hadn't planned on watching it, and suddenly I was on my knees, praying along with it. I must have passed out or something, because suddenly I was crying. I just sat there and cried for fifteen minutes, and then I found myself sitting there talking to them on the telephone. . . . I didn't even know what had happened. The lady on the phone . . . explained to me that I had given my life to Christ and that I was now a new person. I was healed of everything, in an instant. I was healed of smoking cigarettes, alcohol, drinking, in a matter of seconds, it went away, just like that.

As striking as his experience was, Ed is quick to point out that he was not new to Christianity. He had been raised in a home where religion was important.

> It was in the back of my mind, all the time. I never talked to anybody about it, but it was always in the back of my mind. I always prayed. I never just took it for granted. I always believed that there was a Jesus Christ, and there was a God, you know. My grandma, she was a Jehovah's Witness, and she used to bug me to death. And I'd say, "hey, when I'm ready, I'll . . . ."

So, for years, he led a life that now embarrasses him, a life where formal religion played no part.

His experience with the *700 Club* led Ed to join a conventional church. "I talked to a counselor at the *700 Club* and she said I should go around and find a church I could be comfortable with." This was not an easy task for him.

> I tried all the denominations, and the differences bothered me. I didn't go to the Catholic church, though, because after reading the Bible, there are so many discrepancies they have, like confession. . . . I know that the only one you should confess to is Jesus Christ, to God, and not to a man. So there were so many fallacies I saw. I went for twelve years to a Catholic church as a kid, and never had to read the Bible, so that made me not really consider them.

Finally, he found a church he liked, one he went to because his ex-wife had been sending their daughter there for Sunday school. "They come over and pick up the kids for Bible study. . . . I said to myself, 'My daughter is going to Bible study there, and I don't even know where she is going.' So I went there and I really liked it."

Among the things he liked best about this church was that he was made to feel welcomed and was noticed by the pastor. "I really got involved, the pastor was so friendly, he called me up after the first time, and came by and talked to me." Ed sees this experience very much as a conversion, even though he can point to much previous interest in religion and in the development of his beliefs. For one thing, he says that he was instantly healed of some of his worst vices (though he has begun smoking again).

His family was understandably surprised, after his years of noninvolvement in church, that he now considers himself "born again."

> My mother was a Catholic, still is . . . and she can't believe it. My brothers couldn't believe it either. One of them, in Phoenix, said, "If it could happen to you, it could happen to me," [because] he has a lot of problems himself. . . . It was so unbelievable, that the Lord told me to go to Phoenix and talk to him and show him.

The opportunity to share his experience with his brother was important for Ed. At first, after calling several airlines to ask about fares, he thought he could not afford to go. But then an airline called him back and told him about a new fare that was within his reach, so he went. He says that God paved the way for him to witness to his brother.

While he was visiting his brother, Ed was tempted to "backslide" into his old ways.

> We used to party all the time, [and] to go to bars. He wanted to do that, and I wouldn't. I told him that bars have nothing for me. I used to raise some Cain before I got born again, and that is one of the things I've gotten out of, and I wouldn't go back into it. . . . I've basically made the change. My brother is on the way, but it will take time.

Ed's interest in the *700 Club* is far different from that of the Baldwins, the Wilsons, or the Duncans. They see the program as one way that evangelical or fundamentalist Christianity can witness to contemporary life. For Ed Horne, the program's potential impact on viewers' faith is central. The *700 Club* intervened in his troubled life and made a difference. Ed is not a lifelong conservative Christian as were the others. While churchgoing was part of his childhood, as an adult he was only vaguely concerned about religion.

Ed's trajectory (Figure 7.1[3]) highlights the difference between the faith histories of the longtime evangelicals and fundamentalists we met in the last chapter, and someone like Ed, who comes to the *700 Club* from a different religious background. Whereas the Duncans see the *700 Club* and the *PTL Club* as consistent with their pasts (in the case of the Duncans, as representative of a past they feel they have left behind), Ed comes to these programs with a fresh perspective.

The most striking difference is Ed's perspective on social and political issues. He takes a politically liberal stand on capital punishment, homosexuality, control of pornography, and premarital sex.

"I guess I'm a very liberal person," Ed explains. "I say, 'To each his own.' . . . If you want to look at pornography, even though you know what the Bible says about it, who am I to judge a person and tell them that that is wrong?" Ed seems not to have thought too much about the contradiction between his position on these things and the professed political views of Pat Robertson and most other viewers of the *700 Club*. Reflecting on this, he says, "Pat Robertson is there to do that, to encourage people not to do those things, like that is his job. I've got a job I go to everyday, and that is his, . . . to stop abortions, pornography, adultery, and all, but that is not for me to do."

Ed's relationship to the *700 Club* in many ways is the converse of that of the Baldwins and others from whom we have heard. The program confirms for them the value and permanence of their social and religious worldviews. Its spiritual value *to them as individuals*, however, is far less pronounced than it is for Ed, who seems to be on the verge of a religious awakening that the others felt years earlier.

Crises of faith and involvement

Sally Horton is a surprising woman. Short and rather stocky, with frosted hair, she looks very much like a typical suburban housewife in the working-class neighborhood where she lives. Most of her neighbors own their modest homes, as do Sally and her husband, Jim. She decorates their home in a way that does not suggest that she is in any way unique, except that the

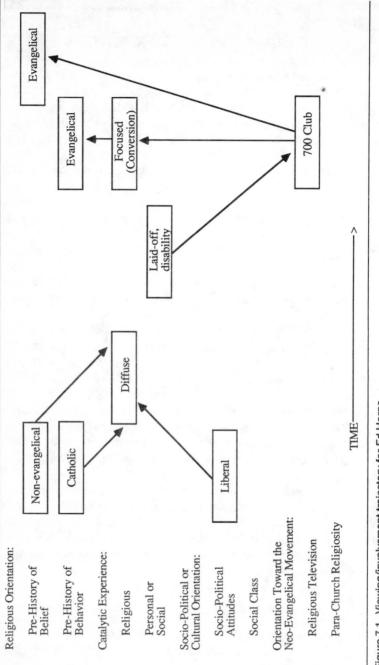

Figure 7.1. Viewing/involvement trajectory for Ed Horne

bookshelves are filled with books about religion and the Bible and the coffee table and end tables in the living room are stacked with religious pamphlets and periodicals.

What is surprising is that, aside from being a homemaker and an avowed evangelical, Sally also is an ordained minister. Her parents were Sunday school teachers in the inner city, in a black church (Sally and Jim are white). "I'm very drawn to minister to the black community. That is something God has called me to do," Sally says. "They are more poorly taught, on the whole. . . . black Christians tend to have less good Bible instruction, and careful, systematic teaching, than do Christians at large." Sally (with Jim's strong support) now is heavily involved in ministries both within churches and in a parachurch operation. Her heaviest commitment is to a ministry of her own creation in a county women's prison nearby.

Sally and Jim both have faced personal crises in previous marriages. This is the second marriage for both. Sally described the place that problems hold in the development of their faith.

> I had all my dreams and hopes pinned [on] my first marriage. It was a shock for me for it to break, and a horror, and very humiliating because now I was a divorced woman and that was horrible. I had to go through a long process of pain and inner healing.

Sally's marriage was annulled after she discovered that her husband was a bigamist, but spiritual growth followed her crisis.

> After that trauma, the Lord went to work. I had a dramatic time of inner healing of memories and scars, a very dramatic release, and an understanding of my dead father, and mother, and my dead sister, and all these traumas I'd been through, very severe deep things, and then I was filled with the Holy Spirit—I was baptized in the Holy Spirit.

Sally contends that she knew, because of her experience, that a new phase of her religious life was beginning. "I couldn't wait to have God use me to touch other people, in a whole new dimension. He'd bring suicidal people to me, and all kinds of troubled people to me and train me how to listen to his spirit and minister to them." Her newly intense faith also brought her into contact with Jim.

> When I heard from my family that Jim had been through this horrible thing of his wife killing herself, I really felt there were few people who could identify with him like I could . . . and I prayed in a really strong fashion, with tears, that God would give him a whole new life, and ministry, and make him fruitful.

The Hortons renewed their earlier acquaintance at church, and later married.

The Hortons' daily lives, aside from Jim's factory job and Sally's homemaking, revolve around Sally's ministry. Both of them acknowledge that theirs is an unusual relationship, at least among conservative Christians.

Sally says of Jim,

> I've found over the years of our marriage that he is very unusual for a Christian man in that he is not intimidated by a wife who is a preacher, and more cultured and educated than he is. He's an observer of what I do, I am more the vocal person. We've looked at it that this is the way I am gifted and that is the way he is gifted. It doesn't fit peoples' stereotypes.

Jim adds, "My wife is such a great communicator. She's intelligent, and well versed, and I get blessed just listening to her."

Sally and Jim are somewhat isolated, despite her prison ministry, the counseling she does at home in the evenings ("Young women in trouble with drugs and other things are drawn to me for help," she says), and other religious work. They are not currently members of a local church. "We recently left our church," Jim says at one point, while discussing the problems with conventional churches. They see most churches as too restrictive and too concerned with petty legalisms.

"My favorite thing," says Sally, "is to have a large gathering where people aren't concerned about their labels, and where they are concentrating on their one-ness in joining that fellowship. It hurt to leave our church, we didn't want to." Jim adds, "Our pastor was very legalistic, and he was putting us in bondage. . . . At first we didn't know he was like that, . . . but when we got into the inner-workings of the church we learned that that was the case."

"Let me describe this," Sally continues,

> because I was the object of most of it. We were both officers in the church, and loved the pastor and loved the people. Quite suddenly, he began to preach on things such as "Women shouldn't wear pants, because that is ungodly." We had just, as a congregation, gone to a ball game, I had organized it, and I wore pants. So everyone in the church saw me like this. I had privately asked him on other occasions if I was offensive to him, wearing pants, and he had said, "No." So when he spent half an hour haranguing on that subject . . .

Jim breaks in, tears filling his eyes, "He was attacking my wife. It upset me a great deal, . . . you can see that, he was zeroing in on my wife."

Sally becomes more philosophical.

> It was mainly painful, not only on the personal level, but because I felt bad for him. . . . We had a good relationship with him and we were giving—it was a tiny black church, and we were the only white people other than people we would invite sometimes. The problem was, it became all legalisms. He preached about

makeup and about tithing to the local assembly only. All of this seemed directed at us because we give so much money to the [prison] ministry God has given us.

The Hortons then have had personal crises in both their social and their religious lives—crises that they feel deeply about. Unlike Ed Horne, though, they do not feel the *700 Club* is crucial to their faith. They appreciate and support religious programming, but for them the *700 Club* is related more to their sense of themselves as ministers and their need for information than it is to upbuilding of their own faith. They enjoy evangelical programming, they explain, even though they do not always agree with what they see.

"We'll watch something to see what they're teaching, how they're coming across, even how they're coming across to other people, . . . we get concerned, pro and con, about that," says Jim. "Whether they're helping or hurting . . . we watch, not for food for ourselves, but out of curiosity to see what kind of programming they're doing for the country. And then for the fellowship and inspiration."

They also find it useful as information, in much the same way many of the viewers we met in the last chapter did. Sally notes,

> I use it to keep on top of world situations from a Christian viewpoint, industry, technology, government, everything. . . . We've always been fascinated with what the Lord is doing in the lives of other people, so the human interest stories, I watch them, and make notes and report them. . . . Since CBN isn't on cable anymore [here], we've really lost touch with things in the world. We really depended on it.

Sally and Jim report that the crises in their own lives convinced them they were chosen to minister to others. They are more than superficially similar to the Baldwins. But their ministry, specifically to black churches, has been costly for them. Their trajectory is shown in Figure 7.2[4].

The dramatic sort of personal religious experience that Ed Horne reports is in the past for Sally and Jim. Day-to-day struggles with acting on their faith occupy their time. They seem drawn to the *700 Club* for moral support of the conservative Christianity they espouse, for its social and political messages, and its "Christian perspective on things." Pat Robertson and other electronic church ministers also exemplify for them the most sophisticated spokespersons for their kind of faith. The *700 Club* is consistent with their view of the world, and its social outreach emphasis reinforces their commitment to a parachurch ministry of their own.

The *700 Club* as a help in personal crisis

June Mason also works in a parachurch ministry, but of a different kind. She is a telephone counselor for a local CBN counseling center, and

162

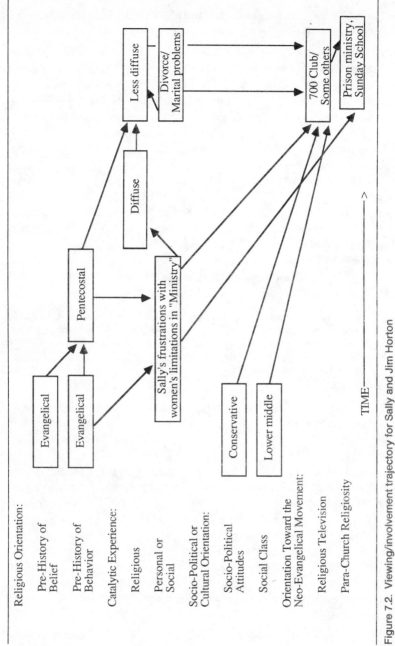

Figure 7.2. Viewing/involvement trajectory for Sally and Jim Horton

through that, she has come to feel that religious broadcasting can "link up" people in need with people who can help. June lives in one of the wealthier areas of the city in a large, finely appointed house. Her husband is religious and a regular churchgoer, but he has not been born again as she has, and he is not a regular viewer of the *700 Club*.

What led June, who lives a comfortable, even affluent, life to volunteer time to counsel by telephone?

> I began to realize that there was such a need for counselors and I just couldn't sit and not help. I realized that there was such a need when Pat [Robertson] said so on television. When I became a Christian, I realized that there are so many people who need to talk to people, and they have no one to talk to. There are hundreds of people who call up and say "I don't have anyone to talk to about this." I'd get a black girl who'd call up and say, "My husband is living with another woman, and pray for her and pray for him"—and I'd give them prayer. You see, they can talk to me because they don't know me, and they can talk about things they couldn't say to anyone else. I'm always there. They can't pay for a counselor, they don't have any money. You just don't know what good you can do. We all need people who can really hear you and listen to your needs.

June has always been a faithful churchgoer, but felt "in the back of my mind" that she was somehow not quite a Christian. She was "just kind of in church, not a real dedicated Christian. I was singing in the choir, just there, but not really close to God." This began to bother her, she says, but she always knew that someday she'd become a "real Christian." She used to fear that she'd be killed in a plane crash and that God wouldn't let her into heaven.

In 1976, she was listening to Pat Robertson on the *700 Club*, and decided that she just had to try.

> So I got down on my knees and prayed with Pat, the "sinner's prayer." And God must have known I needed to be prepared because a few months later our son died . . . committed suicide. . . . It makes me cry to talk about it even now. So in those six months I needed a strong faith badly. . . . If I hadn't had God, I wouldn't be here today. He pulls you through, and you just melt, you just can't get away from God, He pulls you through. There's really no way I'd be here today, if it weren't for God.

The tragic nature of June's loss has been made somehow more bearable through her newfound faith, a faith that stemmed from a commitment made while viewing the *700 Club*. She sees the *700 Club* as a source of both inspiration and solace (see Figure 7.3[5]). Her feelings are quite different from those of the Hortons. She appreciates the information on the program, but its primary function, as she sees it, lies in its ministry to those who are in need.

164

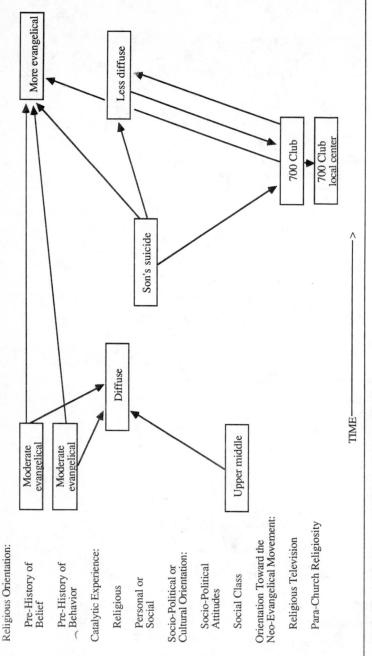

Figure 7.3. Viewing/involvement trajectory for June Mason

June's feelings about the *700 Club* fall somewhere between those of Ed Horne and of the Hortons. Like Ed, she feels the program has been a major turning point in her faith. Like the Hortons, she sees the program as part of a larger institutional religious reality, and she gives time as a volunteer so that others can be helped as she was.

A mystical experience

Ralph Ritter has been a Catholic all his life. His wife and his children also were raised Catholic. The Ritters moved to their present near-suburban home (and current parish) about 15 years ago, after living in an ethnic neighborhood. They live in a simple twin house in a blue-collar neighborhood. Ralph has time on his hands now, having taken full disability due to a chronic disease of the nervous system. His wife works full-time.

The move to the suburbs was a turning point in Ralph's religious life, in that he began to attend evening meetings of the Catholic charismatic movement in the new parish. "We're now spirit-filled Catholics," he says, "but we're still faithful attenders at Mass."

Ralph feels that the major events of his life have all led him to this religious development. Moving to a new parish and joining the charismatic movement has helped him to deal with his disability.

The Ritters' experience with religious broadcasting actually began with the *PTL Club*. They were drawn to this program, which they consider to be more "spirit filled" than the others, after being told about it by friends. They were occasional viewers until a problem came along that they now consider providential. They were about to lose their house after Ralph was laid off and before disability payments started.

"I decided, 'Well, I've tried everything,'" Ralph recalls,

so I called the PTL prayer line and asked for prayer. I had tried everywhere I could—family, friends, everywhere—to borrow money. The Lord gets you to a point where you can't go any farther, and then snaps you in. Well, I called, and a couple of days later, I was worried because I needed the money on a Friday. On Thursday, I said, "I've got to have the money by five o'clock." My wife prayed to the Lord, that he should speak and whatever he wanted, it should go that way. I was about to make one last desperate call to her sister, when—and I'll never forget this as long as I live—this voice said to me "You doubt me, you doubt me" almost like a deep, male voice, and I was looking around the room to see if anyone was in the room speaking to me.

Ralph continues,

I was about to make the call, when the phone rang, and it was a woman I had only known for three weeks, through a prayer meeting. She said that they had been praying for our financial situation, and asked what I needed. I said I needed $500. She said "I was praying, and the Lord told me to call you . . . I don't know why." I said that the Lord had just spoken to me a little earlier, and she began to weep. I said, "Why are you weeping?" and she said "Because the Lord is using me. You see, I have this money, $500, that I don't need." So she said I could have it and that I could pay it back whenever I wanted. I paid it back in two months.

As hard as this all must have been for the Ritters, a worse blow was to come. Three years later, one of their daughters came down with incurable leukemia. Ralph is convinced that, on more than one occasion, her disease was put into remission or possibly removed altogether as a result of healing services to which they took her. Doctors would not believe him, he says, and continued her treatments, which depleted her immune system. As a result, she died of a childhood disease contracted at school (under circumstances the Ritters believe were negligent and they are pursuing legal steps). "I am sure she is with Christ now," Ralph notes, adding "and you know, there was not one trace of leukemia in the autopsy."

Ralph and Jane are regular contributors to both the *PTL Club* and the *700 Club*, in spite of the financial stress they continue to feel. They are convinced that the financial assistance they got came as a result of their faith and involvement in the *PTL Club*, and they continue to contribute. Ralph recounts a similar experience with the *700 Club*.

> I had this car, and I was thinking of selling this car, and Ben Kinchlow [the cohost of the *700 Club*] said one time that we should call in things we could contribute to this "Operation Blessing," so I called and offered my car, and they found a mission group here that needed it.... Sometimes the Lord uses people just like me. Ben said, "You have something you know you want to get rid of, call Operation Blessing." ... I felt he was talking directly to me, so I called and offered my car, and they came and got it. The guy said, "We've never had a car before" but they needed it. They found a use for it and for me that way.

Unlike the Baldwins, the Duncans, and even the Hortons, the Ritters' religiosity is heavily dependent upon the *PTL Club* and the *700 Club* (see Figure 7.4[6]). "We watch both of those shows regularly, and we give what we can. Both shows have blessed us greatly." In addition, the Catholic charismatic movement has them heavily committed to a variety of activities in their local parish, including a Catholic marriage enrichment program. Their viewing of the *PTL Club* and the *700 Club* have coincided with turmoil in their conventional religious lives (their coming to be involved in the charismatic movement) and with a series of personal crises. Their relationship with the *700 Club* apparently helped in one of their crises, thereby reinforcing their newly found charismatic faith.

Finding meaning in crisis

Helen Purton, whom we met in the previous chapter, also had a story of crisis and loss to share. Her faith and religious activities flowed from

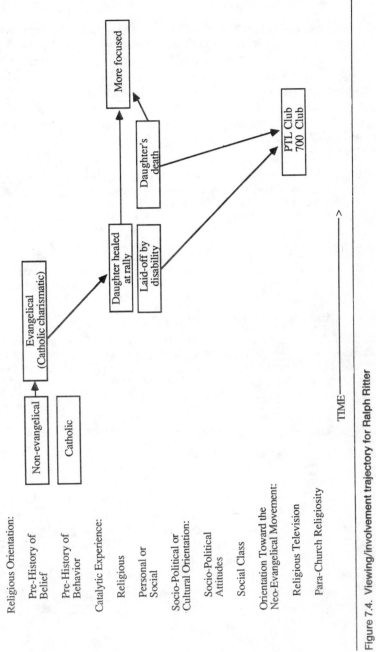

Religious Orientation:

Pre-History of
Belief

Pre-History of
Behavior

Catalytic Experience:

Religious

Personal or
Social

Socio-Political or
Cultural Orientation:

Socio-Political
Attitudes

Social Class

Orientation Toward the
Neo-Evangelical Movement:

Religious Television

Para-Church Religiosity

Non-evangelical → Evangelical (Catholic charismatic) → More focused

Catholic

Daughter healed at rally

Laid-off by disability

Daughter's death

PTL Club
700 Club

TIME ———>

Figure 7.4. Viewing/involvement trajectory for Ralph Ritter

167

long-standing commitment to evangelical witnessing in a mainline church, and later a set of independent, free-lance personal ministries. Her viewing of the *700 Club*, we saw then, seemed to be coincidental with these activities. The *700 Club* also appears much less connected, for her, with her personal loss, than was the case with either the Ritters or Ed Horne. The death of her husband in an automobile accident, however, is just as compelling as the others. She tells the story of the aftermath of the accident, in which she was driving the car.

> We were hit head on, and the car was totaled, and my husband was hurt. I learned later that his head went through the windshield even though he had a seat belt on. Well, they came and got us and put him in one ambulance and me in another, and in the emergency room he was in one end, and I was in the other. They x-rayed my ankle, I had a broken ankle. After five hours a doctor came and said, "Your husband died, but we don't know why." And I said, "Well, I guess that was in the hands of the Lord.". . . At that point, there was a sort of a cloud above me and out of that came the words that I haven't forgotten in ten years, "This was the way it was supposed to be. You take it and do the best you can with it.". . . And by morning, I just couldn't weep and say, "Why did this happen to me." Because I knew that was the way it was supposed to be.

Helen took this revelation seriously (Figure 7.5[7]). The role of her personal loss in stimulating her religious activities is important, though obviously not the complete cause. It is clear, however, that religious broadcasting is, for her, far less important an aspect of her religiosity than is the case for the Ritters or Ed Horne. Unlike them, Helen does not connect her crisis either with her viewing of the *700 Club* or with her other religious involvements. Her faith is largely lodged within *her*.

Viewing as independent of faith tradition

Shelley Browne is very different from Helen Purton and the others we have heard from in that she is a devout, practicing Jew. But she has one thing in common with the Ritters, Ed Horne, and the Hortons: She is a supporter of the *700 Club* and originally became involved due to a personal crisis. Christianity was not a precondition for her, but a crisis was. A married woman in her 30s, Shelley began watching the *700 Club* when she became physically disabled and was home a great deal.

She and her husband were both raised Jewish and had become more active after marriage, attending synagogue regularly. They planned to have a family, but her disability has made that doubtful. They also have economic problems because of losing income from a job Shelley no longer holds.

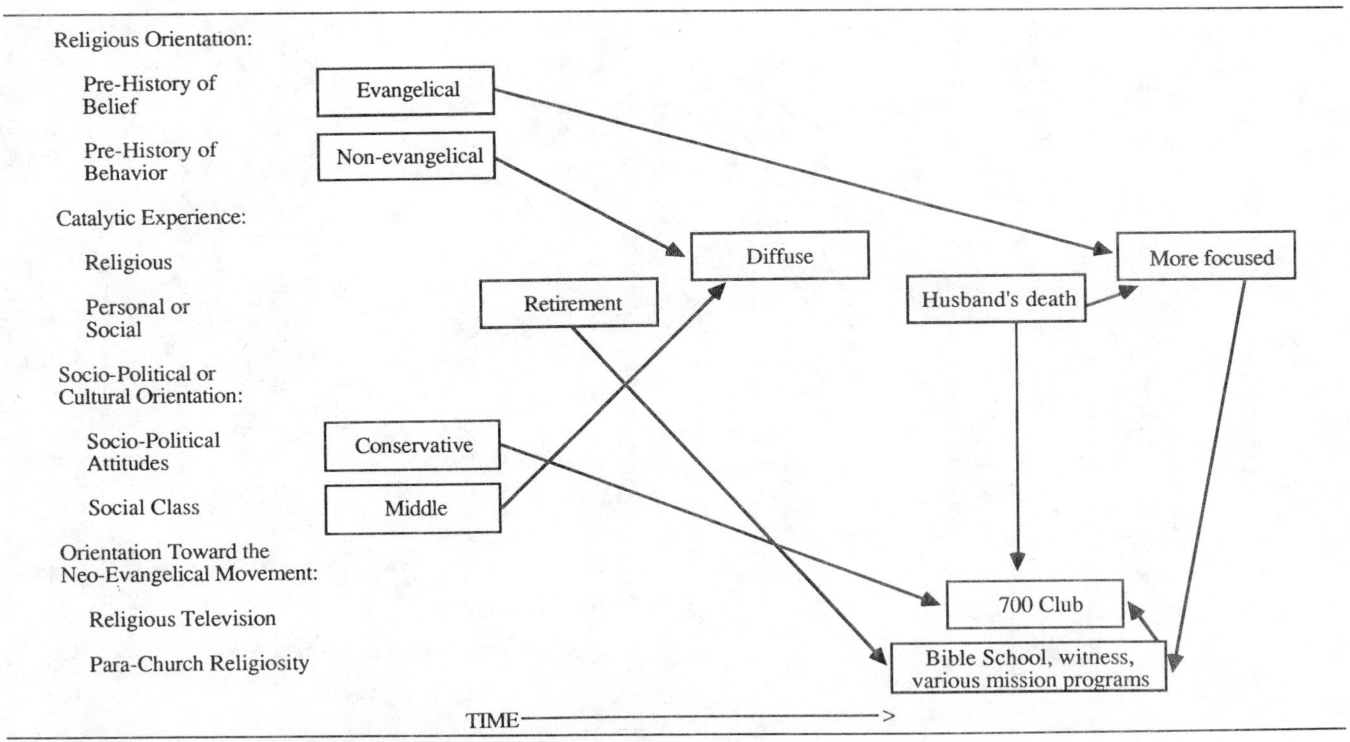
Religious Orientation:
Pre-History of Belief
Pre-History of Behavior
Catalytic Experience:
Religious
Personal or Social
Socio-Political or Cultural Orientation:
Socio-Political Attitudes
Social Class
Orientation Toward the Neo-Evangelical Movement:
Religious Television
Para-Church Religiosity
Evangelical
Non-evangelical
Diffuse
More focused
Retirement
Husband's death
Conservative
Middle
700 Club
Bible School, witness, various mission programs
TIME ——————>

Figure 7.5. Viewing/involvement trajectory for Helen Purton

"I was depressed, so I started watching TV, and ended up with Pat Robertson," she says.

> He kept talking about God and Jesus, so I listened, because I believe in God. I believe in the values and morals of the show, besides its being an informative show. I was depressed, I had no feeling in my legs. . . . Pat Robertson was instrumental in pointing me back to God.

Shelley first saw the *700 Club* while watching conventional television shows. She remembers being instantly attracted to it. "I had been watching [Phil] Donahue, but he doesn't discuss anything important. . . . I was looking for substance, I needed something real, something to hold onto. . . . There was no way I was going to get better. I wanted something that made sense to me."

Unlike others who believe that religious television may have healing powers, Shelley does not view the program in order to improve her health. Instead, she sees it as a source of comfort and inspiration that has helped strengthen her Jewish faith. "It pointed me back in a direction I leaned on, but I needed it more [then] than I had anything in my life."

The obvious dissonance between the *700 Club* program and Judaism will be addressed in the next chapter, but the prima facie relationship between Shelley's disability and her viewing of the *700 Club* presents a parallel to the cases of the other viewers we have spoken with here. As with the others, her viewing began in a period of great personal crisis and loss (see Figure 7.6[8]). It seems not to have had a clear theological impact on her (she has not, after all, become a Christian), nor has it helped explain her disability, or ease her physical suffering (i.e., she has not been "healed").

From viewing to believing

Carole Fox is in the midst of a family crisis brought on by business and financial problems. She has felt lonely and isolated since she moved from a former home for financial reasons. Away from her friends, she reports that she was brooding a great deal until she encountered the *700 Club* on television one day. She was nominally a Catholic, but her church had not helped ease her loneliness and isolation.

> I guess I was searching for something, some help, and I'd go to church just to pray. I had a lot of time on my hands, and not much money, so I'd watch television a lot, and I guess . . . like you hear so many people say, "I just turned the channel and the *700 Club* was on."

Carole was immediately drawn to the program. "I watched from that day forward. . . . They did just what I needed. I talked to the prayer

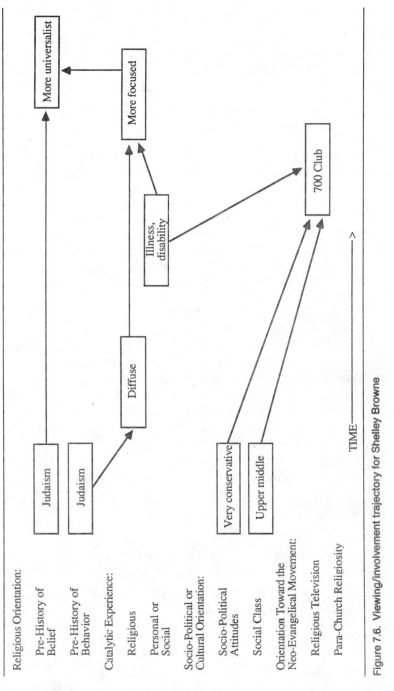

Figure 7.6. Viewing/involvement trajectory for Shelley Browne

counselor about my problems. I learned to pray." As with others we have heard from, Carole began to see her previous religious activities in a new light.

> You always think you're a Christian. I went to Sunday school, I played the organ in church, I read the Bible. So if someone would say "Are you a Christian?" I'd say "Yes," but when I started watching the *700 Club* . . . I realized I wasn't reading the Bible like they say to read the Bible. I've never read it all the way through, for instance. They said things that came right to my heart, and I think they made me feel better. They were teaching how to pray.

Carole is someone else who turned to the *700 Club* for help in a time of crisis, perhaps the best example we have seen. For the others, their viewing was more "accidental," or even tangential. For Carole, while she may have "stumbled onto" the program in a sense, she was actively searching for help in understanding her plight. "I was just having such a horrendous experience that I was searching for anybody or anything," she notes. "I'd go anywhere and listen to anybody."

Carole's search did not end with the *700 Club*, however. As we saw with Ed Horne, June Mason, the Baldwins, and others, viewing of the program led to broader religious involvements. At the suggestion of a prayer counselor at CBN, Carole sought out some previous acquaintances who she knew were involved in religious activities, consonant with her newfound interest in the *700 Club*. She found out about a variety of activities to which she could go, including Bible studies at a church nearby. Her husband, however, turned out not to be as enthusiastic about her newfound religion as she was.

> A girl I met started to have a Bible study, and I asked him to go with me. He said he did not want to go. I was shocked. I think that was the first time he had ever refused me anything. So, I went myself, and he didn't mind. I wanted my husband to be part of this new life I was experiencing. Finally this friend and her husband came over, and my husband got comfortable with them, and he's gradually coming along.

Carole clearly feels that the Bible studies and social activities at nearby churches and the *700 Club* were there to help her in her moment of need.

> As I look back, I think that God must have a plan, because I can't believe all of these awful things would have happened to us if God doesn't have a plan. Anyway . . . a long time ago, I had been invited to one of these Bible studies, but I didn't have time. Last year, all of a sudden, I got an invitation again, and I went this time. The invitation said "How to be happy in spite of . . ." because everybody has their own reasons for being unhappy. Anyway, I had lots of time, and no money so I went this time.

Carole had known several people in the evangelical parachurch long before her personal crisis and so was familiar with the evangelical world.

Still, it seems that the *700 Club*, the Bible studies, and the local church combined to help her.

Carole is clearly the most politically liberal respondent in our sample. She did not vote for Ronald Reagan in the 1984 presidential election (see Figure 7.7[9]). She favors choice in abortion, a nuclear weapons freeze, and opposes capital punishment. Like some other respondents, she feels that her faith was rather laissez-faire until she encountered serious problems.

Yet her gradually increasing involvement in evangelical church and parachurch life exerts a powerful influence on her. That cannot help but move her more in the direction of political and social conservatism. She is, of course, aware of these pressures, and takes pains to describe herself as "not a prude," as we shall see later.

The majority of these viewers, even those for whom crises have proven to be pivotal in connection with their viewing of the *700 Club*, come from conservative evangelical or fundamentalist backgrounds. Carole's personal crisis seems to have been a far more important motivation for her *700 Club* involvement than for the others.

Other viewers we have spoken with also had had health and other personal crises, and related this in concrete ways to their faith. The Baldwins, for instance, became increasingly involved in the *700 Club* following the death of their son. Ed Horne, June Mason, the Hortons, the Ritters, Shelley Browne, and Carole Fox all have found the *700 Club* to be central, even integral, to their coming to understand, accept, or evade personal crisis. The difference is a matter of focus. For Helen Purton, on the other hand, viewing of religious television is secondary. For Ed Horne, though, the program has been the basis of an entirely new religious consciousness.

There are those, like Helen Purton, for whom crisis and a change in faith were coincidental. There are others, like Shelley Browne and the Ritters, for whom the resolution of personal crisis and involvement in the *700 Club*, or the broader parachurch or conventional religiosity, seemed linked. For some, like June Mason, there is a feeling that the *700 Club* prepared them for the crisis. For others, like Carole Fox, the crisis led to a process of "seeking out" new input and new ways of conceptualizing and dealing with their lives.

The lack of consistency in these relationships is significant for understanding the role these broadcasts play in the lives of their viewers. The claim that the electronic church meets real needs for its audience seems partially justified in light of these interviews. But it is unclear exactly how the purveyors of these programs might plan their ministries to enhance this aspect of their work because these programs relate in highly idiosyncratic ways to the lives of their viewers.

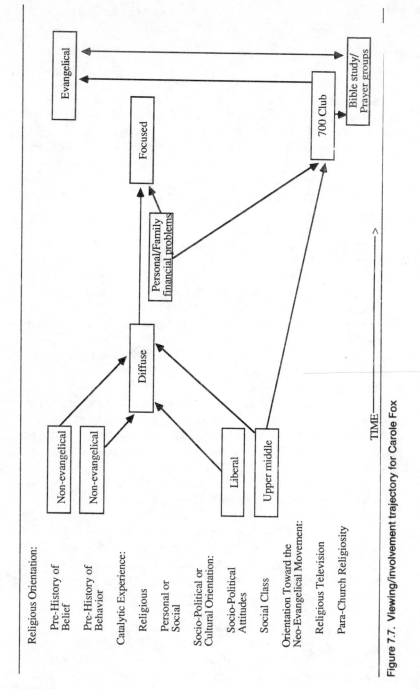

Figure 7.7. Viewing/Involvement trajectory for Carole Fox

Religious Orientation:

Pre-History of Belief — Non-evangelical

Pre-History of Behavior — Non-evangelical

Catalytic Experience:

Religious

Personal or Social — Personal/Family financial problems

Socio-Political or Cultural Orientation:

Socio-Political Attitudes — Liberal

Social Class — Upper middle

Orientation Toward the Neo-Evangelical Movement:

Religious Television

Para-Church Religiosity

Diffuse → Focused

700 Club

Bible study/Prayer groups

Evangelical

TIME →

Crisis as an explanation for membership

Among the most prominent explanations for the power of religious broadcasting always has been its potential for precipitating personal "conversion" experiences. Second only to that rationale has been the supposed power of religious broadcasting to "break in" on otherwise lonely and isolated lives, bringing solace, meaning, and revelation to people in crisis.

In this chapter, we looked at the extent to which religious programming might have an independent, substantive religious meaning; that is, the extent to which we might find viewers who had experienced the sort of "conversion" so often stressed as an important component of these programs. Where we have investigated just these sorts of experiences we have found a complicated and inconsistent picture.

First, the one viewer for whom viewing may have led to actual "conversion," Ed Horne, is quite honest about the fact that Christianity was, in fact, nothing new to him, so that his was not, strictly speaking, a classic "Pauline" conversion.[10] But this should not detract from the testimony of the others for whom the *700 Club* has served as a catalyst for new religious awareness.

Second, viewing of the program, in some cases (for some viewers), came *before* the catalytic experience itself. The model of a viewer turning to the *700 Club* for solace and meaning in times of crisis does not fit someone like June Mason, who began watching the program *first*, before the life crisis with which it has helped her to cope. Instead, she sees her having begun to watch the program as *preparation* for the crisis to come. One thing that can be said, then, is that religious broadcasting seems to have been religiously useful for these viewers because of its *availability*. It is there, in the homes and lives of viewers, on a day-to-day basis, and when crises occur, it can be there for them. As with the viewers in the last chapter, the program seems to have its greatest effect in helping its viewers to find other resources in the evangelical parachurch.

Finally, these viewers tend to agree that the *700 Club* is not the most "spiritual" of major religious programs. It appeals to the intellect more than to the emotions, they contend. We heard much of this in the last chapter, but will look at it in more detail and depth in the next.

Notes

1. See discussion in Chapter 5 (Peter Berger, "Some Second Thoughts on Substantive versus Functional Definitions of Religion," *Journal for the Scientific Study of Religion* 13, no. 2 [June 1974]: 125-33).

2. As with the last chapter, explications of the Viewing/Involvement Trajectories appear in the notes. All are drawn from Stewart M. Hoover, "The *700 Club* as Religion and as

Television: A Study of Reasons and Effects" (Ph.D. diss., Annenberg School, University of Pennsylvania, 1985).

3. Ed Horne's childhood religiosity was varied. He attended three different nonevangelical churches as a child. He had a vague personal interest in religion. He had not had any particular religious experience before he encountered the *700 Club*. His social and political attitudes have always been generally liberal. The crisis in his life came with the breakup of his marriage, but, more important, with his disability and layoff. With time on his hands, he began viewing television a bit, and encountered the *700 Club* on a day, Christmas Eve, when single people are prone to feel quite lonely. He had a strikingly focused religious experience while viewing, and became an evangelical through involvement in a local church. He may be moving toward a personal evangelicalism, as well.

4. Both Sally and Jim Horton come from evangelical and charismatic backgrounds. Both were involved in the same Pentecostal church, where they knew each other even before Jim's wife's death and Sally's annulment. Both shared the conservative social and political attitudes typical of the blue-collar class, though Sally eventually earned a master's degree in social work. The major crisis in their lives has been Sally's difficulties in maintaining her own "ministry." The crises of their first marriages were equally important. Problems with churches accepting Sally's ministry have led them away from direct involvement in church and in religious activities of a formal sort. The time that has elapsed since each of them was "born again" leaves them with a more diffuse type of "religious experience" than someone like Ed Horne, who feels he recently had a "Pauline" conversion. Viewing the *700 Club* helps them understand their own marital problems, supports Sally's commitment to ministry, and has reinforced her commitment to a prison ministry.

5. June Mason was raised as a moderate to conservative Christian, both in membership and in beliefs. She was raised Southern Baptist, which is a moderate denomination in the major cities of the south. She and her husband are upper middle class, and generally moderate in political attitudes. She reports that, prior to the her son's death, she was not a particularly intense believer and had never had a real religious experience. Her son's suicide was the major crisis of her life, and led to many changes in her beliefs and self-understanding. She had begun watching the *700 Club* before his death, and was led to an emotional healing by a prayer counselor on the program. She has become gradually more and more evangelical in orientation in the intervening years, continues to view the program, and now she often volunteers as a prayer counselor at the local center.

6. Ralph and Jane Ritter were both raised Catholic, but became involved in the Catholic "Holy Spirit" (charismatic) movement after moving to a new parish. This led to a more evangelical personal religiosity. Once his daughter became ill, Ralph's belief in the "healing of the Holy Spirit" led him to take her to a number of healing services. He believes that she ultimately was healed at one of them. Ralph's disability and related financial problems led him to search for meaning and help. They had encountered PTL through their charismatic involvements, and Ralph turned to it for help during these crises. He also began to watch other programs, especially the *700 Club*, and found solace there, as well. The daughter's eventual death, along with her earlier healing, and the fact that they had been helped out of their financial crisis at a critical moment, all have reinforced Ralph's faith. He now reads intense religious meaning into this series of crises.

7. Helen Purton is a classic "stranded evangelical." She and her husband continued to attend, and be involved in, a mainline church even though they held more fundamentalist beliefs themselves. She does not report that she had any particular religious experience prior to her husband's death, though she certainly feels that God is active in speaking to her. She and her husband were middle class, and were rather conservative, politically. Retirement was a major break for them. They moved to the suburbs and their involvement in their former

church fell off. Helen was able to begin teaching Bible school near her vacation property, and took on a variety of personal evangelical activities (such as baking cookies to give away to strangers to break the ice). Her husband's death was a major crisis, but her faith was strengthened, not weakened, by that experience. She had a revelation at the time of his death. Viewing of the *700 Club* is not, for her, a major determinant of or precursor to any of these other things; it is simply related to them as another parachurch activity. She does not view the program on a regular basis.

8. Shelley Browne represents a very unusual case. Both she and her husband were raised Jewish, and are now devout, practicing Jews. She has not had any particular focused religious experience. Their political attitudes are quite conservative. Before her illness, they had had an upper-middle-class income. Her illness, disability, and possible infertility were a major turning point in her life. She began to search for ways to understand what was happening to her, and was drawn to work toward greater religious consciousness after having begun to watch the *700 Club*. She has, as a result, become more universalist in her personal religious awareness, finding herself open to understanding faiths outside her own Judaism.

9. Carole Fox is the most politically liberal person with whom we have spoken. She and her husband lived an upper-middle-class life-style until financial crisis ensued. They had been members of a mainline church before the crisis, but she does not feel that she was a particularly intense Christian. She certainly does not report having had any religious experiences. The financial problems she encountered changed all of this. She reports having had a vision around the time of these crises, but does not look on it as a "conversion" or a being "born again" type of event. She found the *700 Club* during her time of crisis and found that it helped her a great deal. As a result of recommendations made by *700 Club* prayer counselors, and because of her new motivation to explore religion as an answer to her problems, she has become involved in a variety of evangelical church and parachurch activities. She now is in transition to a more evangelical religiosity, and is moving into a new circle of social contacts.

10. The term *Pauline* refers to striking substantive experiences of awakening, such as that experienced by the Apostle Paul on the Damascus road. He was struck down and blinded by a revelation that led him into active Christian witness.

8

Being Evangelical in
Mainstream America

For many viewers, the *700 Club* is merely consistent with their faith backgrounds, which are evangelical or fundamentalist. In those cases, the program is primarily valued for presenting religious information and entertainment. For other viewers, the program speaks to basic values and beliefs, but again, beliefs that have found their source elsewhere.

There are others, though, who watch the *700 Club* because they need help with health or financial crises. Because the electronic church can "be there"—in the home, at moments of great need, easily accessible, ever ready to offer consolation (even directly, through telephone-counseling hot lines)—it offers hope and solace to a great many viewers.

For most viewers, the program "just fits." It is based in, and evocative of, a subculture of neoevangelical and fundamentalist religiosity that is familiar and comforting. The Viewing/Involvement Trajectories[1] included in preceding chapters indicate that most viewers are evangelicals or fundamentalists for many years before they become involved in the *700 Club*. This seems typical of the audience as a whole.[2]

Most observers assume that the electronic church has a "social" or even "political" agenda that really motivates program producers and viewers alike. This assumption underlies the major concerns about this media phenomenon.

The "new right," of which the electronic church is considered to be a prominent part, has won and held important political power with the aid of some religious broadcasters. Leading figures of the electronic church, notably Jerry Falwell and Pat Robertson, have not disguised their political intentions and motivations. Meanwhile, powerful political figures and organizations, like Norman Lear's "People for the American Way," point to these developments with alarm, decrying the blurring of constitutional separations between church and state.

It is clear that many viewers do, indeed, embrace the social and political aims of the *700 Club*. But as with many other aspects of religious broadcasting, the myths may far outstrip the reality. Religious political activism could be channeled off in two directions. First, viewers might wish to see the power of religious programs used as a theological force against mainline religious institutions at the national level. Government is not the only arena where political power and prestige are on the line. We have already seen how the two parties of American Protestantism are struggling in an inter- and intradenominational search for identity and ascendancy.

Viewers might also mobilize behind the *700 Club* for a "purely" sociopolitical struggle between the "new religious right" and the forces of "secular humanism" that are said to be its primary foe. The *700 Club* was not as eager, in its early years, to tackle these issues as were Jerry Falwell's *Old Time Gospel Hour*, and James Robison, a television evangelist from Dallas, who ran afoul of his syndicating stations because of anti-gay statements. The *PTL Club*, the *700 Club*'s major daytime competitor, also has tended to avoid political content, but Jimmy Swaggart, the only other national daily electronic church program, has been vociferous about his sociopolitical agenda.

Still, the *700 Club* always has made a case for the "social issues" agenda of the new right. Shriver[3] reports that Pat Robertson's position was clear all along, with him making political appearances such as the watershed 1980 "Washington for Jesus" rally where the religious right' first burst into the national consciousness, and his association before that with the influential "Religious Roundtable" political lobby.

The *700 Club* may not always have been as overtly political as the competition, but Pat Robertson's political views and ambitions never have been hidden. In 1986, Robertson began raising money for a presidential bid. To comply with federal campaign finance laws, he withdrew from hosting the *700 Club* in late 1986, and shortly before formally announcing his candidacy for the Republican presidential nomination in October 1987, Robertson resigned his ordination as a Southern Baptist minister.

Long before 1986, however, his political views were apparent on the program. Monitoring by "People for the American Way," begun in 1982, found the *700 Club* commenting on political issues, such as Supreme Court decisions, defense policy, and (Robertson's personal favorite) banking policy, regularly throughout the mid-1980s.

700 Club viewers regularly see programs laced with political and social commentary. Their reactions to this content vary greatly. These reactions also give us some insight into the cultural meaning of the program as viewers struggle to reconcile traditionally irreconcilable values—the "spiritual" (and thus personal and nonsocial) realm of their evangelical and fundamentalist roots, and the "sociopolitical" (and thus dangerously close to the "social-gospel" wing of the "two-party" dimension) face of the new religious right and its television ministries. As we shall see, this reconciliation is not an easy one for them to make.

In the process, we will learn some things about how these viewers see themselves in the larger society and in their own social networks. Along with the traditional disapproval in the evangelical and fundamentalist circles of politics has run a class-associated self-concept of "old-time religion" as a non- or even anti-intellectual subculture. The "symbolic cast" of fundamentalism and traditional evangelicalism has always been one of simple living and simple thought. A major new dimension of the neoevangelical movement of the past decade then has been its development of an intelligentsia and its movement away from its lower-class roots.

An evangelical "social gospel"?

700 Club viewer Harry Baldwin, the stockbroker we met in Chapter 6, feels strongly that the traditional gulf separating the "spiritual" and the "political" has been bridged by Pat Robertson's skills as a political and social commentator (he is "on top of things"). He also spoke approvingly of Robertson's newsletter as being competitive, in content and interpretation, with the best of those produced by the "secular" media. Harry is aware of the traditional conservative Christian criticisms of such social awareness on the part of religious figures. "I certainly would not agree with that criticism because the gospel is political, and the more well-rounded a program is, the better." His daughter Julie notes that it depends, for her, on what is implied by the term *politicization*. "If you mean he'd start endorsing candidates, and things like that, I'd have a lot of trouble with that, and he's not about to do that." She adds that she sees no necessary contradiction between the "religious" and the "political."

Jim and Sally Horton, longtime evangelicals and charismatics, say that the *700 Club* is an important source of inspiration and information about "current issues." Their evaluation of the program seems to reflect their awareness of the lower-class roots of the evangelical and fundamentalist subcultures. In comparing the *700 Club* to the rival *PTL Club*, Jim observes that "the caliber and type of programming and the level of spirituality is much higher on CBN." Sally adds,

> I feel that CBN appeals to a better educated person on the whole, it is very carefully formatted. I really feel that they have an excellent, high quality on their program, that compares favorably with the commercial networks, whereas I can't say the same thing about PTL. It's more of a "down home," "folksy," "informal thing." I can enjoy watching it, but I can't respect it from a commercial, television, communication standpoint as much. I think that new believers, those that are immature . . . would lean more to PTL.

Sally goes on to an observation about the specific issue of social class.

> I don't want to be condescending about this, but I think it has to do with the cultural and educational background of the people involved. Pat Robertson is an intelligent, well-educated, widely versed man; Jim Bakker, and Tammy, are sweet people, and they simply are not any of those things. They're kind of simple,

down home, country church, hand-clapping, jumping, "holy-roller" types. I've heard her say, "I'm a holy roller and I'm proud of it," and I thought that was kind of sweet, because I understood where she was coming from, but I couldn't imagine Pat or Ben [Kinchlow] saying that.

The Baldwins and the Hortons don't limit the power of the *700 Club* to its potential for cultural ascendancy. It also has religious meaning and force. Sally Horton assumes that, for some viewers, the *700 Club* helps set the standard for what effective evangelical ministries should be.

How many people in this area have a church like Rock Church [another religious television program] to attend, and just to watch it and see the congregation worshiping, and praising, and entering into the whole service rather than sitting rigidly in rows. . . . Most local churches aren't giving that kind of food from the pulpit or [getting that] participation from the pew and therefore a person might benefit more from watching that programming than from a local church. Local churches do offer personal contact and all, but many of them don't do that well. Anyway . . . do you say, "Just go to church because you're supposed to," when people could be home watching some terrific program?

An evangelical revival

Sally and Jim Horton see the *700 Club*'s presence on television as signifying a change in society and politics, a new openness to Christianity.

I think that God has used Christian programming to stir up the religious climate in America. Bringing Steve Bartkowski right into your living room and telling how Christ is now more important in his life than football, I think that has a subtle effect on local Christians. To hear Julius Erving say, "I've been born again." He's willing to come out of the closet, and speak boldly, and say, "I'm a Christian." That does have a big impact. It becomes *less objectionable to talk about those things in public.*

Sally continues,

When I was a little girl growing up, you were really weird if you walked around talking about being saved or born again, or said "Jesus" except as a swear word, or something, you didn't do that. Now, it's quite accepted. It gives me a climate where I can be very bold with my proclamation of the gospel. It's less objectionable to talk about sex, politics. You never used to talk about those things, religion, cults, whatever. There's more openness in society about all sorts of controversial subjects. Certainly, if they can shout "gay freedom" from the housetops, we can shout "Jesus is Lord" from the housetops.

Sally clearly feels that the lower-class roots of the evangelical subculture and its concomitant sociopolitical cast has been modified, and that religious broadcasting is both a measure and a cause of these developments.

We're very proud of Christian programming. We use it ourselves, in our witnessing, we're very proud that instead of just "Bible thumping," as it used to be in the old days on TV—which was mostly embarrassing, really not that great content, it was mostly the salvation message and nothing much more, or something negative, something out of touch with society—now we're not ashamed because now there is excellent Christian programming that is very much contemporary, and in touch with society, and not afraid to discuss controversial issues. Hollywood and Madison Avenue will still try and make us look like a bunch of Elmer Gantrys and weirdoes in general, but basically speaking, people think it's OK.

Joe and Doris Parker are also longtime evangelicals who perceive a new attitude in the nation toward religious broadcasting and neoevangelical revival. Joe's recollection of his first exposure to the *700 Club* reveals the cultural power the program has come to have for him. After his first exposure to Pat Robertson in which the topic was Israel and the Six-Day War, Joe says, "I went to work the rest of the day and thought about it, and said 'boy, there must be a lot of these announcers who are Christians but they just don't come on because of circumstances.'"

Joe and Doris began watching regularly, and subscribing to *700 Club* newsletters and magazines. They became "members" of the organization, and soon were heavily involved in its network of "special friends." This status has given them access to the higher levels of leadership in the CBN organization. Joe observes, "I like where there is *administrative* type of leadership, persons who can interpret the position we have as Christians." They have been recipients of calls and letters from the *700 Club*, and are pleased by this level of involvement.

The Parkers take obvious pleasure in being invited to seminars at the CBN center itself. One such invitation came in a telephone call. Joe recalls it, "Yes, Pat himself, boy, I could of . . . my hair stood on end. I don't know whether it was a recording or not." During their seminar trip, Joe went forward for an "altar call" and had his first experience of the "baptism of the Holy Spirit."

The trip also gave Joe and Doris an opportunity to meet CBN leaders, evangelical leadership that is far different from the stereotypic conservative Christian figures who, in their view, have often lacked the education, eloquence, and sophistication to speak to the modern world. Joe recalls this experience with some excitement.

We went down and stayed for three or four days. I was excited to meet a man face-to-face who has the education, and degrees, who is so pleasant, and humble, he's a servant of the Lord, not a "somebody" to show off his abilities or anything like that. He called people to come forward, and my heart was ready. I went forward and I was there, and there must of been 5,000 people there, and I said "I'm not going to be embarrassed." These people *love* me. They don't know me, but they love me, and I thought I should go up and make a public confession, and the first thing I knew some sounds were coming out, and what I was thinking of when they come out was the sixth chapter of Isaiah, with the angels and seraphims, and all . . ., and I just felt like there was the Lord, and I didn't know what vocabulary to use, to glorify, to worship the Lord, and just using pure English language wasn't good enough, and I thought I was using a heavenly language. I don't know what I said, but I was worshiping.

This spiritual transformation notwithstanding, Joe's and Doris's recollections of their first experience at CBN are peppered with concrete "social" satisfactions. What they found at CBN represented a reality removed from the class-based roles and social and intellectual realms of the traditional evangelical and fundamentalist subculture. Their home, in its appointments and decor, suggests that their own tastes and lives are still grounded in that subculture. What they experienced at CBN contrasts sharply with the way they live every day.

Doris describes with pleasure the sophistication of the physical arrangements of the visit.

> The whole trip was fantastic, from the time we arrived at the hotel, the best there is, and they paid for it, and they called us over and gave us name tags, and they gave us a schedule, and we were busy every minute. What impressed me was this whole thing was so organized, and yet the Holy Spirit was in control. Everything was done top-notch. Nothing was left to chance, from the entertainment, the food, the service, you stayed in the best hotel, you really felt like you were "king's kin." We especially enjoyed touring and going into the buildings.

Joe was more impressed in the intellectual environment.

> They'd say, "Praise the Lord," and it's not that they were fanatical, these were people who had college degrees and had been in manufacturing. As you got into conversation, they were people who could express themselves, and for the first time I said to myself, "This is a taste of heaven," *every* person, *loving* you, smiling, you felt free, you felt like flying around. Occasionally, I'd pick out a couple of people who had just met, and I'd overhear, and they were talking about *Jesus*, about how great he is . . . and there was this sense of "melting to Christ."

Joe Parker is convinced that CBN members and leaders represent a "new class" of evangelicals. The intellectual and sociocultural sophistication once eschewed by fundamentalism (and to an extent by evangelicalism) now are seen as positive attributes in a new era for conservative Christianity.

"At CBN you're getting *leaders*," Joe emphasizes.

> There's a difference. Humility is important, but here you could tell by the people and the way they talked, the vocabulary and everything else, the things they expressed, and their spirituality. I like dedicated hearts, and people with degrees, who can say and believe these things. I was at Wheaton College when Billy Graham was there, and his wife was there and both of them were walking around and dealing with people . . . wow. And here to listen to a consecrated woman

[with] a college degree, and she's winning souls . . . you suspect, but her presentation was simple and to the point, and the blessing I had from this woman was incredible. I get a blessing from people with degrees, top people, who are servants. I love people with degrees, consecrated. And the other brothers and sisters, too, of course, but there's something special about these top people.

Joe and Doris Parker see this as the crucial difference between the *700 Club* and the *PTL Club*. They agree with Jim and Sally Horton that the latter program is more representative of the lower-class "past" of evangelicalism.

You're appealing to two different types of people. Some are *leaders* and not that there are no leaders among the PTL, but there're more leaders, people with college degrees, and people who have the gift of leadership [at CBN], than with PTL.

Doris quickly adds that CBN is spiritually powerful, in spite of these more "social" or "temporal" qualities.

When Pat talks about the gift of discernment, that's very Holy Spirit oriented. I would say PTL is more *emotionally* charismatic, but *700 Club*, you can't watch it without realizing that that's the power there, that you *know* that the Holy Spirit is doing something *out of this world*. That is not the average thing, and in that way, I think CBN is better. Even though *700 Club* has more news, and all, I still think it is evident that the power of the Holy Spirit is there.

A sophisticated evangelicalism

The Parkers also agree with Jim and Sally Horton that part of the *700 Club*'s value lies in its setting a sophisticated standard for local evangelical churches. "I think the *700 Club* helps the local church," Doris says.

The average minister just doesn't have what it takes to prepare heartfelt sermons. You have to put together four or five hours of reading in order to get together good sermons. One of the main reasons people watch these programs is for the sermons, and then they'll go to church for the same thing.

June Mason agrees that the *700 Club* is a "higher order" of religious program. Her husband watches the *700 Club* because of its more "intellectual" content. After observing that the *PTL Club* appeals to audiences of a different educational and social class than does the *700 Club*, she goes on to say that all of the current major programs have strengths based on their level of sophistication and the prominence a national television presence gives them. Her husband, she says,

watches Robert Schuller with me sometimes, but that's about all he'll watch except Pat. He'll watch Pat because he likes his intellect. He's really intelligent. I could listen to anyone, but I'd be more impressed with someone who really knew what they were talking about. Jerry Falwell is fantastic, he is one of the most dynamic men in America, and look at who he brings in; and Dr. Schuller, look at who he brings in; and Scott, he brings in a different group, so each group, certain men appeal to certain groups. Jim Bakker, he appeals to certain people, and no one else. God uses them all, and I would never, never criticize them.

All of these viewers seem to agree that a kind of power, status, and credibility goes along with being on national television. There seems to be, for June, a further credibility that goes with being a Christian who can speak to world affairs and current issues. She tells the story of the daughter of a friend who began to watch the *700 Club*, and was attracted first to this aspect of the program, rather than the "preaching" typical of earlier forms of religious television.

She saw Pat Robertson coming on and giving world events . . . appearing knowledgeable in world affairs, in history, in things happening in the Middle East, and she sat up and took notice, and said, "Mom, this is the most interesting program." And she found the content so interesting and enjoyable, where if someone was just preaching, preaching, preaching, maybe it would have turned her off.

A rather complex picture of the public, social, and political role of the *700 Club* for its viewers begins to emerge. There are the purely political implications, the fact that Pat Robertson and the *700 Club* can and do bring an evangelical view on world affairs to the nation. There also are social implications, with the program's power to state the particular social agenda of the new right.

But most important is this sense that Pat Robertson can, more effectively than the evangelists of the past, argue on behalf of the evangelical or fundamentalist worldview on an equal footing with other media figures. The electronic church in general, and the *700 Club* in particular, provide a public context for an alternative agenda, one that achieves a certain credibility and momentum through its mere presence on the public, thought-to-be-powerful medium of television. The program can be said to be as important for what it *represents* as for what it actually *says*.

Evangelical universalism

There are a number of viewers of the *700 Club* who are not evangelical, or even Protestant, but for whom it is a source of identification anyway. For all of the viewers we have heard from in this chapter, the program does have a broadly *universalistic* character. Those evangelicals who identify with its sociopolitical worldview support its interpretation to a heterogeneous public. June Mason's story of her friend's daughter's attraction to the show is not unique. June correctly concludes that the program's message is stated in a way that attracts attention without repelling viewers by stressing idiosyncratic styles, claims, or beliefs.

Even viewers like Joe and Doris Parker, who find its spiritual (as opposed to social or political) power its most important dimension, see that the program draws around it people from outside the normal lower-class boundaries of evangelicalism and fundamentalism. For them, this is not a rejection of particularism, so much as it is a transcendence of the particular, claiming a place for their faith in a broader public realm.

We saw in Chapter 4 that the producers of CBN's programs and others responsible for its ministries have intentionally made the program broadly palatable in this way. Its relative liberalism in theological terms is tied to conservative strictures on the social and political issues. But this particularism is not necessarily binding on its viewers (as we shall see). This point should not be missed. Regardless of what we may have come to assume about the "jingoism" or "insularity" of conservative Christianity and its relationship to religious broadcasting, programs like the *700 Club* have developed a certain universalist appeal through a careful crafting of content to make it more generally accepted and acceptable.[4]

Viewer Ralph Ritter has found both the *700 Club* and the *PTL Club* to be powerful and helpful in his moments of need. As a Catholic, however, even a charismatic Catholic, he also feels some need to understand and explain his attraction to programming that is Protestant. He has adopted a self-consciously open mind about relations between Protestants and Catholics.

> Most Catholics are Catholic just because they always were, and many people call these programs and criticize the Catholic church, but Pat says you can work within the Catholic structures, in spite of the doctrinal differences. I don't really care about things like intercessory prayer through the saints and like that, but that bothers many Catholics about Protestantism. I think like Pat does, that you can work within Catholic structures, for the Lord.

The electronic church does take a critical attitude toward Catholicism, though, and the differences between faiths are common themes in most of the programs. Ralph finds support for his views by watching fellow charismatic Catholics on the *700 Club*.

> I deal on a one-to-one basis with the Lord through prayer. Most Catholics would disagree that you can do that, but when you look at these programs, you see Catholics there, you see Catholic priests and nuns on the show, spirit-filled people, so there is more openness for this kind of interrelationship, than before. Jimmy Swaggart, and all, they are pretty critical of Catholics, and I don't like that.

Ralph is more committed to the *PTL Club* than to the *700 Club*, and lays this to the conscious politicization of the latter show.

I respect the *700 Club*, I support it. I think that they don't espouse an anti-Catholic message as much as Swaggart and that is good. They emphasize that we are all *one*, that we are all Christians, and that I like. They've had good Catholic priests, good spirit-filled Christian priests and nuns on the show and that inspires me. But Pat deals more with the political aspect now in the new format, and I just have the opinion that there should be more prayer and Bible teaching.

The *700 Club*'s universalism is important to Ralph, as is the sense that he is part of a larger reality of religious renewal and revitalization.

They reach a large audience, they reach a diversified audience. They reach into homes probably that never would have been reached otherwise, that never would have thought of going to church. They break the old taboos.

We as Catholics are taught that it is wrong to go to a Protestant church, that it is evil to do that, and these programs show us that we're all "brothers in Christ." People growing up today with this knowledge will make a better world. I see it all around me. My own life story is typical, many people are like me, and many people are now in church, or are now back in church. Lots of Catholics are now learning what the faith actually is.

Universalism and parachurch activities

These viewers clearly feel that factionalism and denominationalism have been an absolute detriment to Christianity in the past, and that it is time to throw off their shackles. This anti-institutionalism seems to be based as much in a feeling of personal spiritual autonomy as it is in a rejection of previous forms, though the latter is certainly present.

Helen Purton notes, for instance, that such things as which biblical translation to use and specific doctrinal disputes pale in comparison to the overall "great commission" of Christ. "Jesus said, 'Anyone who's not against us, is for us,' so when you criticize other groups, you turn off people who do not listen to what *you* have to say."

She shares the pragmatism of other viewers who have suggested that discretion with regard to doctrinal disputes is necessary when carrying a religious message to a pluralistic society. Noting the activities of "Jews for Jesus," a sometimes confrontational organization aimed at proselytizing among Jewish students in particular, she says, "That's no way to do [it] . . . because they immediately are on the defensive. You have to be very gentle."

Universalism as an end in itself

Jake Stone is unmarried and retired from a blue-collar job. He has lived alone since his mother died some years ago. He is the least religious of all the viewers we have spoken with, at least in a conventional sense. He describes himself, however, as always having been religious. He was raised in a nonevangelical home and church, and attended Sunday school regularly. In adult life, he rarely attended church, and is quite skeptical of the church to this day.

> When I was four or five, I used to go to Sunday school or children's Bible class and I used to study the children's Bible. I went to Sunday school off and on in later years . . . until I was 13 or 14. Then I just stopped. Never stayed with it. On occasion, when someone invited me, I did go. It didn't matter what church. Even though I didn't attend during those "middle" years, I still believed in God, and I still said my prayers and everything. As far as church, I never went to church. Of course, a lot of people who go to church are hypocrites anyway.

Jake has always held to a sort of "baseline" religiosity (see Figure 8.1[5]). Before retirement, he regularly discussed religious issues, such as the existence of God, with co-workers. But he does not describe himself as particularly religious.

A turning point came for Jake when he picked up a hitchhiker, a young woman, who was on her way to a meeting of "The Way International," an evangelical group that stresses encounter-style therapy for drug addiction and other personal problems. Jake was so taken with the idea that this organization meant something to this hitchhiker, that he went along. At nearly the same time, he also began to watch the *700 Club*. The *700 Club* was more attractive to Jake than "The Way International," which he found too restrictive and legalistic.

Jake's worst problem is loneliness. The *700 Club* eases his loneliness and is an acceptable way (to him) of spending his time when the rest of television is not attractive. "Its all garbage," he notes.

Jake does not consider the *700 Club* "religion," but rather as an overall worldview. He does not watch it for religious reasons, he notes.

> I just put it on for that other stuff that they have. It's not a matter of religion anyway. "The Way Ministry" for instance, is *not* a religion, it's [a] *personal* relationship with Jesus. A lot of people say as soon as you talk about *Jesus* you're talking about "religion," but most of religion is just *tradition*.

The *700 Club*, Jake says, is not just hidebound religious ritual, but is something different—a source of information that is independent of the dominant commercial media. "I turned on the *700 Club* and he [Pat Robertson] had something there from overseas. They were telling how it was really happening and in the newspapers it was altogether different."

Jake understands the program's purpose in larger, universalistic terms, as have others from whom we have heard. Jake sees its role to be almost education of a kind. Reflecting on a common criticism of the electronic

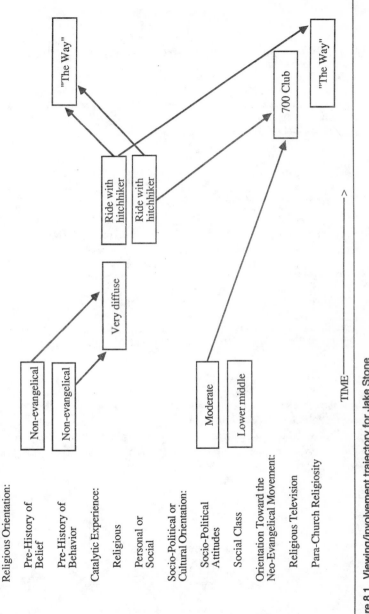

Figure 8.1. Viewing/involvement trajectory for Jake Stone

church, that it puts fund-raising and building ahead of spiritual pursuits, he observes:

> They're [the *700 Club*] building to learn people the way they *should* be. In other words, some churches and places, they take the money and all they're doing is making the place *bigger*. They're *not* learning the people what they're *supposed* to. Like a rabbi here in town who's been saying a Jew can't be a born-again Christian, I don't understand it [a reference to a local controversy in the Jewish community over the activities of the "Jews for Jesus" organization]. Why don't they leave them go? One fights against another and that's no good.

Jake also is aware of growing public concern that television evangelists like Pat Robertson may be more interested in personal power and prestige than in the greater good. "How do I know to trust Pat Robertson?" he asks. "I don't know for a *fact*, I don't know how the people are going to come out of CBN University." Still, Jake is inclined to trust that the motives of Robertson and CBN are the *best* particularly because their intentions run contrary to what he has seen in conventional churches.

> CBN says that they're building a university to teach people to live up to the standards of the Bible out there in the real world. Conventional churches are *not* teaching people how to do that stuff outside the church. That university will learn you the way you should do, to treat the other person right. The church will just tell you to love your fellow man, but not that particular *item*, . . . you don't know how to apply Christian principles to your field.

Universalism beyond Christianity

Jake's perspective on the *700 Club* as a more universalist, less insular witness is shared by Shelley Browne, the Jewish woman in the last chapter. Her primary attraction to the program lay in its solace to her in her crises of loss and loneliness over her physical disability. And because she is a Jew, the program's tendency to avoid judgmentalism and insularity appeals to her.

Shelley shares Jake's appreciation of the "public witness" of the *700 Club*. Like other viewers, she values the *700 Club*'s programming dealing with current events. She feels more keenly than others that news served up by the major networks is inadequate and biased.

> My husband and I have little regard for commercial TV, we prefer public TV—the *MacNeil/Lehrer Report*, the music programs, the nature shows. Network news is too one-sided, not objective. They only report what they want you to know. "MacNeil/Lehrer" is better, but still not totally free. The world news on commercial television never tells you what the *real news* is.

Shelley is convinced that network news fails to contend with moral and ethical issues, which suggests a clear ideological bent in their reporting.

I don't see how you can separate morality from politics, but they're scared to talk about abortion, at least they have been until recently. I'm more worried about abortion than I am about prayer in the school, but that's what they're concentrating on because they don't understand it [the abortion controversy]. I don't see anything wrong with prayer in the schools. I had to pray in school when I was young, and read the Bible, and I was all right. I don't understand what the media are all upset about. And no Jewish "leader" can speak for me about prayer in the schools. None of them is objective about Israel. The network news has just refused to see the whole story there.

Shelley has become more universalist in her beliefs since she began watching the *700 Club*. She maintains a strong commitment to Judaism, however (along with rather conservative political attitudes). Her universalist attitudes come to the fore in her description of her reasons for viewing the *700 Club*. "We all worship the same God, don't we?" she asserts.

But there are things that she doesn't like about the program.

It makes me uncomfortable when they have someone who was born Jewish, and then "accepts Jesus." I *understand* that, but it makes me uncomfortable. I think they [Jews] are in need of something *tangible* when they go this way. When we're in desperate shape, we need something tangible, and therefore, Jesus, who is tangible to so many people, may seem attractive to Jews. I believe that we're all here, Jews, Christians, and Islam, for a reason. We all have something to share, and all have a part in God's plan to eventually redeem the world.

This does not mean Shelley accepts the particular vision of contemporary Judaism projected by some sectors of Protestant evangelicalism. "I don't accept Messianic Judaism. We learn that Elijah will come before the Messiah, and will tell us he's coming. I expect, any day, to see Elijah at the door, but the Messiah has not come. Elijah will tell us, and the Messiah will bring peace."

Shelley disputes claims that religious programming converts people of other faiths to Christianity.

I don't think that Jewish believers would be converted *just* by watching Christian broadcasting. If you're secure in what you believe, you can't be converted. You can co-exist. Jews must plant the seeds at home. It's not the churches and synagogues that are failing, it's the homes. I tell people at my synagogue this, "Why worry about 'Jews for Jesus'? Just plant the seeds at home."

Far from being shy about her interest in the *700 Club*, even among members of her temple and her family, Shelley says she discusses the program. "I talk to neighbors, to people at temple, to people on the street, to friends. In the beginning they were hostile, but I say, 'Wait a minute, look at all the good it does.'" She is convinced that the program's ministry is needed because of the state of contemporary society. She believes that the time is short, and that people of different faiths should work together, not separately.

People are more afraid than they used to be, of everything. The last 25 years of liberalism in this country have destroyed the family. If you don't plant the seed right, you don't get a strong tree. A Catholic friend and I discuss our faith and learn from each other, even though we're from different faiths. We're both still believers in family structure and place. I'm afraid of hate and bigotry. That's what all this liberalism has brought about.

Shelley's curious combination of religious tolerance with a less tolerant, even strident political attitude has not been challenged by the *700 Club*. Rather, she sees her involvement, however small, in the "religious revival" represented by the *700 Club* as supporting Judaism and her conservative political views. The fact that the *700 Club* does not undermine the beliefs of even so unlikely a viewer as Shelley fits the producers' concept of the program. By attracting large numbers of diverse people to the message without "turning them off," the *700 Club* stays on the air (or cable). Shelley Browne's allegiance to the *700 Club* is evidence that many types of viewers may be tuning in, financially supporting the program, talking about it, learning something from it, and yet not accepting, or even relating to, its evangelical and fundamentalist roots.

Liberal social attitudes and the *700 Club*

While Shelley Browne offers evidence of theological looseness among viewers of the *700 Club*, Carole Fox exemplifies the same phenomenon with regard to the program's views on political and social messages. Also originally attracted to the program in a time of financial crisis, Carole holds relatively liberal political attitudes in contrast to the program's well-known conservatism and the conservatism of the majority of viewers. For example, Carole describes herself as "pro-choice" on abortion, as favoring a "nuclear freeze," as against capital punishment, and likely to vote Democratic in upcoming elections.

Carole is well aware of the divergence between her political beliefs and those of the *700 Club*. She attributes this difference, in part, to varying approaches to biblical authority, and, more important perhaps, to a different personal background.

I think Pat Robertson is just taking the Bible literally. Sometimes you come across some things in the Bible, like your whole life is in there. There's one verse in the Bible that says, "don't charge interest." Now if someone asked me, "where did this come from?" that would have been the last place I would've guessed. Now abortion is wrong, technically, and Pat Robertson is very clear on that. I myself, if I was raped by a black man, I would not want to have that baby. My niece has had an abortion. In her case, I don't know what else I would have done. My stepdaughter has adopted a baby. And if someone would not have given that baby away, then she would not be so happy and have a baby now. It sounds awful to say, but I don't think I could have a baby and then hand it to someone. I think if I had the two choices, I'd have the abortion. That's terrible. I haven't come to any clear-cut position. I don't know. People have died from off-street abortions. I think it is better that people can go to hospitals and have safe ones, yet in my heart, I know that if you're going to believe, you believe.

Carole sees the abortion issue as one on which she and the CBN can disagree, even though that causes her some concern. On other political issues, she is more definite. While Pat Robertson and other ministers may have some say about abortion, she does not think they are wise to take positions on things such as nuclear weapons policy. CBN takes a fairly consistent "strong defense" position.

I don't think so on issues like that. He can lead me along through the Word and the Bible, but I have my own ideas, and to me, the nuclear freeze was a vital thing and it is not a theological issue—though the Bible says, "Thou shalt not kill," and my husband and my son were in the service, so I'm conflicted.

Carole feels strongly that there are issues that are clearly religious and those that are not.

I feel as if he [Pat Robertson] can lead me into the Bible, and he can explain things to me and I love what he says, but I just feel like anybody, you have your own opinions. I feel like I like to have him explain things to me, that is valuable, because he really does know the Bible. He has the right to say what he thinks the Bible is saying about things, but just because he's a religious figure, he can't say, "Follow my path."

Carole shares with most other CBN viewers a distaste for conventional television, though she is quite open about her viewing.

I watch a lot of television, a lot of junk, and I think there is a lot of junk on television. Everybody I know watched *Dynasty* last night. I think that's junk and I watched it anyway, and I'll continue to watch it. I think that the kids' programs are a disgrace for their violence, but nursery rhymes are also violent. I watch soap operas in the afternoon, and that is junk.

She also shares with others a distrust of television news, but from the opposite political perspective of that expressed by Shelley Browne.

I watch the news, and you don't even know if it is true. Sometimes the network news is slanted according to who is putting it out. Up until just a couple of years ago, I would have just said that I didn't think the United States government ever did anything wrong, and I don't feel that way anymore. I really do think that the CIA has done wrong. I always felt that you believe in God and Country. I don't feel that way anymore. I think that the news is slanted toward the "God and Country" viewpoint.

She also feels that the news segments on the *700 Club* are slanted to support the views of Pat Robertson, but sees that as just being typical of the all of television.

Now Pat Robertson, I have the feeling he agrees with Ronald Reagan, and I don't. Now you have your own feelings and I don't think anyone can say anything and not have their own feelings come through. I say they all "frame the news." I mean that if you leave out a little something and you don't say the beginning part that that person did say, but you didn't show them saying this part first, I mean if you just switch channels you can see that, the same story told by two different people. Now with the Middle East, I think the *700 Club* is not slanted. On the networks, I think yeah, you get whatever the government gives out.

Although Carole Fox and Shelley Browne both dislike popular culture and the conventional media, Carole has her own reasons. Her relative liberalism spreads to this area as well.

Now don't get me wrong. I'm not a prude, by any stretch of the imagination. But I don't think some of the violence and sex is necessary, and it does not do anything for me. I went to see *Deep Throat* [a well-known pornographic film], and I was stunned, but I went to be able to say that I went. I will never go again. We just went to another film and it had a part where the girl was nude at the top, and I said, "That's just ridiculous, unnecessary," they just put that in for effect.

Carole also departs from the stereotype of the religious television viewer in her attitudes about sex education in the schools.

I believe in sex education—young—because as a child I never had it in school and felt I needed it. I favored it when the teachers asked about it for my son who was in first grade. I had forgotten I said that one time and he came home, and his homework was "Seven Methods of Birth Control," and I was startled. But I was in favor of it. Now I don't think he should see *Deep Throat* in sixth grade, but as an adult, why not? I would hate it if they made a practice of it. And I feel very offended that down in the shopping center here there is a theater that shows X-rated films.

Carole maintains that individuals should take responsibility for their own lives and own actions and that even Christians cannot insulate themselves from the realities "out there."

I don't think you can insulate yourself and just say, "Here are all the good people. We're all good and everybody out here, they do terrible things." How do you know they're doing terrible things unless you're out there yourself. Now, like I said, you don't have to stay. As far as pornography, it shouldn't be around, and child pornography, I don't favor it. But you can't get too upset. Like I found *Playboy* under my kids' beds. I think all kids are curious, and do it. When *Hustler* came out, my nineteen year old had that and it was open on the bed and it was disgusting, and I said, "This offends me. As a woman, and as your mother I am telling you I don't want you to have that in the house."

Carole Fox's self-assurance is perhaps unique among viewers of the *700 Club*, especially given that she so often is at odds with its evangelical subculture. Other viewers also openly express their misgivings about the

700 Club in stark contrast to the stereotype advanced by those who only see an irresistible manipulative political force in the *700 Club*. How long, of course, Carole can "hold out" against the social ideals of her new culture remains to be seen.

The *700 Club* as a public witness

Jeff and Joan Wilson, whom we met in Chapter 6, both were from conservative, Pentecostal backgrounds, and described their viewing of the *700 Club* in terms of its openness compared to the denominations they came from. They also appreciate the program's "public" or political side, which is consistent with the Baldwin's and Jake Stone's feeling that CBN reaches out in a way conventional churches do not and cannot. The Wilsons recall that their original impression of the program was based on this perception.

"When we first saw it the truth, the wisdom, and the work that they do around the world, as well as in this country, just impressed us," says Jeff. Joan adds, "The spiritual aspect of it, plus they keep you informed of everything that is going on around the world, so [that] you're not getting just one view of it." Jeff sees the *700 Club* in pragmatic terms.

> One other thing we felt is that dollar for dollar they were accomplishing more than probably local churches were accomplishing. We saw that it was just in addition to local churches. We wanted to see that work go forward because they were reaching people the local churches couldn't reach.

The fact that the *700 Club* appears on television gives it special immediacy and power for the Wilsons (see Figure 8.2[6]). They also say that the program itself is more effective than a typical local church.

"I think it's both a matter of the quality of the presentation, and the fact of the technology." Jeff notes.

> Obviously Pat Robertson can reach more people, because [he uses a] satellite and he's worldwide. But I think that the quality is better, too, because in my denomination—which [consists of] small churches, and mostly farmers, and workaday people, and not doctor-lawyer-Indian chief, college professor type, you know—small churches are always struggling, and they don't have the wherewithal to do big things. The *700 Club* can do a lot of things a small church can't do, and it can do them well.

This emphasis on "quality" certainly seems to put local churches, particularly small local churches, at a distinct disadvantage. But Jeff doesn't seem concerned that local church pastors cannot compete effectively against someone like Pat Robertson.

In fact, Robertson's power and prestige are essential to his role in public

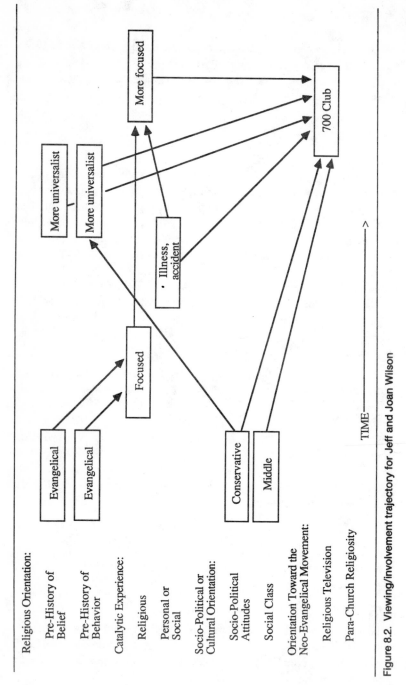

Religious Orientation:

Pre-History of Belief

Pre-History of Behavior

Catalytic Experience:

Religious

Personal or Social

Socio-Political or Cultural Orientation:

Socio-Political Attitudes

Social Class

Orientation Toward the Neo-Evangelical Movement:

Religious Television

Para-Church Religiosity

TIME ──────→

Figure 8.2. Viewing/involvement trajectory for Jeff and Joan Wilson

life, as far as Jeff is concerned. Jeff's feelings echo Joe Parker's self-consciousness about the lower-class aura that has long surrounded conservative Christianity. "I think it's the quality of Robertson's teaching, wisdom, his exposure personally to a lot of people and a lot of events that the poor local pastor somewhere, you know, Timbuktu, Iowa, just doesn't get," Jeff explains.

> Robertson is a "high vis" person in America. He's well educated, his father was a senator, his wife is a nurse, he has a law degree from Yale. It's just that echelon he travels in, his exposure to the things that come back to the local church through the people who watch, and I think that that's the kind of quality you just don't get when you're pastoring a local church. I watched the program when I was a pastor just to inform myself . . . you don't have time to read everything, the newspapers, the magazines.

Jeff takes a utilitarian approach to these factors. Noting the success of the *700 Club*'s fund-raising for relief, he observes:

> It all translates into *power*. They're able to feed many more people, because here again, he got hooked up with these big supply houses of food and he was able to start these big warehouses of food. The little old local church, what's he going to do, he's going to go to the local supermarket and get dented cans. . . . And I think that's [Robertson's efforts'] quality as well as quantity.

For Jeff and Joan Wilson, the power of the *700 Club* is based on more than its mere presence on television and satellite hookups. When comparing CBN with the troubled *PTL Club*, they do not see the same purposes. "Robertson is into making extreme incursions into the government, into economics, to change a whole system, whereas PTL is not into that. They're into hotels, and other things," Jeff says. "Robertson is building universities, and one of the finest libraries." Joan adds: "It's [CBN] more of an intellectual thing, I think. PTL kind of deals with basic day-to-day problems."

For Jeff and Joan Wilson, the overall importance of the *700 Club* seems to be based on putting the concerns of the evangelical community onto the national political agenda. Pat Robertson is "their man in Washington" and "on television."

An entertaining alternative

Blanche Murphy is rather loosely associated with television religion, though she is a regular churchgoer. Her husband Bob attends church, as well, but does not watch religious television. Blanche seems to watch the *700 Club* and other religious programs for entertainment. Her reactions to the programs are offhand, evaluative, not those of a clearly committed viewer, or a viewer for whom any of this has made a great personal difference.

She describes her viewing as just "switching on" the programs.

> Jimmy Swaggart, he gives you an interesting, a more instructive show. The *700 Club*, I do watch that if they have something interesting or I switch off. Now they have more money drives, they've had a money drive the last couple of weeks, so you get fed up with that and switch it off. Then they have topical shows, often, interviews, or maybe historical things. Of course, if I'm home on Sunday, I watch Jerry Falwell. I like to just turn on different ones because they give you the whole thing, you know, even some of the wild ones, like Portee, and the Bakker's. I put them on this morning, and they're still asking for money. You get a little tired of the money stuff.

Blanche was not raised in an evangelical household, though she would describe her home as "religious" (see Figure 8.3[7]).

> We all went to Sunday school and Bible class. It was just the thing we were supposed to do. As I got older it was more and more interesting, at least it was to me. I was just starting to learn. . . . There were so many things that you thought you understood before, that you don't really understand until later.

Blanche watches the *700 Club* primarily because she helps finance its projects for needy children, which she feels are extremely important. "I'm very concerned about children," she says. She also occasionally sends money to other religious programs, including a local faith healer, but she describes most religious programs as being "too emotional" for her.

She comments on the programs she has seen with an almost cynical air.

> I like to hear the sort of information they can bring you, studies of current events that are connected with things in the Bible and things like that. The *700 Club*, sometimes they'll have on a whole lot of people who've been healed and like that, and they come on and tell their stories. . . . Sometimes the same people they had on six months before.

Like other viewers we have heard from in this chapter, Blanche is primarily attracted to the information and news on the *700 Club*, its "public face." She describes other religious programs as being "mostly Baptist, mostly spiritual content."

She appreciates the *700 Club* for its diversity and attention to current events. At the same time, however, her descriptions lack the intensity of Jeff and Joan Wilson, or Jake Stone.

> The *700 Club* is a good variety of things. There's news, and then some Bible teaching, and all of those reports from around the world. It could be depressing, they have a lot of guests who could be really depressing, but its on the up side and never gets too depressing for me. Lots of information. They go in spurts, though. Sometimes the interviews are the same old thing. It is a current, up-to-date show, though, like they cover Lebanon, it's a good place to get that sort of information.

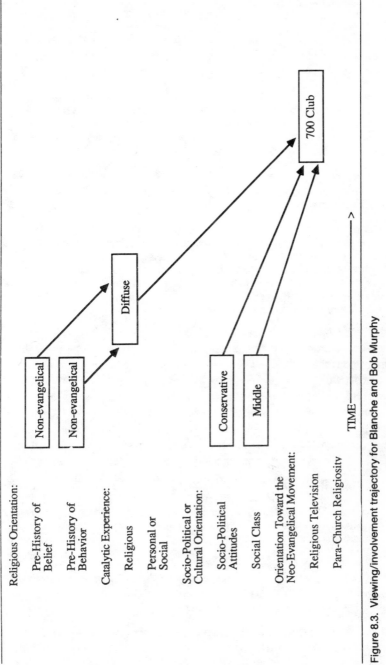

Figure 8.3. Viewing/Involvement trajectory for Blanche and Bob Murphy

Religious Orientation:

Pre-History of Belief

Pre-History of Behavior

Catalytic Experience:

Religious

Personal or Social

Socio-Political or Cultural Orientation:

Socio-Political Attitudes

Social Class

Orientation Toward the Neo-Evangelical Movement:

Religious Television

Para-Church Religiosity

Non-evangelical

Non-evangelical

Diffuse

Conservative

Middle

700 Club

TIME——>

199

Blanche is well acquainted with many religious and conventional television programs, and is clear in her preference for the *700 Club* over other programs that she describes as more "wild."

> By "wild," I mean jumping around, healing, [the] strange things that people do and say on some of them. I watch for the sake of seeing what they do. Portee, he says its OK for him to have all of those fine clothes, and things, and people believe him. I think they are more "showmen" than anything else, but I watch some of them anyway.

Blanche is remarkably nonjudgmental about conventional television and catholic in her tastes, even allowing that she likes *Late Night with David Letterman*.

> Most of conventional TV is just fair. A lot is not too great. . . . I'm not great on car races, shooting, and stuff. The violence is really bad. I like mysteries and comedies, but most stuff is noisy and confusing. A lot of that has to do with the time of day things are on. Even David Letterman has improved, it's funnier humor now. He could do the same things in the morning and they wouldn't be nearly as funny, but when they're on at night, he's real humorous. I like him a lot. Timing is very important, the time of day things are on.

As a viewer who is more "entertainment" oriented and less oriented toward "commitment" to the program, Blanche might not be expected to talk about the *700 Club* with others a great deal. She does, however, talk about it with people, including her own pastor.

Bill Duncan shares with Blanche Murphy a less intense religiosity than some of the other viewers. His viewing of the *700 Club* and his church participation are important to him, but in a general or universalist sense, not for dogmatic reasons. The religious programs he appreciates most are those that stress *general*, not *specific*, questions of faith and practice.

> Charles Stanley is directed more toward maturation of believers in Christ, building up their capabilities in light of their daily lives. The Christian way to do things is through a church, but there are people out there who he can help move along in their development, who aren't in churches. Robertson looks into current issues the world over, world problems, current problems. He has a wider appeal. Non-believers might enjoy his program more than they would Stanley's. The *700 Club* is being true to their mission. Society is very pluralistic and diversified; there's need for a variety of evangelistic approaches. Pat Robertson has a more general audience.

Bill clearly believes that the *700 Club*'s primary claim is to this more general, universalist turf. What is interesting about Bill, in particular, is the extent to which the *700 Club* is not his favorite, yet he appreciates precisely this same "public," "current events" aspect of it. His own inclinations are more spiritual, more insular, but he nonetheless perceives the *700 Club* as providing a different sort of service to its viewers.

Viewing as a "subversive act"

Phyllis Stover is an unusually conservative and judgmental person. She is a lifelong Catholic and is the only respondent who is not currently a member of the *700 Club*, due in part to her family's opposition to her viewing. She has watched religious television for a long time, however. "I started watching religious television years ago. I've always liked programs that had lots of prayers and healings in them, and I used to watch programs just for that. It's something I enjoy watching, like other people like sports or something."

Phyllis also attends all of the healing services in her home parish (see Figure 8.4[8]), so faith healing is not something she gets from religious television alone.

There is an obvious conflict raised for a devout Catholic who views such programs. Phyllis feels this conflict most keenly in her relationship with relatives and friends in her parish. She resolves this conflict through the same universalism that is important to the other Catholics and Jews who view the *700 Club* regularly.

> My neighbors and relatives, they say, "That's Protestant programming, and you're a Catholic." But I watch for interest and inspiration. It's Christian programming, not just Protestant programming. They just criticize it for raising all of that money. That bothers me, too. Some people resent it when you mention the programs to them. They mind being told to watch, so I try to be careful.

Phyllis sees the objections of her friends and relatives as ill informed, based on their failure to recognize that a universalized religious expression is possible. These sentiments are remarkably similar to those of Shelley Browne, who looked on the *700 Club* from the perspective of devout Judaism, just as Phyllis encounters it from her devout Catholicism.

> I don't think my Catholic friends and relatives would really see anything specific to complain about if they watched. They just say "It's Protestant, and we have our own religion," but you know how it is when people just don't want to listen to something; they'll give you any reason for not doing it. I just think that we're all Christian, aren't we, and we all worship the same God and believe in the same Christ.

The seeming affluence of the *700 Club* and other religious programs is the main objection Phyllis has to these programs.

> The affluence, the furnishings on the *700 Club*, and the others bother me. There's just so much money involved, I don't approve of that. I don't see how people could watch two of these shows and contribute to both. I think that would be sinful. It's just so much money. They should be giving that money to the poor.

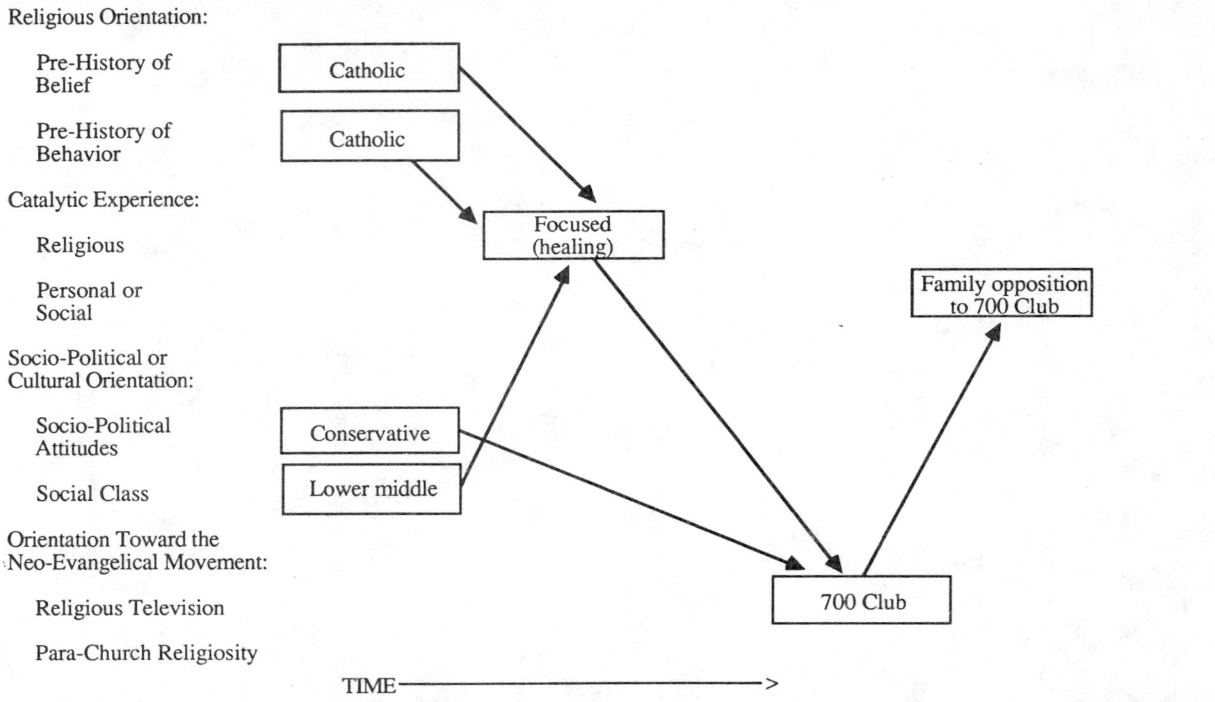

Religious Orientation:

Pre-History of Belief

Pre-History of Behavior

Catalytic Experience:

Religious

Personal or Social

Socio-Political or Cultural Orientation:

Socio-Political Attitudes

Social Class

Orientation Toward the Neo-Evangelical Movement:

Religious Television

Para-Church Religiosity

Catholic

Catholic

Focused (healing)

Conservative

Lower middle

700 Club

Family opposition to 700 Club

TIME

Figure 8.4. Viewing/involvement trajectory for Phyllis Stover

Phyllis does not, in the final analysis, see her viewing as something substantively religious for her. "I don't watch it *purposely*, you know. I just watch it for a *change*. I'm tired of looking at games and everything else. Television's terrible, most of it. Informative things about health, and education, I think are great, and religious television, of course."

Phyllis is typical of other viewers in this chapter in that she sees in the *700 Club* a universalist symbol system, one that, due to its national prominence, speaks for a more broadly defined worldview than might be expected given either its roots or those of most of its viewers.

The *700 Club* as religion's voice of public affairs

For these viewers, the *700 Club* is a sounding board for their values and priorities. Because of their omnipresence, the mass media carry with them a presumption of power and impact, an ability to "confer status" on those figures and ideas they present.[9]

Most observers understandably assume that the mere presence of a figure like Pat Robertson on television gives him enormous power.[10] Indeed, the "status" conferred by virtue of mere presence on TV can be great, as can be seen in specific cases of electronic church figures who have gained prominence and influence because of their presence on a "national" medium.

What we have learned from viewers in this chapter is that this "conferred status" assumption is shared by *700 Club* viewers as well. In terms of the ideas of *communitas* and *societas* that we examined in Chapter 5, it is clear that viewers see major differences between where they live and what they believe, and the wider, national, heterogeneous realms of television, mass media, and politics. Their local realities (including family, church, school, and other local communities of reference) are clearly different from the *trans*local realities of the *700 Club*. They perceive Pat Robertson and the *700 Club* as being from outside their own frames of reference (and, by implication, all other local frames of reference), yet entailing values they consider to be important and positive.

There are some variations here, though. Certain viewers focus on the assumed meaning of the *700 Club*'s ministry. Those who do not come directly from evangelical or Pentecostal roots focus on the question of whether the *700 Club*'s claims are hegemonic or proselytizing. Shelley Browne and Phyllis Stover, along with Bill Duncan, focus on whether the program's theological message is loose enough to be relevant to people from a variety of backgrounds and viewpoints. Carole Fox, being politically liberal as well as not coming from an evangelical background, clearly considers the program to be advisory only, and she need not follow

Pat Robertson's particular political line simply because she appreciates his biblical teaching.

The evangelical and Pentecostal viewers, on the other hand, accept the theological content as a given and focus instead on the "public social witness" of the program and its host. Jeff Wilson stresses Pat Robertson's "incursions" into "centers of power." Joe Parker is stimulated by the fact that these "people with degrees . . . top people" are identified with evangelicalism and Pentecostalism.

By appearing on and being part of television (secular modernism at its most profane), the *700 Club* transcends the lower-class origins of the evangelicalism and fundamentalism out of which it springs.

Notes

1. As with previous chapters, trajectory explications appear in notes. For a complete discussion of viewers' Viewing/Involvement Trajectories, see Stewart M. Hoover, "The *700 Club* as Religion and as Television" (Ph.D. diss., Annenberg School of Communications, University of Pennsylvania, 1985).

2. See the discussion of these issues in Chapters 3 and 4.

3. Peggy L. Shriver, *The Bible Vote* (New York: Pilgrim Press, 1981).

4. Louise M. Bourgault observes precisely the same tendency with the most insular of the viewers of the *PTL Club*. See Bourgault, "The '*PTL Club*' and Protestant Viewers: An Ethnographic Study," *Journal of Communication* 35, no. 1 (Winter 1981): 132-48.

5. Jake Stone reports growing up in a nonevangelical household, though one where religion was an accepted part of life. He has had no catalytic religious experiences and has a rather diffuse faith. His political attitudes were and are rather moderate. A change happened when he gave a young woman hitchhiker a ride and she invited him to a meeting of "The Way International," an evangelical encounter-group type of ministry. This awakened his interest in religion. Loneliness has been a problem, and a sense of belonging is important to him, though he has drifted away from "The Way" more recently. Soon after he became involved there, he also began to watch the *700 Club* and other religious programs, and continues to watch them.

6. Jeff and Joan Wilson both were raised in conservative evangelical households. They had classically focused faiths and had catalytic experiences of faith and of social or personal crisis. Both came from socially conservative backgrounds, as well. The story of their development has been one of growth outward to a more accepting, universalistic faith. They have become convinced that religion must transcend petty disagreements about dogma. The *700 Club* fits perfectly with this worldview for them, and represents a religious and social witness with which they can be quite comfortable. They have grown more focused through the course of their lives. The thing they appreciate the most about religious television, particularly the *700 Club*, is its ability to bring a Christian witness to the wider world in a sophisticated and powerful way.

7. Blanche Murphy has never been an evangelical. She attends a mainline church. Her faith has been classically diffuse—she reports no catalytic personal experiences. Her social and political attitudes are rather conservative, and she has worked outside the home, contributing to a middle-class life-style. Her viewing of the *700 Club* appears to be almost an entertainment activity for her. She reports no particular religious insight or effect from it.

8. Phyllis Stover has always been a Catholic, and remains devout. Her lower-middle-class life-style and ethnic background have contributed to an outlook on life that is quite

conservative, even reactionary. She has always been interested in healing, possibly undergirded by her class associations. She was drawn to religious television due to this interest. Her continuing viewing of religious television is contributing to a potential crisis in her life, because of the strident opposition of her family and friends to her viewing of "Protestant" programming. She holds fast to the universalist idea that these shows are Christian, and therefore acceptable for Catholics, but she has not been successful in convincing her family and friends.

9. For a complete discussion, see Charles R. Wright, *Mass Communication: A Sociological Perspective*, 3d ed. (New York: Random House, 1986).

10. See Chapter 3 for a review of evidence on the actual audience size and composition of the *700 Club*.

9

Evangelical Identity in the
Electronic Church

In their analysis of contemporary American social development as an individualistic search for "meaning," Robert Bellah and his associates conclude that most of us yearn for a lost sense of "belonging," of "community," of rootedness in a past embedded in our collective memory.[1] Each of the viewers we have met is on this same quest. In a secular world where "meaning" is most often sought in therapy, materialistic individualism, or in the artificial communities of work or vicarious escape, many of these people seem grounded in "community" of a sort that is only a memory to most Americans.

It is tempting to think that such "traditionalism" (or "antimodernism," as Berger and his associates have called it[2]) born of basic fundamentalism is at the heart of the electronic church for most viewers. It is tempting to see the fundamentalism of Esther Garnet and John and Martha Hand as nothing more than social anomie or dissatisfaction. These viewers do share with many Americans, evangelical and not, a sense that something has gone wrong with the promise of modernity. As such, they form a fertile field for the early stages of revitalization as described by McLoughlin.[3]

There is more going on here, though. There is a substantively religious or spiritual basis for these life experiences, a personal dimension that underlies the more social or political ones. We set out to look at religious culture in general, and that corner of it represented by the evangelical and fundamentalist electronic church in particular. Recognizing that there is nothing necessarily unique about these viewers' sense of frustration with modern life's atomism and secularism, we can nonetheless see in their faith histories the specifically religious (and communicational) character of their consciousness and experience. A number of the issues we introduced in Chapters 1 and 5 can help in our analysis of what we have seen and heard, and now is the time to draw them together.

The development of faith

Consistent with what Fowler might have predicted, we can see from these faith histories that the religious consciousness of these viewers has evolved in an evolutionary, developmental process.[4] Each viewer readily describes stages, or points, or key incidents, or (significantly) "crises," that led them to new understandings and meanings. There are some things all of these stories seem to have in common.

For all of them, religious consciousness *began* somewhere. For most, it began at home, in childhood, and is remembered now as part of the fabric of that past, central to memories of family, friends, and neighborhood, and central to their memory of who they "were" at that time and who they have become. They were "raised fundamentalist," some say. Their home was a loving one, but not enough attention was given to religious instruction in the "basics," say others. Still others describe their background as being in a "liberal" church, or one that did not stress the "Lordship of Christ."

It is important to all that their religious consciousness has *changed* over time. Some viewers speak of actively searching for religious meaning as part of their growth. For some, a failure to develop spiritually for periods of their lives is important to their sense of "salvation" more recently. "I really fell away from religion," said Jeff Wilson, "until I met my wife." Following that, he had "a wonderful, startling, conversion experience." Standing still is not allowed; "growing in faith" is the norm.

Their change in religious consciousness has taken place in *social* as well as *religious* contexts. Viewers live in a heterogeneous, secular society. They are aware of the social and class significance of religious expression (particularly fundamentalist or charismatic expression) and of denominational membership. They are conscious of the political ramifications of the evangelical "new right," and generally find it necessary that authentic religious communities have a social outreach. Whatever disagreement may have existed between the modernist and conservative wings of Protestantism over the appropriateness of social involvements by the church, it is not an issue for these viewers. Some of them are even activists in a classically political sense.

Their religious consciousness is *not tied* to *formal religious institutions*. There is no clear boundary between "religious" and "secular" fields of experience and meaning. All of life's experiences carry with them the promise of some new insight or some new affirmation that they are on the right track. They do not share with some observers and some church leaders a preoccupation with defining what are appropriate contexts (church, "religious education," and so on) for the development and expression of faith. They can find religious community nearly anywhere, and the fact that their faith can be built up from a variety of sources and in a variety of ways is, in itself, important to their religious identities.

The *universalism* (their openness to input from outside their own "home" faith and culture) that underlies their experience with religious television, the parachurch, and the wider society is consistent with the notion of faith development described by Fowler. Each successive stage of development involves, for the individual, an ever-widening awareness that faith traditions and experiences outside his or her own exist, and can be authentic.[5]

A structure thus emerges. All of these viewers describe a process of religious development that is undergirded by a widening of the frames of reference for their beliefs. For some of them, this came about as a result of religious television. For most, they were in a process of looking outward (they were "searching," they say) before they began to view, and their exposure to these programs has reinforced this openness. For all of them, religious television is an input in their lives on which they have a sense of *perspective*. Few, if any, of them can be said to be unthinking or naive consumers of its messages.

Symbols and values of religious television

We have discussed how symbols serve the formation and reformation of cultures. The "liminality" of the television viewing experience is an important context where shared symbols can be experienced in modern life. Electronic church broadcasting represents a particular cultural reality, as discussed in Chapters 3 and 4, and thus presents a specific set of symbols and values to its viewers. The following are the key symbols and values that emerged from these faith histories of involvement.

Recovering authentic faith

They feel that they are *recovering* the *authentic religious faith* of their individual and cultural roots. Some, like Ed Horne before his "conversion" experience, admit to having drifted away from the true faith themselves. In other cases, they see their current involvement with the *700 Club* and the parachurch as a rejection of religious institutions that have drifted away from authenticity into empty rituals and self-preoccupation. This more universalistic understanding was clearly illustrated by Shelley Browne, a Jew, and Ralph Ritter, a Catholic, and was also the position of Helen Purton, who was a "stranded evangelical."

A voice of conservative Christianity

In spite of the comparative universalism of the *700 Club* for some viewers, the *religious gestalt* it represents for most is *conservative* and *fundamentalist Christianity*. The electronic church is a phenomenon of the conservative wing of American Protestantism, and derives its major symbols and values from that realm. The conservative political message comes through loud and clear. Even Carole Fox and Ed Horne, the two most politically liberal viewers, understand that the program has a specific position on moral, ethical, and political issues—the position of the new right. And, for both of them, it is beginning to challenge their contrary beliefs.

The dislocation of modernity
All of these viewers share the feeling that contemporary America is in the midst of a crisis brought about by the secularism and atomism of modernity. Most agree that "authentic" religion is the answer. There has been too much hubris involved in religious institutions, they feel, and the time has come to allow powerful, incisive expressions of true religion to "cut through" to individuals and to society at large and make changes. Religious television seems to them to be the ideal vehicle for this revitalization, because it can bring together a modern means of communication with a powerful expression of traditional values.

The modern, "worldly" evangelicals
For most viewers, the *700 Club* serves many of the classic "functions" of mass media. It provides news and information. It orients them to the wider range of activities and involvements of the evangelical parachurch. It introduces them to other evangelicals, fundamentalists, or charismatics with whom they can identify, and from whom they can learn. It provides entertainment in the form of music and "good preaching." It gives them another concrete avenue of involvement in addressing a world they see as badly in need of the "good news."

It does these things in a specific *way*. The *700 Club* is (they believe) a sophisticated, effective, and powerful forum for expression of symbols and ideas they can affirm. It has within it—because of its national reach and focus, its manipulation of modern technology for the meeting of the challenge of Christ's "great commission," and its refusal to recognize the traditional turf of the traditional churches—the essence of their particular vision of Christ's church.

The "political" aspects of the program, its most controversial elements, are seen by these viewers as positive. The program is, for them, a higher stage in the evolution of evangelicalism, where its worldview finds expression in a national, public forum.[6] It fits the vision of the "worldly evangelical"[7] that has evolved in the past decade.[8] In an era when they feel themselves under siege, all tools, especially powerful ones such as religious broadcasting, can and should be put to use, they say.

The "two parties"
Most of these viewers are conscious of the evangelical contention that conventional churches, particularly the establishment, mainline denominations, have failed. Helen Purton and Esther Garnet feel that their

fundamentalist beliefs were not welcome in the mainline churches to which they have belonged. Ed Horne found little that stimulated him in the churches he attended in his youth. Ruth Jackson expresses appreciation for her mainline pastor in her disabled son's times of need, but is critical of the liberal theological bent of her congregation. Ralph Ritter and Phyllis Stover criticize their Catholic parishes for being too insular and self-preoccupied.

The viewers who have never been mainline or establishment church members are even more vociferous in their criticisms. Jeff and Joan Wilson feel that establishment, mainline religion is simply "dead." The Baldwins reject out of hand the very idea of denominationalism, feeling that individual church communities are more biblical.

The recovery of authentic community

One of the most compelling dimensions of these stories is that these viewers have been able to find a kind of community in their lives that is lost to most of their contemporaries. The Baldwins have found themselves in the community of CBN, in their prison work, and in a vibrant evangelical church. Carole Fox's loneliness has been replaced by her involvement in a number of prayer and Bible study groups. June Mason has recovered from the loss of her son through volunteer work directly with CBN. Jake Stone found, then rejected, the community of "The Way International." Ed Horne has found a church where he feels welcomed and challenged. Shelley Browne has been in contact with Christians with whom she discusses scripture and theology.

It is not the case that the *700 Club* is the only authentic community of involvement for these people. Instead, each of them has found some other context of community involvement as a result of their initial contact with the program. Ed Horne was put in touch with a local church by a CBN phone counselor after his initial conversion. The same thing happened to June Mason and Carole Fox when they called the program during crises. In all the cases where a catalytic experience led viewers to the *700 Club* for help, an enviable and unusual level of direct, personal contact for support, human relationship, and help has come along with their involvement.

Religious universalism

As we have seen, most of these viewers embrace a kind of religious universalism that is surprising considering the evangelical and fundamentalist particularism at the roots of the *700 Club* and other religious programs. As they see it, the crying need of contemporary America for intervention calls for serious measures, and the traditional insularity of denominational labels and interfaith disagreements about polity and theology must stand aside. While the mainline denominations seem particularly to have failed, these viewers criticize all churches for their preoccupation with legalisms and empty structures. Before we become lost in their euphoria with them, however, we should note that their universalism is *relative*. These people by and large come from exceedingly insular and particularistic backgrounds. The universalism to which they ascribe, when compared to society in general, is limited indeed.

The power of this universalism can be seen in viewers' reactions to the generality of the theology of the *700 Club* itself. Far from feeling that it "waters down" key elements of conservative Christianity, they feel strongly that the program should be seen and appreciated by people from a variety of walks of life. The "authenticity" of its appeal can be allowed to come through, they believe, but it must not too quickly turn people off with the more demanding claims of fundamentalism or evangelicalism.

As Fowler observes, adult religious development occurs when individuals broaden their focus to account for people and cultures and beliefs that are outside their own local frames of reference. Most of these viewers feel that even nonbroadcast religion can and must find ways to witness without raising unnecessary boundaries. Observing that mainline and evangelical Protestants have often been at odds, Joan Wilson wonders why they cannot work together. When criticized by her Catholic friends and family for watching a Protestant program, Phyllis Stover exclaims, "but we're all *Christian,* aren't we?" When explaining to her rabbi that she watches the *700 Club*, Shelley Browne asserts that Christians, Jews, and Moslems all worship the "God of Abraham."

Localism and translocalism

We said, in Chapter 1, that the development of community identity and meaning depend to a great degree on the individual's consciousness of the fact that his or her communities of reference exist alongside of, or within, other communities. Anthropologist Robert Redfield has said that nearly all societies—developed and preindustrial—derive a large measure of their identity from the awareness that there are other communities within which they, their village, or their clan find themselves.[9] They are "communities within communities." The ritualized process of reorganization of symbols and paradigms that structure consciousness, as identified by Turner, rests on the distinction between the individual's home community and others outside the most local one. McLoughlin's early stages of revitalization arise out of conflicts between authentic, "core," local beliefs, and contexts where those beliefs are found to be inadequate. Fowler's cognitive stages of development occur in adulthood when such locally based beliefs are challenged by ever-widening circles of contact with other individuals and communities.

In many of our interviews, this awareness of distinctions emerges. Chaplain Jeff Wilson, for instance, identifies in the *700 Club* a ministry that can transcend the limitations of the "local pastor in Timbuktu, Iowa." His declaration that Pat Robertson represents the evangelical worldview to "centers of power" recognizes that a larger context of centralized political power exists. Many other viewers, particularly those mentioned in Chapter 8, have similar ideas about the role of the program in transcending traditional religious and social boundaries.[10]

This translocal awareness seems to function on three levels for these viewers. First is the *physical* or *geographic* level. They clearly recognize the fact that this program comes from a place distant from their homes. Television has an ability to draw geographically disparate people and places together. Pat Robertson "comes from Virginia, and used to live in New York." He is different from most of them because of this fact, yet comes into their homes, bringing them values and symbols they consider to be authentic and meaningful. It is also significant that major electronic church ministries and other parachurch agencies offer concrete geographic linkage through their "pilgrimage sites," such as Oral Roberts's "Prayer Tower," and PTL's "Heritage USA" theme park.

Translocalism also seems to have *cultural* referents. These viewers recognize that the program represents, and puts them in touch with, people from a wide variety of backgrounds and beliefs. Viewers who are drawn to its universalism see people from all walks of life and representing different faiths interviewed and talked about. The program has presented rock 'n' roll music and sacred dance, much to the displeasure of the Wilsons. It has presented "spirit-filled" Catholics, to the satisfaction of Ralph Ritter. It has presented "remote" news stories from across the world, usually focusing on the affect of evangelical witness on some local or national issue.

Finally, translocalism seems to function to clarify positions in the *social structure*. The Hortons and the Parkers, for instance, recognize quite self-consciously the fact that conservative Protestantism tends to be a class-identified phenomenon. Constantly referring to "people with degrees," Joe Parker speaks glowingly of the *700 Club*'s ability to bring all classes and educational backgrounds together. The Baldwins, June Mason, and the Hortons all contrast the *700 Club* with other programs (such as the *PTL Club*) in terms of its attractiveness to "better educated" or higher-class viewers.

The evolution of religious consciousness through viewing of the *700 Club*

Chapter 1 suggested that religious and cultural consciousness evolve within contexts of *the individual, local communities of reference*, and the broader *social and political environment*. We have evaluated these three contexts for each type of viewer, using analytic frameworks that place them in social, cultural, and theological perspective. We have looked at *individual* experiences as catalysts in faith development. We have examined *local communities* in terms of their cultural rites of passage to new levels of consciousness. Finally, we have considered the *social* and *political consequences* of the electronic church as a potential organizing force for movements of revitalization and reformation.

The individual context: "Prehistories" of belief and behavior

The *700 Club* is involved in the "faith searches" of its viewers. For most of them, the program (and its other ministries, in some cases) serves to enlighten them on their "faith journey." It provides inspiration, information, support, and insights. Typically, however, their individual faith was well developed in far more traditional settings *before* they ever encountered the *700 Club*. Faith development is a powerful, preoccupying process, and most of those we have met here ground this aspect of their lives in far more tangible contexts than a mere television program.

Most of these viewers grew up as evangelicals or fundamentalists. While some of them were not involved in a church that supported these beliefs, all of them found ways, along the way, to participate in conservative Christianity, primarily through "parachurch" activities. For all of them, the powerful, universalist reality that the *700 Club* represents is an important confirmation of, and inspiration for, a faith that has not changed much at its core. What has changed is their openness to celebrate cultural and religious diversity to a greater extent than is common in some conservative religious circles.

They have developed more religious tolerance because they have grown beyond the contexts of local church, family, and community within which their early faith was formed. All of them have lived in urban or suburban settings where cultural and religious diversity is the rule, not the exception. Most of them have dealt with a range of new experiences brought on by careers, military service, marriage, relocations, child rearing, and "life crises."

Most of them also are convinced that, because of these stresses, they had "drifted away," to a greater or lesser extent, from their roots. Their social commentaries suggest that such "drifting" is widespread in society at large as well. The values of modern life are far removed from those of traditional, Christian America. What evangelicals seek is a way to reconcile their initial (and still compelling) faith with a world that constantly challenges their beliefs. They have found, in the *700 Club*, and in their new religious communities of reference, a return to their roots that permits them to retain something of the identities they have found in modern life.

The catalytic experience and the context of local community

Many of these viewers report having had some sort of a catalytic personal crisis that relates to their viewing of the *700 Club* and their subsequent religious development. Frequently, these crises put them in a new social and community context that resolved the crisis for them. Whether the crisis was one of faith, as in Ed Horne's reported "conversion" while watching the *700 Club*, or a crisis of a medical or social nature, as reported by Ralph Ritter and Carole Fox, it evoked a new set of relationships for each of them, through which help was made available.

New personal relationships and communities of reference seem to evolve as a means of handling these crises. Their "drifting" thus ended, they begin participating in these new communities. These communities also undergird and support further development of religious consciousness on their parts. However important the *700 Club* may have been in meeting their needs in times of crisis, none of them now depends on it entirely for "community." Religious television is only one of the many communities, church and parachurch, in which they find themselves.

Indeed, community identification can shift rapidly in times of crisis and need. For Carole Fox, Ralph Ritter, and others, times of physical and spiritual testing have stimulated profound shifts in loyalty and behavior. Community is a sense, not necessarily a place.

The *700 Club* and sociopolitical context

How does the *700 Club* come into viewers lives? It is a remarkably casual affair for most of them. Many hear about it from others. A friend told Mabel Baldwin. Helen Purton's daughter told her about it. Martha Hand's mother first told her about the *PTL Club*, and then Martha noticed the *700 Club* as well. Ed Horne and June Mason just "stumbled onto" it. For Ed and June, this presaged major catalytic experiences—a sudden faith conversion for Ed, and the death of June's son. Most of the others were well along in the development of their beliefs when they first encountered the program, and its consistency with their personal histories of evangelicalism or fundamentalism further added to its attractiveness for them.

It is not only the program's consistency with traditional evangelicalism and fundamentalism, however, that is the key to its attractiveness. It is important, even vital, for viewers to realize that the *700 Club* extends beyond their community of reference and gives them a broad, universal cast for their religious experiences.

The decisions of the producers and managers to couch the program in a broad, socially, heterogeneous context (after all, it appears on television) lead to programming content that stresses the commonalities of Christianity in general and within evangelicalism, in particular. Further, the direct involvement of CBN officials in the broader "new evangelical establishment" (evidenced by such things as the cross-promotion of each other's books and rallies, and the appearance of people like Billy Graham at CBN functions, and vice versa) leads to a generalized, not particularized, vision of neoevangelicalism.

There is much yet to be seen about the role of the wider sociopolitical context in these developing faith histories. The *700 Club* and other religious programs bring a conservative Christian witness to bear in centers of power where such voices have not traditionally been present. Jeff Wilson, Helen Purton, Joe and Doris Parker, and Jake Stone all point to this as a significant part of the program, even more important than any "catalytic" event that may have accompanied their viewing.

Pat Robertson symbolizes the sociopolitical power of neoevangelism for them. "He is into radical incursions into the centers of power," says Jeff Wilson. He is the embodiment of a new brand of evangelicalism, one that is sophisticated, even urbane, that can "stand up to" the secularized, humanistic worldview that they believe dominates government, the schools, the commercial media, and business. Secular society serves as a foil for these viewers' evolving communities of reference.

The differences between "believing" Catholics, Protestants, and Jews pale in comparison to the moral and theological challenges posed by the broader society. The "social issues" of concern to those on the "inside" become more meaningful when seen in contrast to the general trends in society. Without secular society's movement toward women's rights, for instance, the neoevangelical social agenda of "family values" would not have been as focused (or would have evolved in a different way). The U.S. Supreme Court's school prayer and abortion decisions also provide rallying points for these values. As we saw in Chapter 2, fundamentalism has always defined itself partly by its opposition to social change. In the era of accelerating change, this "against-ness" sees more and more enemies in society and, consequently, seeks out allies among other faith traditions.

The *700 Club* as a factor in new consciousness and revitalization

The life trajectories we have seen and the faith histories we have heard do not fit neatly into a model of gradual evolution. While consistent with the progression of broadening and universalizing stages predicted by Fowler, we have seen a variety of ways in which new religious awarenesses has "broken in" on these people's lives. In nearly all cases, there is a story to share, one of stark differences in attitude, of powerful personal crises, and of vital loyalties to evolving institutions. Fowler's scenario is consistent with what we have heard, but it does not account for sudden shifts in the speed and direction of the development of religious consciousness.

What we have seen are lives and consciousnesses undergoing dynamic change. McLoughlin's notion of a "social movement" of revitalization is near the mark. The sense among viewers that the *700 Club* and neoevangelicalism represent a "new," "sophisticated" form of Christianity that can authentically face the trials of the present age is precisely the sort of sensibility observed in the earlier Awakenings of American Protestantism. As explained by Joel Carpenter and George Marsden, in Chapters 2 and 3, those movements, after some initial reservations, moved aggressively to take command of the most powerful communication tools of their own day.

700 Club viewers feel a strong dissonance between their basic beliefs and the society and culture that surround them. They have found in religious broadcasting an institution that addresses their concerns. The *700 Club* and other religious programs purvey symbols, codes, and leaders that speak to the crisis of modernity and thereby revitalize fundamentalist values. Whether that constitutes a Fourth Great Awakening, either in and of itself, or within the broader neoevangelical movement, awaits further evidence.

The *700 Club* as a liminal ritual of pilgrimage

We have considered the role that might be played in the neoevangelical movement by the sort of ritualized religious experience and the social and cultural liminality identified by Turner. Turner based his theories on his observations of rituals of kingly ascension and individual rites of passage in a number of traditional and newly industrial societies. As we discussed in Chapter 5, the notion of liminality is central to his system.

Liminality is a state of "in-betweenness," where the individual is helped to transcend the pragmatic structures of everyday life through the ritual suspension of those structures. The structured, rigid part of life, which Turner came to call "societas," can be seen in full relief through such rituals. The effect on participants is a transcendent understanding of a wider, more universal "world of meaning," which Turner calls "com- munitas." *Communitas* is the sense of each individual that he or she is "one with a larger reality," after having been through an experience where the petty and everyday realities are suspended. Through rituals of this type, says Turner, individuals in traditional societies travel through liminality to communitas.[11]

Recently, this idea of liminality has been applied to television viewing. As we noted earlier, Bernice Martin,[12] Horace Newcomb,[13] and Dayan and his associates[14] have discussed the extent to which the mass media and other popular arts provide the space and freedom in which to suspend old beliefs and reorganize worldviews. There is evidence of such situational (framed) liminality in the experiences of viewers of the *700 Club*. The ideas of liminality and communitas emerge from some of the accounts of our viewers in tangible ways as well. For instance, Joe and Doris Parker's trip to CBN headquarters (indeed, their entire experience with CBN) evokes imagery consistent with Turner's more recent work, where he began to consider these processes in more modern societies.

Turner came to feel that *pilgrimages* generate liminality and communitas among those who no longer live in traditional sociocultural settings. Through a pilgrimage, strangers join in a collective search for religious meaning that transcends not only geographic, ideological, and cohort boundaries, but class boundaries, as well. As Turner points out:

> I myself tend to see pilgrimage as that form of institutionalized or "symbolic" "antistructure" (or perhaps "metastructure") which succeeds the major initiation rites of puberty in tribal societies as the dominant historical form. It is the ordered anti-structure of the patrimonial-feudal systems.[15]

Turner has studied pilgrimages to sites such as Santiago de Compostella, Guadalupe, and Czestochowa. The pilgrimage becomes ritual liminality because the pilgrims forsake their homes, families, and communities for a rigorous, and sometimes dangerous, journey. During the journey, they encounter other pilgrims, from other places, and from all walks of life, all of whom are on the same quest as they are. The general sense of universalism that ensues gradually builds until, at the site itself, huge numbers of vastly different people converge to share a common "center." The ritual suspension of everyday social structures through pilgrimage thus includes each of the contexts of "translocalism" we have discussed. Pilgrims come together from different *places*, different *cultures*, different *classes*, and even (to an extent) different *religions*, around shared symbols and beliefs.

The potential for the *700 Club* to induce liminality among its viewers is obvious from the example of the Parkers, who made a physical pilgrimage to CBN. They seemed to be particularly attuned to the lowering of class and culture barriers among viewers, referring to "people with [academic] degrees . . . top people," Joe seemed clearly moved by the type of gratifications described by Turner:

> We went down and stayed for three or four days. I was excited to meet a man face-to-face who has the education, and degrees, who is so pleasant, and humble, he's a servant of the Lord, not a "somebody" to show off his abilities or anything like that. . . . And the thing that shocked me, but I expected it, *every* person loving you, hugging you. . . . They'd say, "Praise the Lord," and it's not that they were fanatical: these were people who had college degrees and whatever, and had been in manufacturing. . . . They were people who could express themselves . . . and for the first time I said to myself, "This is a taste of heaven."

The parachurch and localism-translocalism dimensions describe mechanisms within which *pilgrimagelike* functions might flow from physical involvements, such as Harry and Mabel Baldwin, in actual travel and nontelevision activities. Such functions, further, *may* flow from viewing itself. Viewers might be said to travel, in a sense, from their "home" contexts of family and culture "through" a cosmopolitan, even potentially dangerous, medium (in that it is at least potentially threatening to their basic values and beliefs because of the content of commercial television) to a "center." At the center, they find a wide variety of other people, often different from themselves, with whom a shared set of symbols and beliefs is celebrated, and thus communitas is affirmed.

The unfolding of "new lives"

Viewers' experiences with the *700 Club* play an important, if not central, role in their evolving religious self-understanding. We have caught these people at a particular moment in their faith development. We see these things in a specific sociopolitical context that is challenging their traditional faith. But we see evidence that major changes in evangelical consciousness are taking place.

These changes have antecedents: Most viewers have strong "prehistories" of belief and behavior on which the core values they identify in the *700 Club* are based. These processes can also have a dynamic, catalytic dimension: Many viewers have experienced crises that the *700 Club* and other parachurch involvements have given specific meaning.

Finally, these changes in consciousness have consequences. We can see in the trajectories interactions of belief and behavior with dimensions of personal experience that lead in new directions. The "effects" of these interactions of prehistory, catalytic experience, and broadcast- and non-broadcast-based religious "community" are not necessarily consistent. Instead, we see a wide range of changes among these viewers. In general, however, each change seems to be one that broadens, rather than narrows, personal identity and group identification.

We see evidence of transformations of *class* and *general social identities*. Some viewers find themselves drawn in more "liberal" directions because of the electronic church. The very "universalism" and generality of the approach of the *700 Club* is broadening for some viewers, especially those who come from the most traditionalist and particularist backgrounds. Esther Garnet, for instance, finds herself challenged to reevaluate her traditionally literalist stance on the Bible by the teaching of electronic church ministers. Carole Fox and Ed Horne, on the other hand, the most politically liberal of those from whom we have heard, may be being drawn in a more conservative, or "traditionalist," direction by their involvements in the *700 Club* and the parachurch.

We also see evidence of transformation of *sociopolitical attitudes*. In nearly all cases, viewing of the *700 Club* seems to go with expanded horizons and greater involvement in the "social" witness of the neoevangelical movement. For the Baldwins, the *700 Club* has opened up avenues of ministry and advocacy that can bring their values and beliefs to bear on concrete community and individual needs through their prison work. The new evangelicalism espoused by the *700 Club* and its related parachurch institutions allows them to be evangelistic and social reformers at the same time, something novel in the history of fundamentalism, at least.

The program adds momentum in this direction by providing information and insight about contemporary social and political issues, albeit with a neoconservative slant. Viewers see themselves as part of a larger social movement supported by the core values and symbols of their native faith. Jeff and Joan Wilson and Sally Horton feel strongly that a religious revival is overtaking America, a revival based on social outreach as much as it is based in merely personalistic or "spiritual" transformations.

Finally, there is a *growing identification with the parachurch* by most of these viewers. The electronic church is one component in a larger, long-standing network of parachurch agencies that work in a loosely coordinated way to bring neoevangelicalism and its message of personal transformation to as many people as possible.

The main reason many viewers progress from simply watching the *700 Club* to broader involvement with the parachurch is that the program cannot (and does not claim to) serve as a real "community" for its viewers. The whole logic of the program is to encourage what its producers see as a revitalized nonchurch evangelicalism. Viewers who encounter the program are first put in touch with local, independent congregations, prayer groups, and other ministries. This is what happened to Ed Horne, Carole Fox, and June Mason.

The process can move in the other direction for other viewers. Helen Purton, for instance, encountered the *700 Club* as a result of her financial support of other parachurch ministries.

The fact that these viewers, by and large people who grew up with a faith proud of its insularity, have come to accept ministries with a broader, more universalist appeal indicates a certain fluidity of community in contemporary evangelicalism and fundamentalism. Whereas local communities of church and family may have been the sole source of religious identity in an earlier era, the evolution of the evangelical parachurch has encouraged individuals to identify with a variety of religious organizations that share the core values they hold dear and directly apply them with the goal of transforming a society gone out of control.

The "worldliness" of evangelicalism in recent decades can be seen in the ready identification of these viewers with the universalism of the *700 Club*'s witness. The times are critical, say many of these viewers, and authentic Christianity must adapt its appeals to attract as wide a range of adherents as possible. This universalism is the essence of the evangelical parachurch.

Myths of power, credibility, and ascendancy

Religious broadcasting is driven by a powerful mythology about its importance and effects. These myths deserve scrutiny, and some of them can be evaluated from what we have seen here. Religious broadcasting is thought to be a powerful new force on the national and international religious scene. Proponents and critics alike attribute to it a power far beyond that of conventional churches and conventional religious expression. Any religious medium that can claim to reach millions of people in their homes, on a daily basis, is a force unique in all of recorded history.[16]

Many of these claims and fears are clearly unfounded. There has been no major change in the way people perceive reality or in the ways in which they search for meaning that has allowed a basically mechanical process to intervene in what are first and foremost *human* endeavors: the search for, and cultivation of, transcendent meaning. As we have seen in these accounts, people are still religious in ways that are traditional and human. Television is not an adequate substitute.

In fairness to the majority of religious broadcasters, it must be pointed out that this is not a new insight. Most reasonable observers, both within and outside the electronic church establishment, have long recognized that, for the great majority of viewers, religious broadcasting is not, and cannot be, a church. Its role is, at best, ancillary to the church, though it is clear that the electronic church is far from a neutral participant in contemporary religious-institutional development. The fact that the major religious broadcasters are based in the neoevangelical movement or are historically fundamentalist or charismatic gives an advantage to these groups over others. This is a fact that cannot be denied, regardless of what else we might say about the phenomenon.

While the electronic church is not neutral, neither does it automatically confer religious hegemony. Just because certain of these programs can be heard or seen in most households in the country once a week does not mean that they are actually viewed. The data indicate, in fact, that actual viewing levels are remarkably low, particularly when compared with the numbers who regularly watch or listen to conventional media.[17] Viewing data also show that the *composition* of the audience is not remarkably different from that that has always watched or listened to religious broadcasting, in spite of the brightest hopes of the genre's supporters.[18]

Based on the data we have seen, the ascendancy and power of these programs in terms of numbers of people who are regular members of their audiences is more mythic than real. Based on what we have heard from viewers, their qualitative power is correspondingly weak. The viewers we have spoken to, presumably rather loyal participants in one of the major electronic church ministries, seem remarkably laissez-faire about their participation in what is often assumed to be an influential ritual in their lives. They are offhand, almost matter-of-fact about most aspects of the program, placing more emphasis on the importance to them of the interpersonal, direct-community, and parachurch relationships they have developed (though, for some, the *700 Club*, itself, was their access to these communities).

Furthermore, the content of the program is far less important to these viewers than is the association of the program with their own communities of reference, with their social and cultural backgrounds, and with the dominant symbols and values of their worlds of meaning. This means that, for most viewers, not only is Pat Robertson "preaching to the choir" (in that his audience is already basically convinced), but that they are less interested in what he has to say than they are in associating the program with their other beliefs and involvements. Jeff and Joan Wilson, June Mason, and Sally and Jim Horton, for instance, do not now *need* the *700 Club* for themselves. They support it for "those who really need it." Realizing that they, themselves, may actually be the typical or target audience of the program would belie its value for them.

It follows from this, and is apparent from our interviews, that these viewers are active in constructing meanings out of their viewing that transcend those intended by the program's producers. The program is *symbolic* for them. It is not a package of instrumental, powerful messages so much as it is evocative of dimensions of culture, community, and belief based on their "core" beliefs.

Symbols of power and credibility

Figures like Pat Robertson are far less important as individuals than they are as *symbols*. Robertson represents evangelical ascendancy to these viewers. For Joe and Doris Parker, he is the kind of leader churches need at this point in history. For the Wilsons and the Jacksons, he is a spokesperson for a set of sociopolitical ideas they endorse. For the Baldwins, the Hortons, the Hands, and June Mason, he demonstrates that evangelicals can be literate, educated, and sophisticated, even about secular issues.

Viewers seem to read into electronic church figures as much as they get out of them. When pressed for their evaluations of Robertson and his rivals Jim and Tammy Bakker, for example, many viewers respond with attributes only available by inference (e.g., Jake Stone's descriptions of the high-minded intentions of CBN's expensive building projects), or by glossing over aspects of the ministry that seem discordant (e.g., the Wilson's psychohistory of Tammy).

Unquestioned credibility and respect are the lifeblood of figures like Pat Robertson. This issue of *credibility* was thrown into stark relief by Robertson's presidential candidacy, but it has also been invoked by the financial crises and lurid scandals that periodically rock the electronic church industry. Nowhere is this more evident for our viewers than in their observations regarding Tammy Bakker, who has been an enigmatic symbol for many of them, evangelical and nonevangelical alike.[19]

Even though Joan Wilson is a minister's wife and therefore has a special interest in Tammy Bakker, she is otherwise typical of other viewers, particularly those who come from the most conservative backgrounds— Joan herself grew up in a "holiness" denomination in the south. She observes that Tammy Bakker is a well-known type: A woman from conservative or Pentecostal roots who has taken on the trappings of the secular world but has somehow managed to retain her authenticity.

"Tammy comes from a very closed, holiness background. It's a sociological fact that when people grow up in these holiness churches, they can overdo it when they come out," Joan explains. Still, Tammy has retained her credibility for Jeff and Joan. "She's flighty, shallow, showy, brassy, has identity problems," acknowledges Jeff. But Joan quickly adds:

"She must be a good person under there. She visits prisons, and all."

Tammy is an enigmatic figure for other viewers as well. Joe Parker says: "At one time I didn't care much for Tammy, but now. . . . I really believe she's a woman of God and a child of God. I've never sensed that she's out of the spirit in anything she's had to say. Never. Never."

Ed Horne expresses similar sentiments about Tammy and PTL when he says, "She's too extravagant, with jewelry and all, but she's got to answer to God for herself. It's not for me to judge." He is troubled, however, by the extravagance. "Why would you want to ask people to come down and visit a city and spend their money on that when it should be going to starving people?"

Still, he can forgive Tammy. "They explained one day on the program, where her money comes from, like she sells her own records and stuff, and she speaks around the country, and makes her own money that way. It's like me, I can spend my own money."

Many of the viewers shared these sentiments. Tammy is a dissonant symbol for the evangelical and fundamentalist roots from which these programs and these viewers come. Her flashiness, materialism, and provocativeness clearly are unsettling to them.

Tammy as a symbol, however, is more understandable if we consider her in the context of translocalism and Turnerian ritual processes. She represents the world "outside" in the same way Pat Robertson does. Both Tammy and Pat are evidence that there are people of national importance who are grounded in the same local and particularist values as these viewers. It is important to Joe Parker and Jeff Wilson that Pat Robertson, a Yale Law School graduate, can move in the centers of power in the country.

There is an authentic, religiously credible core to Pat Robertson. The fact that he speaks with authority and sophistication and relates to the rich and powerful makes him all the more compelling as a symbol. He may look like other Yale-educated lawyers, but inside, at the core, he is "one of us." In the same way (and possibly to viewers of different social classes), Tammy Bakker is compelling as a symbol because she too is authentic at the core. In a sense, the more outlandish and dissonant she appears on the "outside," the more compelling becomes the knowledge that she is authentic on the "inside." Once viewers have accepted the basic proposition that either of these figures is authentic and credible, the *more* they appear to be different, the more they come to carry the trappings of the translocal and the cosmopolitan (within reason), the more powerful becomes the message that their brand of Christianity can and does have force and effect far beyond the local settings where it originated.

There is a sense in which television itself shares this legacy. As we saw in

Chapter 2, it has not always been a foregone conclusion that conservative Christianity would find a comfortable place in media dominated by debased "entertainments." This threshold was crossed by the fundamentalist movement in the 1920s. It has yet to be crossed by other groups. The mere presence of a fundamentalist or neoevangelical message on television carries with it the implication that the "dangerous," "debased," medium is being transformed. This conclusion is implicit in many of the stories we have heard.

The power of television and religious television

The compelling image of television that comes through here is one of power. Television has intrinsic power due to its assumed persuasive effects. It is attractive and influential to most of its viewers. Television also has power due to its presence in the everyday lives and consciousnesses of its viewers. It is not like education, or government, or even the church—sociocultural institutions whose presence is felt in individual lives only episodically. Instead, it is there, in the home or the workplace. If survey data are to be believed, it is one of the most satisfying and attractive activities of contemporary life.

Television also has meaning. It is not merely "doing nothing." Its central role in the key liminal context of daily life—leisure—places it at the heart of contemporary cultural meaning construction. It organizes and defines not all consciousness, but much of what contemporary Americans (and people throughout the world) consider to be symbols and values. It is the "storyteller" of the contemporary age, the most common, consistent, and pervasive cultural ritual of the "global village." It is the primary source of the symbols that might serve cultural revitalization.

All of television thus has *theological* as well as merely *secular* meaning. People do not make institutional distinctions between the parts of their cultural selves that are touched by transcendent as opposed to material symbols. Meaning on both levels can be encountered anywhere, anytime. The popular media of mainstream America affirm this. The *Reader's Digest*, for instance, carries material intended to "inspire" as well as "enlighten." The world of *Saturday Evening Post* artist Norman Rockwell is a world inhabited by rituals that have both religious and secular connotations.

Individuals develop their religious consciousnesses out of inputs that are both self-consciously "religious" and self-consciously "secular." Television cannot escape a role in these processes. People read meaning into all of television and, to the extent that they are open to transcendent or "religious" insight, it should be available to them nearly as readily on *Dallas* as on the *700 Club*. These processes of cultural meaning involve the celebration of a number of the dimensions and processes we have seen, regardless of whether it is "religious" or "secular" programming being watched.

When people watch conventional television, they also do so with an understanding of its more universalist, translocal context. They are aware that it is produced in Hollywood or New York. They identify with or reject its values with an eye to this awareness. Many of them have expressed great frustration with the "secular humanism" of it. The relationship between the rich and value-laden world of the local community of reference and the colder, more remote and possibly value-threatening world of the television box is an important dimension of its meaning for viewers.

We also have seen that all of television influences, in important ways, these viewers' relationship to religious television. Conventional television is the standard, in technical and other ways, by which more specialized television is gauged. Major television "personalities" set the standard by which personality in the electronic church is assessed. Part of viewers' understanding of Tammy Bakker, for instance, is based on their perception of how she differs from and (more important perhaps) how she is similar to "other" television figures, such as Dolly Parton. The gestalt of conventional television, its basic meanings, are those of the secularized and profane world, the *societas* against which the *communitas* of rich, authentic, local, and familiar symbols are judged.

Neoevangelicalism derives much of its momentum, as we have seen, from the widespread perception that America and the world are in the midst of a moral crisis. Extraordinary measures are necessitated by extraordinary conditions. Conventional television is the basis on which much of this judgment is made. The moral depravity of the "sin capitals" of the world is made real by a variety of entertainment programs. The amorality of the business community and of government is a subtext of much recent news programming. The individualism and materialism that seem to typify human relationships in "the culture of narcissism" is real, in a certain way, to viewers of daytime and evening soap operas.

Television in daily life

The whole dramaturgy of cosmopolitan, secular, translocal American life and culture is laid out, in a sense, before any reasonably constant television viewer, anywhere in the country. Viewers in Aniston, Alabama, Rocky Ford, Colorado, and Albany, New York, share much of the same information about contemporary life. Individual "readings" of this "text" can and do differ. Some of the same meanings are drawn by similar people in all of these settings, however.

Using what we have learned from these viewers of the *700 Club* as a guide to how all of television is infused with meaning by its viewers, we are able to say some things about its role in contemporary searches for meaning. Television acts both as a source of symbols and as a context within which these symbols are evaluated, infused with meaning, used, or discarded. As a source of material from "outside" the local setting, television has great power to convince viewers through its sophistication and its assumed credibility.

This power is tempered, however, by the fact that consumption of television takes place in a specific setting—most often in the context of a local community, a family, or a social network. The "readings" of it in these settings are influenced by these contexts. Contrary to recent speculation about the powerful role that the audience plays in meaning construction, it appears that these readings are contingent, to an extent, on other factors. Perhaps first among these is the perception, on the part of viewers, of the distance between the "local" and the "translocal" cultures. Television is able to bring the translocal home, to local settings, in a powerful, persuasive way. Its values interact with local values. Its information serves the development of cultural conclusions and meanings.

All of these processes derive their momentum and direction, to a great extent, from the fact that they involve television. It is not like other cultural inputs from which meaning can be derived. It is assumed by its viewers to be powerful, persuasive, important, cosmopolitan, dangerous, credible, and questionable, all at the same time. It can be negative, but it can be used for good. It can convey misleading information, but it can also make truth more real. The myth of its power enhances its real influence, which is considerable. The story of the electronic church is the story of the presumed co-optation of this powerful medium by a new, revitalized religious movement, one that can use television to recapture the essential core of authentic religion.

The leisure setting in which viewing takes place is a liminal place. Viewers are drawn into experiences that suspend the structures and relationships of workday life. They are led to see things in new ways. As we have seen, television shares with all of art the ability to function in this liminal way. The process is not that simple, though. Both the local context, the "little community" within which the viewing occurs, and the translocal context where television resides, contribute their own flavor to the experience. Television's sources "outside" the local community give it a special place both "inside" the community and in the lives of individuals.

Watching television often broadens consciousness. It universalizes the individual's understanding of human life and experience. It may lead to whole new levels of consciousness. It can also scare its viewers, and make them want to retreat into negativity and rejectionism. That—in most of the cases we have seen here—viewers took the bad and the good of television and worked with it to paint a worldview that accounts for its input is a testimony to one of the most basic truths about it. Television is a highly satisfying and salient part of contemporary life for most people. Its cultural place is secure. The extent of its cultural power seems wide. There are limits on it, but the typical viewer may be far more interested in excusing its excesses, than in condemning its role in his or her daily life.

Notes

1. Robert N. Bellah et al., *Habits of the Heart* (Berkeley: University of California Press, 1985).

2. Peter L. Berger, Brigitte Berger, and Hansfried Kellner, *The Homeless Mind* (New York: Random House, 1973).

3. William G. McLoughlin, *Revivals, Awakenings and Reform* (Chicago: University of Chicago Press, 1978).

4. James W. Fowler, *Becoming Adult, Becoming Christian* (San Francisco: Harper & Row, 1984). Fowler's work has stimulated a broad and growing literature dealing with the development of faith in psychological and cognitive-developmental terms. Our purpose here has not been to chart the specifics of this development, but rather to take on a prima facie basis the self-described evolution of faith among these viewers. It is worth noting that, by the mere request, "Tell me your faith history," the respondent has been led to the assumption that a historical process must be involved. Enough evidence exists that individuals tend to think of their faith in evolutionary terms that the dynamic characteristics of its development can probably be accepted at the outset, however.

5. Fowler, *Becoming Adult, Becoming Christian.*

6. The electronic church may represent a new permutation on H. Richard Niebuhr's classic formulation of the relations between Christianity and culture. In *Christ and Culture* (New York: Harper, 1951), he detailed the variety of ways various Christian groups have related to culture. Whereas the traditional place for the evangelical worldview has been to see "Christ against culture," as opposed to the mainline or liberal churches' attitude of "Christ transforming culture," the past ten years has found more and more evangelicals, particularly those of the politicized "new right," taking the transformationist position.

7. See Richard Quebedeaux, *The Worldly Evangelicals* (San Francisco: Harper & Row, 1978).

8. It is particularly interesting to observe the extent to which one family, the Baldwins, came to be socially involved in "prison ministry" through the *700 Club*, and may hold a more "liberal" attitude toward criminal justice issues as a result.

9. Robert Redfield, *The Little Community* (Chicago: University of Chicago Press, 1956).

10. This particular line of analysis might also benefit from the concept of "boundary" itself, as a dynamic component of cultural meaning. Mary Douglas, in *Purity and Danger* (London: Routledge & Kegan Paul, 1980) and elsewhere, has done much to extend this argument.

11. See, in particular, Victor Turner, *The Ritual Process* (Ithaca, NY: Cornell University Press, 1982). For application to the special problem of "media events," see Daniel Dayan, Elihu Katz, and Paul Kerns, "Armchair Pilgrimages: The Trips of Pope John Paul II and

Their Television Public" (Paper delivered to the American Sociological Association, San Antonio, Texas, August 1984).

12. Bernice Martin, *The Sociology of Contemporary Cultural Change* (Oxford: Basil Blackwell, 1981).

13. Horace Newcomb and Robert S. Alley, *The Producer's Medium* (New York: Oxford University Press, 1983).

14. Dayan, Katz, and Kerns, "Armchair Pilgrimages."

15. Victor Turner, "The Center Out There: Pilgrim's Goal," *History of Religions* 12, no. 4 (1972), p. 204.

16. For the most comprehensive apologia for the genre, see Ben Armstrong, *The Electric Church* (Nashville: Thomas Nelson, 1979).

17. See Stewart M. Hoover, "The Religious Television Audience: A Matter of Significance, or Size?" *Review of Religious Research* 29, no. 2 (December 1987).

18. For a recent apologia, see David W. Clark and Paul H. Virts, "Religious Television Audience: A New Development in Measuring Audience Size" (Paper delivered at the Society for the Scientific Study of Religion, Savannah, Georgia, October 1985). (Also extensively discussed in Hoover, "The Religious Television Audience.")

19. All of these interviews predated the scandal that rocked PTL in 1987. Some of these opinions may have changed subsequently as a result of that event. It should be remembered, however, that smaller scandals had plagued PTL for its entire history, and many of these viewers referred specifically to those scandals in preface to their remarks here. This discussion of Tammy Bakker's credibility is presented to illustrate the individual and cultural reasoning underlying credibility for electronic church figures, and is undoubtedly the type of reasoning that continued to drive supporters of the Bakkers even after they resigned from PTL in 1987.

10

The Electronic Church and American Culture

The extensive use of television and radio by fundamentalists and evangelicals seems natural, at least to outsiders. Movements that stress revelation are drawn to media assumed to have direct power. The evangelical theology of "the word" assumes that expression, by itself, can have persuasive effects. The grand traditions of the tent meeting and revival carry with them a show-business aura and willingness to adopt contemporary entertainment standards and technology. Those traditions have largely shaped the form and substance of the electronic church. The "popular culture" of rural Pentecostalism and fundamentalism has always straddled the boundary between the religious and the secular.[1] The ministers of the electronic church have capitalized on social and economic circumstances (discussed in Chapter 3) in moving religious broadcasting, thus constituted, from the margins of society to a central place in public discourse.

The popular media have not always been acceptable to conservative Protestantism, however. The frontier experience left many sects and denominations with an abiding mistrust of "entertainments," that later included television because of its pervasiveness, its assumed power, and its secular origins.[2] Therefore, a threshold has to be crossed by evangelists who choose to employ such a "dangerous" modern entertainment medium for religious ends. The history of CBN reflects serious consideration of this issue, involving some self-conscious decisions toward accommodation with a secular, anonymous, national, pluralistic, medium.

CBN is a model of how evangelicalism has come to the modern media. The appeal of broadcasting, with its promises of huge audiences and national prominence, proved attractive enough that major concessions to its form were accepted. For CBN, this has meant taking the edge off some basic evangelical symbols and values. Strict sectarian dogmas have not been allowed to overwhelm television's demands for entertaining and informative content that does not violate its standards of propriety.

From its place within the neoevangelical movement, religious broadcasting has been at the center of reformulation of the fundamentalist worldview directed at social and cultural reform. Religious broadcasting today reflects a universalizing of claims that were once dogmatic. It has been fully integrated into the parachurch, an important institutional base for conservative Christian consciousness.

The electronic church, and the *700 Club*, are transforming traditional symbols, structures, and relationships. They really are new, and that is part of their power and appeal. Their newness has implications in several specific areas, each emanating from the changes in religious broadcasting itself. The new religious broadcasts have implications for the wider neoevangelical movement. They have implications for American religious culture. Finally, they claim to have, and probably do have, implications for American culture and society in general.

The transformation of evangelical broadcasting

Seen in light of the broader cultural analysis we have pursued, the electronic church is more than just a new kind of religious broadcasting. It represents a synthesis of modernity and religious traditionalism. The Christian Broadcasting Network, for instance, brings to television—the very center of secularism in modern life—a set of appeals and claims that contrast with television's own. It uses the medium of modernity to convey the gospel of traditionalism to widely diverse communities of viewers. Such programs thus represent a transformation, not just a new emanation, of evangelical broadcasting. This transformation is evident in several specific areas.

First, a different *infrastructure* is now thought to be necessary for success in religious broadcasting. Technical sophistication in production is the rule among the major electronic church organizations. CBN was the first to start a satellite network; now others distribute their programs this way. Most of these organizations have extensive nonbroadcast services, including schools, ministries, telephone counseling operations, and even retirement homes and hotels. CBN has even recognized that its fiscal security lies in commercially sponsored, not fund-raising-supported, program distribution, and has eliminated many "religious" programs from its cable channel in favor of syndicated "secular" programming.

Second, the electronic church also represents changed *fund-raising* and *direct-contact activities* by religious broadcasting. Major television ministries have established complex systems of direct-mail solicitation, work with major donors, and on-air telethons. The services and "ministries" of CBN and the *700 Club* have been supplemented by a large network of trained telephone counselors both at the headquarters itself and in regional centers. The relationship of the electronic church to the parachurch integrates broadcast ministries into broad networks of other agencies as well.

Third, far removed from the marginality of an earlier era, the new religious broadcasting presents a kind of television that is seen by its viewers as a real *alternative*. It has pretensions to be a complete programming service, providing a wide range of options for its viewers. It presents alternative entertainment for those who might eschew conventional television. It presents alternative, "clean" soap operas, films, and variety shows. It presents an alternative worldview—one steeped in its fundamentalist past. It presents alternative sources of news and information—from a Christian viewpoint. It presents alternative sources of entertainment and identity for youth and other age groups. And it presents alternative leaders, like Pat Robertson, who transcend the boundary between religion and politics.

Fourth, and most significant, the electronic church is clearly *transformationist* in intent. Where fundamentalist radio reached (and may have been intended primarily to reach) those who were already believers, neoevangelical religious broadcasting is intended, in a self-conscious way, for "outsiders," for the American public as a whole. Unlike the fundamentalism of the past, which avoided all but the most basic social involvements, the electronic church promotes a new kind of "social gospel." It has formulated symbols and ideals aimed at revitalizing modern culture—a matter to which we will return.

Transformation of the evangelical tradition

The electronic church, as we have seen, derives much of its clout from the widespread presumption that it has powerful "direct effects" in social, political, and spiritual matters. We also have seen that there is little evidence to support this presumption. Mass media research has shown, for decades, that broadcasting rarely, if ever, has such direct effects.[3] Mass media, in fact, seem to be least effective in contexts where they must provide entirely novel ideas or beliefs, as would be the case were they "reaching the unchurched" or presenting a new political agenda to a dubious audience. The significance of the electronic church is not in its power to change minds and lives.[4] Rather, it represents the transformation of the evangelical tradition itself. Religious broadcasting has helped integrate formerly isolated and dogmatic evangelicals and fundamentalists into the mainstream. By stressing a universal form of evangelicalism, it has moved their consciousness to a plane where a broader witness to the outside world seems possible and desirable.

It also has spoken to those in the mainstream who have felt alienated from their traditionalist roots. There are many outside the neoevangelical movement who are sympathetic to the evangelical critique. Many people, religious and not, are troubled by the rapid social changes of the past decades. Even within nonevangelical or liberal faith groups, there are concerns about modernism, as well. Catholics and Episcopalians who are troubled by the ordination of women or liturgical changes can identify with a generalized call to return to an earlier era, for example. The electronic church helps to reach such people through its projection of a generalized message of reform. It thus appears that it may, at the least, represent a new type of religious consciousness within evangelicalism itself. It supports the wider movement, but in ways that are unique to its own symbols, structures, and practices.

The individual level: A new self-identity

The electronic church serves the evangelical movement through the sense of *self-identity* it supports in its viewers. The traditional insularity of conservative Christians has given way to a sense that they are the "new" evangelicals, able to speak to a wider, more diverse world. The *700 Club* symbolizes the significance, power, and relevance of their worldview. It leads to a broadened affinity with social and cultural groups that previously would have been outside their realm of experience. It demonstrates that the new, diverse, complex world can be mastered by the evangelical and fundamentalist culture. It provides a safe context within which to encounter that world, and builds self-confidence for individuals who formerly may not have been able to see beyond the traditional boundaries of their faith.

The community level: The parachurch

The *700 Club* is not, in itself, a community, even a vicarious one. Its viewers are by and large involved in "real communities" in addition to their religious viewing. Beyond their formal church involvements, they are heavily integrated into a broader system of institutions that form the transdenominational *parachurch*. American secular and religious culture today are typified by a loosening of ties and structures. The "loosely bounded culture" spoken of by Richard Merelman[5] supports a loosely bounded institutional religiosity. The sectarianism of the past has less and less power over the minds and lives of individuals today. The parachurch suits this new cultural reality because it has few boundaries and ties. It eschews the structures of the past in its preference for a new, independent approach to today's challenges.

The parachurch has a number of unique characteristics, as we have seen. Its *institutional claims* are limited. Viewers and participants take only what they want from it, and leave the rest. Pat Robertson's claims on the political loyalties of viewers like Carole Fox are far from profound, for instance. Thus the loyalty we would normally expect to see in religious communities does not seem to hold in the parachurch. Viewers speak favorably of the need for particularistic proscriptions to take a back seat in an era of global awareness. Wider *doctrinal* matters are put in abeyance in the parachurch. Doctrine fades in importance when the real business of reform and witness begins. There is doctrine, of course, but it is a new doctrine that fits a new situation.

The new situation is the recognition of *cultural diversity*. The modern parachurch presumes to speak to a diverse world, as we have seen. Whereas the evangelical "voluntary association" movement has always had social and religious reform as its goal, its overarching motivation during the Great Awakenings of the past was as a *reaction to* the cultural diversity created by the frontier and the new immigrant classes. Today's parachurch claims to *embrace* diversity instead. It has done this by identifying common needs in lives of many classes and groups. It is thus a community of "mutual help."

In response to embarrassing revelations about his personal life during his 1988 presidential campaign, Pat Robertson remarked that publication of such facts would help people identify with him because "they will know that I have hurt.... There are millions of hurting people in America."[6] The commonality recognized by the parachurch is this "hurting," which cuts across cultural and denominational lines. As long as hurting is being addressed, Robertson recognized, his constituency would remain loyal.

The parachurch also has supported the loosening of *class* and *geographic ties*. The translocalism of its appeals derives from both modern communications technology and from pilgrimages to its "shrines." This loosening has reaffirmed a commonality of purpose and worldview, a sense of communitas that transcends the boundaries of earlier times.

The societal level: Transformationism
The parachurch brings powerful tools to its witness in wider society. Whereas evangelicalism and fundamentalism traditionally have been identified with a rejectionist attitude toward culture (H. Richard Niebuhr's "Christ *against* culture" paradigm), neoevangelicalism, the parachurch, and the electronic church are now *transformationist* in tone, as we have said. Christ can transform culture, they believe, through the powerful communication tools of secular society.

The electronic church has given its viewers new confidence. Their new identity allows them—even encourages them—to venture out into the world, and helps them to maintain their authenticity while doing so. It gives them role models in the form of successful Christians who are "in the world, but not of it." Such a role is thus made legitimate and real for them.

The electronic church also symbolizes, in and of itself, the power and ascendancy of the evangelical worldview. It represents the capturing of one of secular society's most powerful tools and contexts by the forces of authenticity and reform. The very danger of television thus serves to enhance the meaning of the electronic church for its viewers. A controversial figure like Tammy Bakker comes to symbolize this as well, at least for some of them.

The electronic church has helped modern evangelicalism move into the secular, public arena in a way that is relevant to its followers. That is, it has "brought them along." Its ultimate meaning for secular society is further enhanced for viewers by the social and political program of reform that has been shaped and projected by the parachurch and the electronic church. The dogmatic and insular sociopolitics of fundamentalism in the past (including its obsession with "fringe" issues like liquor and gambling laws) has been replaced by a call for a return to "traditional values," which has a more universal appeal. The neoevangelical bandwagon is rolling, and its course and progress are being charted for this new and disparate community of followers by the parachurch and the electronic church.

The electronic church and American religious culture

The electronic church has transformed American religious culture in general, primarily through its relationship to parachurch institutions and networks. First, it has reinforced the parachurch's denial of denominational boundaries. Boundary-setting and maintenance are important aspects of the American Protestant experience. The class and cultural bases of these boundaries underline the importance of denominational distinctions. By ignoring them, the parachurch and electronic church run up against powerful interests and traditions, and by projecting this conflict into the national spotlight, the very existence of the electronic church becomes a challenge to the conventional church. Just as the itinerant independent evangelists who ply the Bible Belt are seen to threaten the stability of local denominational churches in the towns where they appear, national, high-profile religious broadcasting raises questions about the power and position of national denominations.

Second, the high visibility of the electronic church has changed the balance of power in the "two-party system." The old structure, described by theologian Will Herberg, of "Protestant, Catholic, Jew" has been undermined. The questioning of old systems that began in the 1960s has continued. The clear distinctions between the various religiocultural groups have broken down as society in general has loosened all of its boundaries. This loosening has allowed new religious institutions to spring up alongside the formerly dominant institutions of the religious culture. Gaps have formed in what was once almost a seamless web. Institutions, even those claiming to be noninstitutional, like the parachurch, have moved in to fill those gaps. Consequently, validation of religious leadership and symbols has become a problem.

The electronic church and the parachurch have reorganized those symbols. For example, Jerry Falwell, a fringe representative of a fringe branch of evangelicalism before the rise of television religion, has become a prominent religious spokesperson. In the place of Marc Tannenbaum, Fulton Sheen, Bishop James Pike, William Sloane Coffin, and Eugene Carson Blake appear figures whose only claim to national attention is that they are on religious television. The secular media, never known for their insight into American religion, easily fall prey to the impression that the "resurgence" of religion they now see (in fact, an artifact of its own prominence and self-promotion) is evidence of a "new type" of religion—media religion—that will hold sway in a "media age."[7]

Third, the electronic church and parachurch have changed the way we see politics and religion. Whereas the mixing of religion and politics was once a major defining feature of modernism's "social gospel," the new evangelicalism of the electronic church has taken on a political prominence. The ground underneath the public perception of religion has shifted.

Fourth, the neoevangelical right thus has been able to claim the broad middle ground in an era where the whole political turf has shifted to the right. The modernist side of the two parties has thus found itself groping for new, powerful symbols, and has tended to be forced to the left (politically) as a result. In the establishment era, the middle belonged to the mainline churches. In the neoevangelical era, those churches find themselves searching for new ways of articulating their worldview, ways that clearly differentiate them from the other "party." This mixing and shifting of the public symbol systems has given some people a new paradigm with which to identify. For others, it has undermined long-held beliefs about the role of institutional religion.

Finally, and perhaps most significant for the establishment churches themselves, the electronic church and the parachurch serve to reinforce the "two-party" dimension *within* individual congregations and denominations. Through the electronic church and other agencies of the parachurch, individual evangelicals, fundamentalists, and charismatics within mainline or liberal churches find a source of orientation, insight, and reinforcement. The result may well be an extension and hardening of tensions within those groups.

Conventional churches are being forced to redefine themselves. Mainline Protestant churches, for instance, must formulate new and appealing "liberal" symbols for themselves to counter the clearly focused, and seemingly effective, conservative symbols projected by the electronic church. They must find new ways of bringing their message to the public.

Conventional denominations and
religious broadcasting

The mass communication activities of the mainline denominations have not been effective in this task. The government-sanctioned sustaining-time system, on which they long depended for access and under which they became complacent, continues to deteriorate. Because of the decline of sustaining time and competition from the electronic church, there have been a few paid-time broadcast and cable television shows produced by the established denominations. There are even a couple of electronic churchlike networks. The Southern Baptist Convention operates one, as does a Catholic, Mother Angelica of the *Eternal Word Network*. But overall, the denominations have continued the search for "alternatives" under way when Harold Ellens studied them in the early 1970s. They have wisely avoided the temptation to compete directly with the electronic church in favor of an approach more consistent with their traditions, but have not as yet found a satisfactory solution.

There is an important theological difference between established churches and the freewheeling, antiestablishment movement of the evangelical parachurch. Most churches of the establishment have a strong theological commitment to local congregational communities as the true contexts of faith development and expression. Catholicism, for instance, holds a set of formal sacraments to be vitally important and only possible within the structure of a local parish. Protestant denominations are less sacramentally elaborate, but nonetheless hold a local fellowship community to be the true church, and the only perfect setting through which individual Christians can come to be assured of salvation.

An evangelical theology that stresses the power of revelation within individual lives—"the word"—and that denigrates the structures of conventional religious institutions plays better on television, which is itself context-less, ahistorical, and unstructured. Mainline and establishment churches necessarily have a different perspective on such a medium.

Mainline efforts to combat the electronic church on its own turf would probably not be successful anyway. From what we have seen here, it is unlikely that such programming would really interest the "core" audience of the electronic church. The largely evangelical and independent viewers who make up the audience for programs like the *700 Club* would be unlikely to watch denominational programming unless it closely approximates the evangelical appeal of the electronic church, something denominations are unlikely to do.

The denominations of the Protestant establishment and the Roman

Catholic church are large organizations. They are largely hierarchical (though some are more so than others) and involve structures of representation, democratic participation (to a greater or lesser extent) by local members, and relatively large bureaucracies for administration and outreach. However extensive an electronic church ministry may be, it will always operate more like an independent corporation than like a church denomination, more closely matching the model of organization of commercial television than it does conventional religion.

Denominations have not made good media producers, by and large. Their structures of representation and participation (not to mention their extensive and often idiosyncratic ideological commitments) bind them to specific ways of making their witness known. Independent religious broadcasters are not bound by their institutions at all. The institutions serve the broadcasts, not the other way around, and therein lies the competitive edge the electronic church may have over the denominational church in the area of communication.

We have seen through interviews with viewers that the *700 Club* is particularly responsive to its audience. Direct access via telephone, as well as frequent "feedback" through direct mail, questionnaires, and personal interactions at sponsored events provide ready opportunities for producers to hear from their audience. For a denomination, the problem is very different. Who is the audience intended to be? Is it members (the actual constituents)? Is it "unchurched" (as is claimed by electronic church broadcasters)? Is it the broad public (an audience already "claimed" by conventional media)?

There is no way that the hierarchical, representative structures of conventional denominations can mimic the structures of the largest religious broadcasters. They cannot yield to one person, or even one small production team, the authority to design and produce their "national witness." Further, they cannot justify for themselves the massive amounts of money involved, even if they were able structurally to account for the independence of vision such a creative process demands.

The result has been that denominational television simply cannot compete with the electronic church in sophistication, reach, and visibility. Denominations have found themselves in a battle for national prominence and attention that is loaded against them. The prominence of electronic church figures is a constant sore point for many denominational leaders, who, believing they can do little about it, go quietly about other priorities. While their churches probably are not being undermined by the evolution of the electronic church and the parachurch (at least not yet), their authority is, and that is a point of discomfort for them.

Insights from the data

There are a few things we could say to these groups, and to other "conventional" churches, as they consider what their options are. It is obvious that their challenge is a large one, for the structural and institutional reasons we have noted. This cannot be ignored. That said, however, there are some insights available from our interviews and other data at hand.

First, broadcast production and distribution is a *creative* process. Art cannot be produced by a "committee" and neither can television. The democratically responsive biases of most denominations put them in a poor position to be able to develop a "creative edge," and to be responsive to the interests and reactions of their audiences. Denominations have often looked on the large amounts of money involved in broadcast production, and loaded on those broadcasts a concomitant weight of expectations— demanding services and results far beyond the wildest fantasies of commercial advertisers and producers. This is a formula for disaster and disappointment.

Second, denominations have often failed to develop a clear sense of purpose for their broadcasting activities. Do they wish to evangelize? To proselytize? To increase public awareness and "name recognition"? To influence behavior and attitudes? Each of these objectives requires a radically different approach, few of which are, incidentally, ideally situated in broadcast television.

Third, denominations often have been unclear about the distinction between their *constituents*—those who pay the bills and sit on boards, parish councils, and in the pews on Sunday—and their potential *audience*, which may be a radically different group of people. The electronic church suffers from no such problems. Their objective is simply to broadcast. No one really questions the mythology of who the audience is, or whether the audience and the constituents are, in fact, distinct (or distinguishable) groups. Too often, denominations must produce to please constituents regardless of audience. The electronic church has devised an institutional and production formula that is blind to these distinctions. The "feedback loop" for a denominational program is input from local churches, pastors, parishioners, board members, and public comment. For the electronic church, with its sophisticated mail and telephone facilities, feedback is more immediate and direct.

Finally, since the advent of the electronic church, denominations have too easily accepted the mythologies of the genre, particularly the myth that a large, anonymous, and needy national audience exists for consciously religious programming, and that churches must begin to compete for it. In fact, the "natural" audience for religious broadcasting may *not* be the one conventional denominations really want to reach anyway. The data indicate that the religious television audience is still made up largely of independent-minded evangelicals and the already "churched." Can denominations justify the large sums necessary to reach such an audience?

The electronic church does represent a real challenge to the denominations, however. In an age dominated by the mass media, the traditional prominence of denominations as the centers of religious authority has been eroded by the emergence of free-lance media ministers. Their authority in social and cultural symbols, values, and norms has been further eroded by the emergence of the "new religion" of media-based interpretations of reality and sources of ideology. Their access to their own constituents has been eroded in an era where those constituents are more likely to be members of the television audience first and members of traditional social and cultural formations second.

The electronic church symbolizes the crisis facing denominations more than it is a direct threat. It presents a clear and forceful articulation of the antidenominational and anti-institutional critique brought to bear by the evangelical side of the "two-party" controversy. It represents an era in which traditional means of communication—the word and the book—are being subsumed by new forms of communication and new means of association. In an era where social anomie has led many to search for meaningful community, conventional churches must reach out to them using means of communication that are largely foreign and untested.

Religious television and American culture

As Tocqueville observed in the nineteenth century, religious symbols have always been, and continue to be, an important foundation of American culture. American public life has always depended on such public religious symbols.[8] There are prayers at major public events. The religious affiliations of political candidates are matters of concern. The basic cultural traditions of mainstream American life can be traced to differing interpretations of biblical values. American higher education has religious roots. And major social and cultural changes of the past, specifically the Great Awakenings of the frontier and industrial periods, were struggles over religious culture that moved out into secular culture.

The evangelical tradition has been deeply involved in such struggles. McLoughlin claims, as we have seen, that each of the earlier Great Awakenings was intended to be both a religious and a *sociocultural* movement of reform. The evangelicalism of those earlier eras promoted reform based on religious premises.

The real significance of the electronic church for American culture may lie not so much in its effects on individuals—on political attitudes, for example—as in its capacity to organize and orient a movement or group of movements under the banner of neoevangelical revitalization. There is a major sociopolitical movement under way labeled the "new right," and evangelicals play a key role in it. The movement has powerful, publicly celebrated symbols, symbols that are projected by the electronic church on a daily basis. Pat Robertson and other religious figures have become such symbols for many viewers, embodying the values of the movement. But Pat Robertson's potential as a political candidate is probably not as great as is his role as a spokesperson for an evolving religious consciousness that has social change and cultural reform as its goals.

Conservative Christianity has always held itself up as the embodiment of traditional American values. Basic American myths are celebrated as sacred by evangelicalism and fundamentalism. The electronic church gives these Christians cause to believe that, after a period of great crisis and stress, conservatism has once again found itself at the center of American culture. Evangelicalism and fundamentalism have reaffirmed their place as the *best* religious expression of American myths and values, casting doubt once again on the formerly ascendant mainline churches.

There is a new kind of conservative Christianity that has evolved, though, if our interviews can be taken as typical of the movement as a whole. It is a conservatism that is more open and more universalistic than before. With the mass celebration and expression of the electronic church has come an openness and tolerance that is new to these religious subcultures. A new "type" of evangelical has come along to fit the new age, and we have met and heard from a number of them.

Jeff Wilson spoke for many viewers when he praised the power of the *700 Club* to address a mass audience from its roots in particularism. He and his wife Joan come from such particularist roots themselves and see reflected in the *700 Club* their own journey from that background to a more open and tolerant attitude.

Sally Horton, a woman frustrated by conservative Christianity's inability to recognize her potential gifts as a minister, sees in the electronic church a powerful affirmation and validation of her beliefs and a source of support she has not found in a local church. Joe and Doris Parker illustrated, through their pilgrimage to the CBN center, that the neoevangelical parachurch and the electronic church bring together their "past" in class and ideological terms with a "present" where all social classes can join in celebrating the evangelical and charismatic worldviews.

Religious broadcasting resolves many such dissonances for its viewers. The Parkers are not the only ones for whom the *700 Club* connects the values of their traditionalist social class with the symbols of a new, more universalist order. Harry and Mabel Baldwin see within the program the merging of the traditional isolationism and personalism of evangelicalism with a pragmatic witness to the wider society. With the electronic church, conservative Christianity has found a fresh approach to American culture. It has always claimed to be the religious embodiment of authentic Americanism, but found itself pushed aside in the social struggles of recent decades. Religious television has come to symbolize a recognition that evangelicals and fundamentalists can have a new and vital access to a secular culture they see as in great need of their ministry.

Television as the new American religion

Television has long been assumed to have great cultural and political power. From the earliest days of commercial television, concerns have been raised about its effects on viewers' beliefs and behaviors. Alongside this "effects" tradition has arisen another, more "cultural" one (as we discussed in Chapter 1) that looks at television in folkloric terms. Television, these observers note, is consumed by the majority of the populace, its messages and stories respond to the demands of the public, and it has become a powerful cultural force.

In short, television is the new "cultural storyteller," an agent of norms and values as much as of news and information. Television fulfills this function very much in the way traditional storytellers did—by a process of dialectic, not didactic—where the stories evolve with the culture, retaining most, but not all, of their formal integrity by changing to suit its audiences and new contexts of expression.[9]

One particular strain of this thinking focuses on the *institutional* implications of such a picture. George Gerbner has said that television is not just a "storyteller," but it is the "new state religion" of the modern era. Whereas the church, in pre-Reformation Europe in particular, was the major arbiter of values, norms, and beliefs—the teller of the stories—that is a role now taken by the industrial process of television production. The basic "stories" of contemporary life—Who has power? Who needs it? How do they get it? How is "the good" enforced?—are the stuff of which institutional religion (in pre-Reformation Europe) and contemporary television are made.[10]

There is evidence to support such a view. The estimable cultural power of television is accepted by most observers, and aspects of this power have been empirically verified. Further, research has shown that "conventional" television could be said to be at odds with the first principles of most major religions. Materialism is the rule in television, not communitarian values of sharing and asceticism. Force and violence dominate the value systems, instead of love and cooperation. Classes of people are objectified and manipulated, not encouraged and cared for. Further, some evidence suggests that television viewing is, itself, negatively associated with conventional religious behaviors.[11]

The most ardent of the evangelical new right spokespersons agree that conventional television and other secular media are part of the new state religion—the religion of "secular humanism." Many of those we interviewed echoed this idea. There emerges the clear impression that these people, standing on the "right bank" of the "mainstream" described by Gerbner and his associates[12] see in conventional television the new "religion" he proposes it to be. The religion of "secularism," to these viewers, is a threat both for its challenge to traditional Christian values *and* for its quasi-religious overtones. They further seem ready to accept the view that television's cultural hegemony spreads beyond the more superficial levels of materialism to deeper, quasi-religious levels of consciousness and ideology. They see the struggle clearly to be between two "religions"—one "authentic" and one "secularist." Religious television, and the wider parachurch, are the tools of the former, while conventional television and other hegemonic (in their view) social institutions represent the latter.

Further investigation of Gerbner's thesis would require more careful consideration of what we mean by *religion*. The distinction between "substantive" and "functional" religiosity needs to be applied both to our contemporary phenomena *and* to the *urgeschichte* of the pre-Reformation era. Presumably, "religion" was not the unitary institution integrating both theological substance and social function we assume it to have been. Religion was probably then, as it is now, a polyglot, a social and material, as well as substantive and transcendent, cultural reality.

Conventional television is an important determinant of electronic church power, however. Television itself has important claims on public consciousness, and the electronic church is built on that base. The presumption of electronic church power and effect derives directly from those same presumptions about conventional television. The electronic church has capitalized on the role of television as a central reality of modern life. Television is a major ritual and a public context, and the electronic church embodies for its viewers and movements the use of that ritual for an alternative vision of America.

Religious television in the postmodern era

The phenomena we have been considering arose in a specific era in American cultural history. The neoevangelical, parachurch-based new right developed during decades when the larger culture and society were recovering from the whirlwind of social and cultural change of the 1960s.

As a revitalizing reaction to that era's permissiveness and liberalism, political and religious conservatism found new favor and new prominence.

The electronic church, both in the way it is perceived as well as in its substance, speaks to certain people in such an era. They are not unlike others in their need for some mode of social identification. Robert Bellah's studies of contemporary meaning and values identify an *anomie* and thirst for communities of meaning even in largely "secularized" classes and social groups. The *700 Club* viewers we have spoken to have always been in, and identified with, a religious community. Yet they are not immune to the broader social self-conceptions of an "era of uncertainty." They are involved in a social process similar to the earlier revitalizations described by McLoughlin.

We have made much of the distinction between the substance of the electronic church—its claims to a powerful role in changing minds, lives, and politics—and the importance that its *perceived* power has had in establishing its role in contemporary religious, social, and political life. Its significance lies more in its perceived roles. As we have seen, the existence of the electronic church within the neoevangelical movement has helped to shape an entirely new environment within which religious and social institutions must work out their relationships. It has shifted the agenda. It has become one vector, one force among many that are drawing the culture in a specific direction. It has helped to shift the center of gravity in contemporary culture, regardless of its verifiable, direct, manifest effects.

We must, finally, look at those claimed substantive effects, however. The electronic church and the neoevangelical movement claim to have a very broad appeal. They argue that the profane and meaningless structures and boundaries of the past are giving way to a new consciousness and a new consensus, built around the evangelical worldview. As we have seen, that universalistic claim is of critical symbolic importance in and of itself. The idea that the appeals of the electronic church find favor with a wide range of people in countless places underlies and reinforces the identity that is central to its type of religious consciousness. The *appeal* of this claim to viewers of the *700 Club* and others in the movement is profound, but the *reality* of the claim may be another matter. In spite of its pretensions, the electronic church may well be severely limited in its power to transcend preexisting class boundaries, social structures, and cultural symbols.

In the nineteenth century, American religious culture was evangelical, and Protestant, and Christian, to a far greater extent than it is today. The traditionalist and nativist appeals of the Great Awakenings had broad potential for support in the society as a whole. When the preachers of the Great Awakenings spoke of reform and return to authenticity, there were clear, commonly understood implications to their words.

The electronic church's call for authenticity and reform is, as we have seen, intentionally more diffuse and less specific. When high-minded appeals for social reform are translated into specific actions and clear implications, the broad consensus of its audience—based on discomfort with modernity—may break down. Protestants, Catholics, Jews, evangelicals, fundamentalists, charismatics, Christian humanists, and secularists have far different agendas in many areas. The vague doctrine of the parachurch—"helping the hurting"—is not an agenda of social reform. The "petty legalisms" that typify American religious and secular cultures are more profound than can be swept away in the blush of triumphalism. Simply put, the symbolic resources of the electronic church may not be broad enough or profound enough to account for a significant portion of American culture.

America is diverse today in ways that few of us fully comprehend. The fundamentalist, evangelical, and neoevangelical cultural critiques speak to a consensus at a certain social level. But at other levels, their importance and ultimate persuasiveness have yet to be proven. The natural constituents of the parachurch and the electronic church—their probable potential following (which we would conclude is a more limited field than the guiding mythologies of the movement would hold)—do share a consensus with individuals in the wider society. There are many, within and outside the movement, who feel the stresses and strains of postindustrial life. They all need help in coping with their lives. But there are so many cultural differences among modern Americans that it is difficult to see how the neoevangelical critique will ultimately prove persuasive to a broad cross-section of society.

We have seen this movement in the appeals of its leaders in the parachurch and the electronic church *and* in the evolving consciousness of a group of its followers. There is a difference between those in the movement, as we have seen it, and those on the "outside," whom the movement and its followers presume to reach. The difference is that those we have heard from have a context, a set of institutional and quasi-communitarian relationships with which to identify. They have hope. Their hope is of a peculiar kind, though. Consistent with their millennarian worldview, these people see hope in both the success and the *failure* of their witness to speak to contemporary society. If they succeed, then America will rise to God's vision, and their whole society will become "the elect." If they fail, that also is a comforting sign of God's judgment—something their particularist beliefs have always predicted.

Their friends and neighbors seek a far more temporal salvation. The dramaturgy of conventional social and cultural theology—the symbolic world in which Bellah's respondents by and large live—celebrates *social* salvation. His interviews stressed a quest for the recapture of lost temporal community. The substantive and transcendent orientation of electronic church members does not depend on things ever working out quite right in contemporary life. The electronic church thus does not seem to hold out promise for satisfying the kind of needs Bellah for the most part encountered. Many contemporary American social movements, including neoevangelicalism, search for a "lost" America of social and cultural connectedness. But at its base, the electronic church remains a particularist vision that may not be shared by many beyond the few who find in it remnants of a remembered, self-consciously religious past.

The empirical data show that, despite its intentions and pretensions, the electronic church holds out promise mainly for those who are most easily convinced, not for a broader society in need of some sort of help. In an era dominated, as Martin Marty[13] has said, not by unbelief but by "other-belief" (that is, belief in ways and contexts and centers other than the traditional ones), the electronic church offers one alternative. That it fails to reach many aside from those who already are adherents suggests that its cultural appeal is very limited, indeed.

Notes

1. For example, most people are surprised to learn that the evangelist Jimmy Swaggart and the pace-setting rock 'n' roller Jerry Lee Lewis are first cousins, and used to perform together in rural churches in their home parish in Louisiana. Their musical styles are quite similar. The content of their music and their public images are not.

2. See William F. Fore, "Broadcasting in the Methodist Church, 1952-1972" (Ph.D. diss., Columbia University, 1972), for a discussion of this phenomenon with regard to the development of broadcasting within a major frontier faith. This is not a phenomenon unique to Christian fundamentalism, either. Fundamentalist Judaism and Islam also eschew such activities, particularly around holy days.

3. For a discussion of current thinking on "direct effects" of mass media, see Charles R. Wright, *Mass Communication: A Sociological Perspective*, 3d ed. (New York: Random House, 1986).

4. We should note here two significant matters discussed earlier. First, while there are those anecdotes of powerful transformation accompanying viewing of the electronic church, they are probably relatively rare overall. Most viewers seem to have been religious for a long time before they began to view. Only one of the viewers interviewed here had such an experience, and while this sample was not a full-probability one, it was drawn with some attention to randomness and lack of bias. Second, it should not be overlooked that many religious television programs, and probably many of their viewers, are members of the charismatic movement in one of its forms. Their experience of religious television is necessarily different than that of fundamentalists or liberals. The charismatics in the sample here, however, expressed the same set of satisfactions with the revitalizing emphasis of the *700 Club* as did the others. They were no more likely than the others to draw a clear boundary between the "spiritual" and the "material" implications of the program, as we might have expected.

5. Richard M. Merelman, *Making Something of Ourselves* (Berkeley: University of California Press, 1984).

6. News Conference on 91 Report, WHYY-FM, Philadelphia, PA, 8 October 1987.

7. Of course, the sensationalism of media religion has justified some coverage on a prima facie basis from time to time. Examples include such things as the 1987 PTL scandal and Pat Robertson's 1988 presidential campaign.

8. Robert Bellah's work on American civil religion has been particularly persuasive. See, in particular, Robert N. Bellah, *The Broken Covenant* (New York: Seabury Press, 1975).

9. See, in particular, Roger L. Silverstone, *The Message of Television* (London: Heinemann, 1981).

10. See George Gerbner and Kathleen Connoly, "Television as New Religion," *New Catholic World* (April 1978): 52-56.

11. G. Gerbner, L. Gross, S. Hoover, M. Morgan, N. Signorielli, H. Cotugno, and R. Wuthnow, *Religion and Television*, technical report of the Annenberg-Gallup Study of Religious Broadcasting conducted by the Annenberg School of Communications and the Gallup Organization, Inc. (Philadelphia: Annenberg School of Communications, University of Pennsylvania, 1984). The study found that heavy viewers of "conventional" television were less likely to report Bible reading, church attendance, and a number of other religious behaviors than were light viewers.

12. See George Gerbner and others, "The 'Mainstreaming" of America: Violence Profile No. 11," *Journal of Communication* 30, no. 3 (Summer 1980): 10-29. The Gerbner thesis vis-à-vis television as religion has come to hold that the ideological ground staked out by conventional television's ideological impact is in a broad "middle" of American polity.

13. Martin E. Marty, "Religion in America Since Mid-Century," *Religion and America*, ed. Mary Douglas and Steven Tipton (Boston: Beacon, 1982), p. 280.

Index

About the Author

Stewart M. Hoover has always been interested in the relationship between local, traditionalist cultures, and cosmopolitan, modern media. He grew up on the edge of the Bible Belt, and was always fascinated by the men, women, and media of the evangelical and fundamentalist subcultures there. The study here continues his research interest in communication technology and culture, which has had him looking at new technologies in Third World countries, religious broadcasting in the United States and Europe, traditionalist attitudes in the United States and Great Britain, and telecommunication policy domestically and internationally. He has given papers, lectures, and seminars throughout the United States and in seven foreign countries. He is a member of the faculty of the School of Communications and Theater at Temple University, Philadelphia. He received his Ph.D. from the Annenberg School of Communication, University of Pennsylvania, in 1985. He has a number of scholarly and other publications, and one previous book, *The Electronic Giant,* published in 1982.

NOTES

NOTES

NOTES

NOTES

NOTES